Options for the Stock Investor

Options for the Stock Investor

James B. Bittman

McGraw-Hill

New York   San Francisco   Washington, D.C.   Auckland   Bogotá
Caracas   Lisbon   London   Madrid   Mexico City   Milan
Montreal   New Delhi   San Juan   Singapore
Sydney   Tokyo   Toronto

McGraw-Hill

*A Division of The **McGraw·Hill** Companies*

This publication is designed to provide accurate and authoritative information in regard to the subject matter covered. It is sold with the understanding that neither the author or the publisher is engaged in rendering legal, accounting, or other professional service. If legal advice or other expert assistance is required, the services of a competent professional person should be sought.

From a Declaration of Principles jointly adopted by a Committee of the American Bar Association and a Committee of Publishers.

Library of Congress Cataloging-in-Publication Data

Bittman, James B.
    Options for the stock investor : how any investor can use options
to enhance and protect their return / James B. Bittman.
       p. cm.
    Includes index.
    ISBN 1–55738–872–5
    1. Stock options.   I. Title.
HG6042.857   1996
332.63'228—dc20

                                            95–21707
                                            CIP

Printed in the United States of America
12 13 14 15 16 17 18 19 20

Dedicated to Lyman and Elizabeth Bittman
who taught me the patience that investing requires and who gave me the
optimism needed to hang in there until patience paid off.

Contents

Section 1 **Option Fundamentals** **1**

Section 2 **Basic Investing Strategies** **77**

Section 3 **Advanced Investing Strategies** **147**

Foreword

Looking back over the 25 years since the Chicago Board Options Exchange was conceived, there have been unbelievable changes in the financial industry. In 1973, who could have imagined that the average daily volume of 16 million shares on the New York Stock Exchange would grow to the 290 million per day in 1994, that mutual fund holdings of less than $100 billion in 1973 would be over $2.2 trillion by 1994, or that the Dow Jones Industrial Average would rise from 960 to over 4400 by June 1995? For that matter, who would have thought on that first day in April, 1973, when 900 options traded on 16 stocks at the Chicago Board Options Exchange (CBOE), that average daily volume would surpass 700,000 in 1994?

Looking forward, over the next 25 years, I believe we will see some equally dramatic changes in the finance and investment landscape. Demographic forces will play a crucial role. First, aging of the world's population will put tremendous pressure on retirement funding. In their twenties and thirties, people generally have a high need for liquidity and tend to invest in safe, short-term instruments. As they reach their late thirties, they start to focus more on retirement needs and tend to shift to longer-term investments with higher expected returns. Another contributing factor will be the tremendous transfer of wealth, which is about to commence and will continue for the next 25 years. This transfer will come about as the parents of the baby boomers start passing on to their children much of the $12+ trillion of net worth that they have amassed. The parents of the boomers are both the wealthiest generation in American history—and the longest lived. As a result of this longevity, the boomers are generally going to be in their fifties when they receive this windfall. Consequently, most of it is expected to go into savings and investment rather than consumption.

Knowing how to invest these funds and knowing how to manage the risk of investing these funds is becoming increasingly important. Although options are complex products, we are approaching the day when it may be considered imprudent if you do not know how to use options. As a consequence, there is a tremendous need and desire for education. At the CBOE, we see this need in the demand for the services of The Options Institute, which is the CBOE educational arm. Over 8,000 investors attend our seminars every year, and thousands more call for information about education.

Although many excellent books have been written on options, few have focused attention on stock investors, many of whom probably do not think of themselves as options users. This book, among other things, explains why long-term investors need options. Many fictionalized, but realistic, situations are presented in which options solve the stock investor's problem. Personally, I have been in several of the situations described and although a fictitious Robert, Susan or Sally is named, it very well could have been me about whom Mr. Bittman is writing. As I read the solutions presented, I was struck by the "real world" value of this information—practical ideas that every investor can use on a regular basis.

Stock investors tend to have diverse goals ranging from buying "good stocks" at "good prices" to limiting the risk of owned stocks or generating income. Although option strategies cannot guarantee that the desired results will be achieved, options do provide investors with a wider range of alternatives. Understanding how options work and what trade-offs are involved are the first steps in learning when option alternatives might be preferred over simply buying or selling stock. This book excels in its explanation of option basics and investment-oriented option strategies. These strategies include using puts and calls to limit risk, to increase income, and to establish a selling price above the current market price. The two chapters on covered writing are a complete and in-depth discussion of this popular strategy. The list of investment-oriented strategies also includes one which adds leverage over a limited price rise in the underlying stock with little or no out-of-pocket expense.

Understanding risk is essential when using options, and Mr. Bittman explains clearly how the risk of option strategies can be managed so as not to exceed the risk of stock ownership. When the risk of a strategy exceeds the risk of stock ownership, investors have crossed the threshold into speculation, something which many investors do not want to do. Mr. Bittman explains how to identify the risk level of a strategy and thereby gives investors the ability to make conscious decisions whether or not a particular level of risk is suitable.

On a different subject, that of technology, some investors have shied away from options for fear of being tied to a computer. Mr. Bittman explains that such fears are unfounded. Computers can, however, help develop realistic expectations about what option strategies can and cannot do for investors. Computers, it is explained, make calculations; they do not make decisions. The computer program which accompanies the text is amazingly easy to use, and shows how option prices can be expected to change with changes in the time to expiration, the underlying stock price, the volatility level or any combination of these factors. Needless to say, such calculations cannot be done on a four-function calculator, let alone in one's head; so the OP-EVAL™ program is a handy tool for experienced option users and newcomers alike.

The section on trading strategies rounds out the complete presentation of the subject of options. This section not only gives hints to short-term traders, it also gives long-term investors insights into how differently traders analyze situations and make decisions. The conclusion is obvious: markets are comprised of three participants—investors, speculators, and market makers—who have different reasons for using the markets and who are not in competition with each other. Given the presence of speculators and the important role of market makers, stock investors have a highly efficient options market available to them which provides more investment and risk management alternatives than those offered by the stock market alone.

Alger B. Chapman, Chairman
Chicago Board Options Exchange

Acknowledgments

This book would not have been possible without the efforts of Lisa Harms who edited the entire manuscript and made numerous contributions to both the writing style and the outline.

Mick Noordewier of Rutgers University wrote the OP-EVAL™ computer program. Ingenious in its simplicity and ease of use, I believe it offers everything that most option users will ever need. Furthermore, the new friendship, alone, has made this book-writing experience worth it!

Harrison Roth also read the entire manuscript and provided valuable advice about strategy concepts and text detail. Sharon Egan generously gave time and effort both in editing and conceptualization. Fred Bruch contributed significantly to the chapter on index options, and Jim Adams reviewed not only compliance issues but also contributed to content and clarity.

I would also like to make a special note of thanks to Libby Heimark, the first director of The Options Institute, who got me started in the field of options education. Libby's vision for this organization, and her emphasis on quality programs and constant improvement, both personally and professionally, led to our worldwide reputation for excellence and has done much to spread the good news about conservative, investment-oriented use of options.

In addition, I would like to thank the following people (listed alphabetically) who, in a variety of ways from feedback to moral support, made many contributions:

Marc Allaire	Richard G. DuFour
Sue Belling	Vicki DuFour
Bob Belling	Greg Ellis
Susan Bittman	Tora Ellis
Tom Bittman	Bill Floersch
Linda Boland	Terry Haggerty
Alger B. Chapman	Felecia Hardy
Darrell Dragoo	Joe Hartzler

Charles J. Henry
Mimi Herington
Clark Heston
Tim Hinkes
John Hull
Ramona Hull
Alex Jacobson
France Kozlik
Sheldon Natenberg
Debra Peters
Don Pinkerton

John Power
Dione Rendo
Harrison Roth
John Rusin
Eileen Smith
Laurel Sorenson
Gary Trennepohl
Sandra Trennepohl
Margaret Wiermanski
Jim Yates
Libbie Yates

Disclosures

Throughout this book hypothetical examples are used. These examples do not represent and are not intended to represent real people, real situations, or actual advice on particular stocks. Although they are meant to be realistic, the examples used are for illustrative purposes only.

In order to simplify computations, commissions, and other transaction costs have not been included in the examples used in this book. Commissions will impact the outcome of stock and option strategies and should be considered in real-world situations.

Options involve risk and are not suitable for everyone. Prior to buying or selling an option, a person must receive a copy of *Characteristics and Risks of Standardized Options.* Copies may be obtained from your broker or from OP-EVAL™, Suite 200, 2501 N. Lincoln Ave., Chicago, IL 60614. The investor considering options should consult a tax advisor as to how taxes may affect the outcome of contemplated options transactions. A prospectus, which discusses the role of The Options Clearing Corporation, is also available without charge upon request addressed to The Options Clearing Corporation; 440 S. LaSalle St., Suite 908, Chicago, IL 60605.

Introduction

Setting Goals

This book is for the stock investor who wants to learn how options can be used to pursue investment goals. Investors, unlike short-term speculators, have several specific goals for improving long-term investment performance. Options can help an investor pursue these objectives:

- Buy "good stocks" at "good prices"
- Sell stocks at "good prices"
- Lower the cost basis of stocks purchased
- Enhance income
- Insure stocks against a market decline
- Insure cash (or liquid investments) against missing a market rally
- Reduce the break-even point on a losing position without increasing risk

This list is enticing to many investors, but it is important not to get too excited too soon. Every successful investor needs to develop realistic expectations about what can be accomplished with options, what the costs are and, equally important, what is impossible. In addition, setting and achieving investment goals involves many subjective elements; the use of options makes the job no less subjective. The chapters in this book are designed to help investors understand, first, how options can be used to pursue stated goals and, second, what the pros and

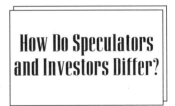

How Do Speculators and Investors Differ?

cons of using options are. With this understanding, investors should be able to incorporate options into their investment decision-making process.

One attribute of options typically touted as an advantage is not on the list of investor objectives. "Leverage" is not on this list because it is not a goal of most investors. While leverage may be useful for some short-term speculators under certain circumstances, the presence of leverage increases risk, which is not a positive for conservative, long-term investors who seek primarily to reduce risk.

Why Is Leverage Not on the List?

To understand what options offer, investors must understand how markets function. One prominent theory about the way markets work is the "Efficient Market Theory." This theory asserts that many competing market participants have taken all available information (company earnings, industry trends, macro-economic developments, etc.) and have translated this information into the current market price of a company's shares. The market has effectively determined the "efficient price" of every security.

Many investment advisors challenge the Efficient Market Theory by claiming that their research (and, therefore, their advice) uncovers "hidden" or "undiscovered" opportunities that are not reflected in current market prices. However, there is not necessarily a contradiction between the general premise of the Efficient Market Theory and the process of researching, selecting and investing in individual stocks. These competing market participants who attempt to gain advantage by researching investment opportunities and making subjective decisions can be viewed as necessary components of properly functioning markets.

Assuming markets present investors with what are essentially "fair" prices, as the Efficient Market Theory asserts, then what adds value when researching and selecting investments is something which increases alternatives. This is what options do—options give investors more investment alternatives.

What Do Options Give Investors?

Alternatives are not necessarily "better;" rather, alternatives offer different trade-offs—a different set of positives and negatives. "Growth versus income" is the classic investment trade-off. Given an investor's specific circumstances and market opinion, an option strategy may be deemed "better" by that investor; but it will not be "better" in an absolute sense.

This book does not assert that options solve all investment problems all of the time. Rather, it is the contention of this book that options help some of the time, that they offer good alternatives to consider and that they add an interesting diversity to an investor's portfolio. To use options wisely and efficiently, however, an investor must understand the trade-offs they offer and when and how those trade-offs fit into the subjective investing process.

The Outline of This Book

This book is divided into five sections: Option Fundamentals, Basic Investing Strategies, Advanced Investing Strategies, Trading Strategies, and Getting Started.

Section 1, Option Fundamentals, thoroughly develops the vocabulary of options, the mechanics of options, and the important concepts of why options have value and how option prices behave. This section is essential for newcomers to options. Chapter 1, The Vocabulary of Options, is important because option-related words are sometimes used in a way which differs from everyday usage. Chapter 2, How Options Work, is perhaps the most important chapter for beginners and shows in great detail how profit and loss diagrams are created. Profit and loss diagrams illuminate the potential profit and risk of various strategies. Potential profit and risk become especially important in later sections when market opinion and investment objectives are matched with the trade-offs of various strategies. Chapter 3, Why Options Have Value, presents the conceptual reason for an option's value and the important components of value. Chapter 4, Option Price Behavior, explains important concepts about how option prices change prior to the expiration date. To say the least, the behavior of option prices seems counterintuitive to many newcomers to options. But this is part of the fun of learning to take advantage of new investment tools, and Chapter 4 is therefore, an essential introduction to the trading strategies section presented later.

Section 2, Basic Investing Strategies, starts with Chapter 5, The Difference Between Investing and Trading Strategies. Contrary to the belief of many, options are not primarily speculative instruments; many option strategies are investment-oriented. These basic strategies are the subject of Chapters 6 through 10 which cover the following strategies in depth: buying calls with a view to buying the underlying stock (Chapter 6); covered writing, which is perhaps the most popular option strategy (Chapter 7); adjusted covered writes (Chapter 8); buy stock with ratio call spread, a strategy with many applications (Chapter 9); and, finally, the protective put strategy, an insurance strategy which many investors will find useful (Chapter 10). The important attribute of these strategies is that all are "investment-oriented" and can be used successfully by traditional stock investors.

Advanced Investing Strategies are presented in Section Three. The term "advanced" does not imply excessive risk. Rather, the strategies presented vary from conservative, stock-oriented strategies, to strategies involving various degrees of leverage. Most important, it is explained and illustrated how an investor can monitor the risk level of a particular strategy in all cases. After defining what an advanced strategy is (Chapter 11), the strategies covered in this section are covered writing on margin (Chapter 12), writing puts and buying Treasury Bills (Chapter 13), and buying stock and writing a straddle (Chapter 14).

Section Four, Trading Strategies, departs from the realm of stock-oriented strategies and examines short-term strategies where understanding option price behavior prior to expiration is of the utmost importance. Chapter 15 explains the need for realistic expectations about what computers can and cannot do. Chapter 16 introduces the software program, OP-EVAL™, that comes with this book. Chapter 17 works through in step-by-step detail some short-term trading situations, examining the important decisions to be made, and illustrating how OP-EVAL™ can be used to assist in the process. The program, of course, does not make decisions for any trader, and it does not in any way guarantee success. The purpose of the program is to get more information and consistent information which can help develop realistic expectations and improve the decision-making process. Chapter 18 compares strategy performance prior to expiration. The theoretical value tables presented are an important tool for any short-term trader to estimate how a strategy might behave. Chapter 19 discusses the unique aspects of index options and what adjustments must be made when using OP-EVAL™ to plan trades.

The book concludes with Section Five, Getting Started, which offers some practical advice to both beginners and experienced option users. For beginners, studying the stock market itself, setting goals and choosing stock-oriented strategies must all be done carefully. For experienced option users, focusing on the proper information—and not trying to do too much—is important. For all investors, a four-step strategy-selection process which matches strategies with specific objectives is presented.

SECTION 1

Option Fundamentals

One

The Vocabulary of Options

Introduction

This chapter defines all of the generally accepted terminology an investor needs to know, but it does not list every term associated with options, as experienced option traders may notice. Options are often considered to be far more complicated than they actually are, a situation exacerbated by industry jargon which is frequently used incorrectly or with conflicting meanings. This book will use all essential terms as clearly defined in this chapter:

- Call Option
- Put Option
- Long Call
- Short Call
- Long Put
- Short Put
- Strike Price (or Exercise Price)
- Expiration Date
- Exercise
- Assignment (and Assignment Notice)
- American Style Option
- European Style Option
- Effective Purchase Price
- Effective Selling Price
- Option Buyer

- Option Writer
- Covered
- Uncovered (or Naked)
- In-the-Money, At-the-Money, Out-of-the-Money
- Premium
- Intrinsic Value
- Time Value
- Cash Account
- Margin Account
- Marginable Transaction
- Initial Margin
- Maintenance Margin
- Margin Call

If you are familiar with these terms, proceed to Chapter 2. For those who wish to review the following definitions, please keep in mind they are written on a basic level. The nuances will be explained in later chapters.

This chapter will first look at call options, then put options. At the end of the chapter, questions (with answers immediately following) will reinforce the reader's understanding.

Call Options

A *call option* is a contract between the call owner (or buyer) and the call writer (or seller). A call option gives its owner the right to buy stock from the call writer at a specified price until a specified date. An equity option contract covers 100 shares of stock (one round lot). The *strike price* (or *exercise price*) is the price specified in the option contract at which stock is traded if the call is exercised. The *expiration date* is the date specified in the option contract, and is the date after which the right contained in the option ceases to exist.

Call Owners Have the Right to Buy

Rights and Obligations

The buyer of one XYZ September 50 Call has the *right* to purchase 100 shares of XYZ stock from the call writer at $50 per share (the strike price) at any time until the September expiration date. The call writer, in contrast, has an *obligation* to deliver 100 shares at $50 per share. If the call owner exercises the right to buy, the call writer must deliver stock. The call buyer is described as having a long call position. The call writer is described as having a short call position.

Call Writers Have the Obligation to Sell

Exercise occurs when the call owner declares the right to buy stock from the call seller and makes the proper notifications. An *assignment notice* is given to a call writer and represents notification that a call owner has exercised the right to buy. The process by which this occurs is as follows: When a call owner decides to exercise, the first step is to notify the brokerage firm. The brokerage firm then notifies The Options Clearing Corporation which is the central clearing house and guarantor of all option transactions. The Options Clearing Corporation then makes a random selection of a brokerage firm with a short call position. That brokerage firm, in turn, selects a customer with a short call position and notifies that customer the option has been assigned. Brokerage firms typically select customers on either a random or first-in, first-out basis. At this point, a stock transaction has occurred: the call owner is the buyer of stock, and the call writer is the seller of stock. The price of this transaction is the strike price of the option (plus or minus commissions). On the settlement date of the stock transaction, the brokerage firms will transfer the appropriate funds to the seller and shares of stock to the buyer.

A call option ceases to exist after one of two events occurs. First, if the call owner exercises the right to purchase stock, then the terms of the contract must be fulfilled by the call writer. After exercise, the option no longer exists, but stock has been purchased, and the exerciser pays the amount indicated by the strike price. If a 50 Call is exercised, for example, the exerciser must pay $50 per share or $5,000 for 100 shares.

Option Owners Exercise

Second, if a call is not exercised prior to expiration, it expires; and the right ceases to exist. In this case, the option is said to "expire worthless."

Calls: Covered and Uncovered (or Naked)

If a call writer owns the stock on which the call is written and can deliver that stock, the short call position is described as *covered*. In contrast, when a call writer does not own the stock, that short call position is described as *uncovered* or *naked*. In the case of an uncovered call, receiving an assignment notice means the investor must acquire stock to deliver. Since it cannot be known at what price the stock can be acquired (or even if it can be acquired), the uncovered, or naked, call writer is taking a risk that is significantly greater than the risk of the covered call writer.

Option Writers Are Assigned

Calls: Investment Position after Exercise and Assignment

Both the call owner and call writer will have changed investment positions after a call is exercised. Figure 1–1 summarizes the changes. For the call owner, the

Figure 1–1 Call Options: Changed Positions after Exercise or Assignment

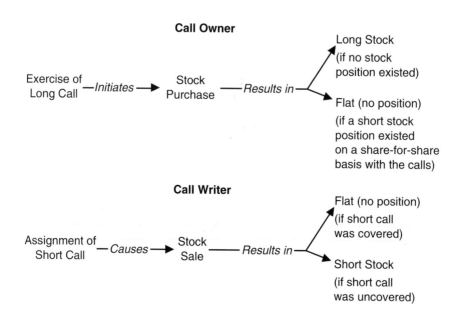

Call Owner

Exercise of Long Call —*Initiates*→ Stock Purchase —*Results in*→ Long Stock (if no stock position existed)

Flat (no position) (if a short stock position existed on a share-for-share basis with the calls)

Call Writer

Assignment of Short Call —*Causes*→ Stock Sale —*Results in*→ Flat (no position) (if short call was covered)

Short Stock (if short call was uncovered)

exercised long call becomes a long stock position (100 shares per option) unless a short stock position existed. If a short stock position did exist on a share-for-share basis with the long calls, then the call exercise initiates a stock purchase which offsets the short stock position and leaves the investor flat (i.e., with no position). For the call writer, assignment of a covered call becomes a flat position. Assignment of an uncovered call, however, creates a short stock position.

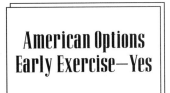

**American Options
Early Exercise—Yes**

Calls: Effective Purchase Price and Effective Selling Price

The price at which the call is transacted is significant, because it is an important factor in the ultimate price of the stock transaction. The *effective purchase price* is the price of purchasing stock which takes into account the price of an option. The *effective selling price* is the price of selling stock which takes into account the price of an option. The following example illustrates this point. If a 50 Call which was purchased for $300, or $3 per share, is exercised, the effective purchase price of that stock is $53. This price is calculated by adding the call price to its strike price on a per-share basis. For the assigned call writer, the effective selling price of stock is also $53: $3 per share is received for selling the call and $50 is received when assignment occurs. The general formula—strike price plus call premium—applies equally to the call writer as the effective selling price and to the call buyer as the effective purchase price.

Types of Option Contracts

An *American style option* is one in which the right granted by the option may be exercised at any time prior to the expiration date. A *European style option* is one in which the right may be exercised only on the last trading day before established deadlines. In the U.S., all equity options are American style. The popular OEX Index options (options on the S&P 100 Index) are also American style. Some index options, such as the SPX Index options (options on the S&P 500 Index) and the XMI Index Options (Major Market Index), are European style.

**European Options
Early Exercise—No**

Calls: In-the-Money, At-the-Money, Out-of-the-Money

The relationship of the stock price to the strike price determines whether an option is in-the-money, at-the-money or out-of-the-money. An *in-the-money call* has a strike price below the current stock price. If a stock is trading at $55, for example, the 50 Call is in-the-money. To be precise, it is $5 in-the-money. This call, however, would not necessarily be trading for $5. In fact, it is very likely to be trading for more than $5, and reasons for this are discussed in Chapter 3.

An *out-of-the-money call* has a strike price above the current stock price. For example, with a stock trading at $55, the 60 Call is out-of-the-money.

At-the-money means the stock price is equal to the strike price. This term has both a strict definition and a looser, common usage. Theoretically, the 55 Call is at-the-money only when the underlying stock is trading exactly at $55. The rest of the time, it is either in-the-money or out-of-the-money. In practice, however, the 55 Call is designated as an at-the-money call when the stock price is closer to that strike price than to another strike price. With a stock trading at $54 or $56, for example, it is common practice to refer to the 55 Call as the at-the-money call.

In-the-money, at-the-money and out-of-the-money are dynamic terms. As stock prices rise, out-of-the-money calls become at-the-money and then in-the-money. As stock prices fall, the opposite happens: in-the-money calls become at-the-money and subsequently out-of-the-money.

Calls: Premium, Intrinsic Value and Time Value

The term *premium* refers to the total price of an option. This premium, or price, consists of two parts: intrinsic value and time value. *Intrinsic value* refers to the in-the-money amount of an option's price, and *time value* refers to any portion of an option's price that exceeds intrinsic value. Consider a situation in which the following prices exist:

	(per share)
Stock	$55
50 Call	6
55 Call	3
60 Call	1

Figure 1–2 Call Options: Intrinsic Value and Time Value

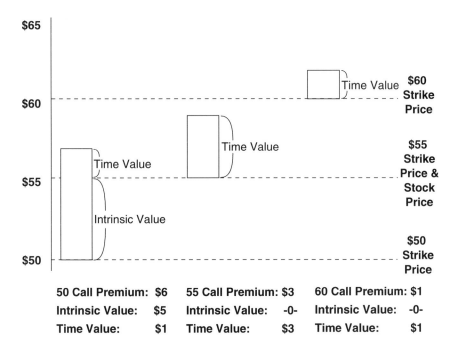

50 Call Premium: $6   55 Call Premium: $3   60 Call Premium: $1

Intrinsic Value: $5   Intrinsic Value: -0-   Intrinsic Value: -0-

Time Value: $1   Time Value: $3   Time Value: $1

An analysis of each option's premium (or price) will illustrate the concepts of intrinsic value and time value. First, examine the 50 Call. The stock price is $5 above the strike price of the 50 Call which is $5 in-the-money, and, therefore, has $5 of intrinsic value. The premium (or price) of the 50 Call, however, is $6. The $1 difference is the time value.

The $3 premium of the 55 Call, consists entirely of time value. The premium of the out-of-the-money 60 Call—$1—also consists entirely of time value. Figure 1–2 illustrates intrinsic value and time value for in-, at- and out-of-the-money calls.

Competition in the market makes it extremely unlikely that in-the-money options will trade for less than intrinsic value. Assume, for example, a stock price of $56. If the 50 Call were trading for $5, investors could buy the call, exercise it immediately and sell the stock for $56. Since the effective purchase price of the stock in this case is $55, the result would be an immediate profit of $1 per share (not counting transaction costs). A profit opportunity of this nature would attract profit-seeking capital. Competition between professional traders would force the call price up and/or the stock price down, reducing the $1 profit per share to an amount slightly greater than transaction costs. For professional traders, transaction costs are very small and, for this reason, options in U.S. markets rarely trade below intrinsic value. When they do, they are very near to expiration and the amount below intrinsic value is only one-sixteenth or one-eighth of a point.

> **Put Owners Have the Right to Sell**

Put Options

A *put option* gives the put buyer (or owner) the right to sell stock to the put writer (or seller). In the case of American style options, this right may be exercised at any time prior to the expiration date. In the case of European style options, the right to sell may be exercised only on the last day of trading prior to established deadlines. The put buyer is described as having a *long put* position, and the put seller is described as having a *short put* position. After exercising, the put buyer must deliver stock. A short put position is an obligation to buy stock if an assignment notice is received. The process by which exercise and assignment occurs for puts is identical to that for calls described earlier.

Puts: Covered and Uncovered

The terms covered and uncovered do not have as precise meanings when applied to puts as they do to calls. If an investor with a short call position actually owns the stock, the short call is covered. By analogy, if there is sufficient cash to purchase stock, one would think a cash-secured short put is covered. In a practical sense this is true. However, it is not as easy for brokerage firms to monitor cash availability as it is to monitor stock holdings. Many brokerage accounts are used like checking accounts and have widely fluctuating cash balances, and these transactions generate little or no fees to pay for monitoring. Stock transactions, in contrast, are relatively infrequent and produce revenue that

> **Put Writers Have the Obligation to Buy**

pays, in part, for the expense of monitoring covered calls. Many brokerage firms, therefore, require that all short put positions be established in a margin account.

Figure 1–3 Put Options: Changed Positions after Exercise or Assignment

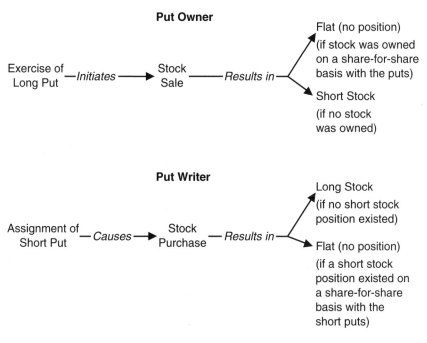

Put Owner

Exercise of Long Put —*Initiates*→ Stock Sale —*Results in*—

Flat (no position)
(if stock was owned on a share-for-share basis with the puts)

Short Stock
(if no stock was owned)

Put Writer

Assignment of Short Put —*Causes*→ Stock Purchase —*Results in*—

Long Stock
(if no short stock position existed)

Flat (no position)
(if a short stock position existed on a share-for-share basis with the short puts)

Puts: Investment Position after Exercise and Assignment

As with calls, the investment positions of put owners and writers change after a put is exercised. Figure 1–3 summarizes the changes. For the put owner with no stock position, the exercised long put becomes a short stock position. If, however, the put owner holds long stock on a share-for-share basis with the puts, then the put exercise sells that stock and leaves the investor flat (i.e. with no position). For the put writer, assignment of a short put requires the writer to purchase stock. If no stock position existed initially, assignment of a short put creates a long stock position. If, however, the put writer has a short stock position on a share-for-share basis with the short puts, then the put assignment leaves the investor flat.

Puts: Effective Purchase Price and Effective Selling Price

The price at which a put is transacted is significant, because its price is an important factor in the ultimate price of the stock transaction. Consider a

50 Put which is purchased for $200, or $2 per share. For the put owner who exercises this put and, consequently, sells stock, the effective selling price is $48 per share. The stock is sold at $50 in accordance with the terms of the put option contract, but $2 was paid for the put; and this reduces the net amount received to $48. Similarly, for the assigned put writer, the $2 per share received lowers the effective price paid from $50 to $48. The general formula—strike price minus put premium—applies to the put writer as the effective purchase price and to the put buyer as the effective selling price.

Puts: In-the-Money, At-the-Money, and Out-of-the-Money

The relationship of the stock price to the strike price of at-the-money and out-of-the-money puts is opposite that for calls. An *in-the-money put* has a strike price above the current stock price. An *out-of-the-money put* has a strike price below the current stock price. Consider a situation in which a stock is trading at $55. The 60 Put is in-the-money. Specifically, it is $5 in-the-money. The 50 Put is out-of-the-money by $5. The 55 Put is at-the-money. The term at-the-money applies to puts in a similar way that it applies to calls. If the stock price is at or very close to the strike price of a put, that put is referred to as the *at-the-money put*.

Puts: Premium, Intrinsic Value and Time Value

As with calls, premium refers to the total price of a put, and it consists of two parts: intrinsic value and time value. Consider a situation in which the following prices exist:

	(per share)
Stock	$72
80 Put	9
75 Put	5
70 Put	2

The 80 Put is $8 in-the-money. It therefore has $8 of intrinsic value and $1 of time value. The 75 Put premium of $5 consists of intrinsic value of $3 and time value of $2. The $2 price of the out-of-the-money 70 Put consists entirely of time value. Figure 1–4 illustrates intrinsic value and time value for in-, at- and out-of-the-money puts.

Figure 1–4 Put Options: Intrinsic Value and Time Value

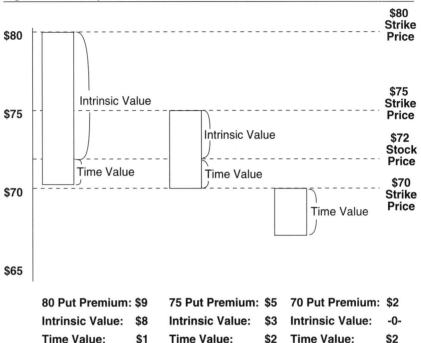

80 Put Premium: $9   75 Put Premium: $5   70 Put Premium: $2
Intrinsic Value: $8   Intrinsic Value: $3   Intrinsic Value: -0-
Time Value: $1   Time Value: $2   Time Value: $2

Margin Accounts and Related Terms

Many conservative investors believe that a "margin account" involves excessive risk. This is not necessarily true, depending on the level of margin debt, if any, and the volatility or "riskiness" of the securities involved. As later chapters reveal, the level of risk of a particular strategy depends on the amount of equity capital supporting that strategy. Paying for stock in cash is the lowest level of risk, because the maximum potential loss is known and fully paid for up front. If the stock price were to suffer a total collapse to zero, the investor would not be called upon for additional funds. In contrast, buying stock "on margin" involves borrowed money which must be repaid in full. If a stock price declines below the loan amount, the investor will be called upon to make up the difference. This potential liability is the reason why margin accounts have a reputation for risk.

Option users need to be aware of margin account procedures because some option strategies are required by regulations to be established in margin accounts. The following overview of margin accounts and related terms is presented for newcomers to these topics.

Cash Account, Margin Account and Marginable Transaction

A *cash account* is an account at a brokerage firm in which all purchases are fully paid for in cash. In a *margin account*, the brokerage firm may lend money to the customer to finance certain types of positions which are called marginable transactions. Different types of *marginable transactions*, according to regulations, require different amounts of equity capital from the customer. This equity capital is called a *margin deposit*, or simply *margin*.

For example, if stock is purchased "on margin," the account equity balance will be less than the value of the stock, and the balance of the purchase price will be lent by the brokerage firm. The investor, of course, pays interest on the loan. The use of margin debt means that market fluctuations will change the account equity balance at a greater percentage rate than the same fluctuation would cause in the equity balance of a cash account. This is called leverage.

Another common marginable transaction is selling stock short. In this transaction, the brokerage firm borrows stock on behalf of the customer who sells it at the current market price with the hope of buying it back later at a lower price. In a short stock transaction, the customer actually pays nothing when initiating the position (except commissions), but a margin deposit is required to provide assurance that the customer will cover any losses.

Certain option transactions are marginable transactions, and certain ones are not. Also, certain option transactions are required to be conducted in a margin account, and others may be conducted in either a cash account or a margin account. Before engaging in option transactions, an investor should be thoroughly familiar with the type of account required for the transactions that are planned.

Initial Margin, Maintenance Margin and Margin Call

A simple formula to remember is: account equity + margin debt = account value. Account value is the total market value of owned securities. The margin debt is the loan to the investor from the brokerage firm, and the account equity is the investor's share after the securities are sold and margin debt repaid.

Initial margin is the minimum account equity required to establish a marginable transaction. Initial margin requirements are frequently expressed in percentage terms of the market value of a position or its underlying security. Purchasing stock, for example, is a marginable transaction which currently has an initial margin of 50%: the purchase of 100 shares of a $50 stock requires an initial margin of $2,500 plus commissions, or 50% of the purchase price plus commissions, and the loan made to the buyer would equal $2,500.

If a margined position loses money, the account equity will decrease both absolutely and as a percentage of the total account value. *Minimum margin* is the level, expressed as a percentage of account value, above which account equity must be maintained. If account equity falls below the minimum margin level, the brokerage firm will notify the investor in a *margin call* that the account equity must be raised to the maintenance level. *Maintenance margin* is the level to which account equity must be raised when a margin call is received. Upon receiving a margin call, a customer may either deposit additional funds or marginable securities or close the position. In the case above, a stock price decline from $50 to $35 would cause a decline in equity to $1,000, because the margin loan of $2,500 remains constant. This $1,000 equity would represent only 28% of the account value (1,000 divided by $3,500 = .28). If the maintenance margin were 35%, the account equity would be under the requirement, and the customer would receive a margin call.

Although many option strategies are marginable, the real point here is that the amount of equity supporting a position is a key element in capital management, and how an investor manages capital is a decisive factor in determining the risk level of a strategy—that is, whether a particular strategy is speculative or conservative in nature. The importance of this concept will be developed throughout the coming chapters.

Summary of Definitions—A Quiz

This chapter concludes with the following quiz. Match the terms below with their correct definitions (some definitions may be used twice). Answers appear immediately after the definitions.

Terms

Long Call _____	In-the-money Put _____
Short Call _____	At-the-money Put _____
Long Put _____	Out-of-the-money Put _____
Short Put _____	Premium _____
Strike Price _____	Intrinsic Value _____
Exercise Price _____	Time Value _____
Expiration Date _____	Cash Account _____
Exercise _____	Margin Account _____
Exercise Notice _____	Cash Transaction _____
Assignment _____	Marginable Transaction _____
European Style Option _____	Effective Purchase
American Style Option _____	Price—Long Call _____
Covered _____	Effective Selling
Uncovered _____	Price—Short Call _____
Naked _____	Effective Purchase
In-the-money Call _____	Price—Short Put _____
At-the-money Call _____	Effective Selling
Out-of-the-money Call _____	Price—Long Put _____

Definitions

1. A form presented to the Options Clearing Corporation demanding that the terms of an option contract be fulfilled

2. A short option position behind which an investor owns the underlying stock in the case of a short call, or has cash to purchase stock in the case of a short put

3. A put option with a strike price above the current stock price

4. The process by which a short option position is selected as the one to make good on its contingent obligation

5. A put option with a strike price equal to the current stock price

6. The total price of an option

7. That portion of an option's total price which is in excess of the intrinsic value

8. Strike price minus premium

9. A transaction requiring a "good faith" deposit

10. A call option with a strike price below the current stock price

11. An account in which brokerage firms provide special services such as lending money, facilitating short stock sales and handling uncovered option transactions

12. A call option with a strike price equal to the current stock price

13. A call option with a strike price above the current stock price

14. An account in which all transactions are fully paid for in cash

15. Strike price plus premium

16. Same as uncovered

17. A short option position behind which an investor does not own the underlying stock in the case of a short call, or does not have cash to purchase stock in the case of a short put

18. An option that may be exercised only on the last trading day prior to established deadlines

19. That portion of an option's total price which is equal to the in-the-money amount

20. A put option with a strike price below the current stock price

21. A transaction in which the full cash amount is transferred to or from the customer's cash account

22. The right to buy

23. The price specified in an option contract

24. Demand that the terms of an option contract be fulfilled

25. The contingent obligation to buy

26. An option that may be exercised at any time up to and including the expiration date (prior to established deadlines)

27. The contingent obligation to sell

28. The date after which an option ceases to exist

29. The right to sell

Answers

Long Call **22**

Short Call **27**

Long Put **29**

Short Put **25**

Strike Price **23**

Exercise Price **23**

Expiration Date **28**

Exercise **24**

Exercise Notice **1**

Assignment **4**

European Style Option **18**

American Style Option **26**

Covered **2**

Uncovered **17**

Naked **16**

In-the-money Call **10**

At-the-money Call **12**

Out-of-the-money Call **13**

In-the-money Put **3**

At-the-money Put **5**

Out-of-the-money Put **20**

Premium **6**

Intrinsic Value **19**

Time Value **7**

Cash Account **14**

Margin Account **11**

Cash Transaction **21**

Marginable Transaction **9**

Effective Purchase Price—Long Call **15**

Effective Selling Price—Short Call **15**

Effective Purchase Price—Short Put **8**

Effective Selling Price—Long Put **8**

TWO

How Options Work—Profit and Loss Diagrams

A basic requirement for understanding and using options is the ability to draw profit and loss diagrams of strategies on the expiration date. Although many readers have seen the standard profit and loss option graphs that are presented and explained in this chapter, there is a difference between seeing them and truly understanding them. If you are not sure of your ability to draw these diagrams, you must take the necessary time to study this chapter. An investor who can draw expiration profit and loss diagrams of option strategies is 90% of the way to understanding options. With a firm grasp of these concepts, you will greatly enhance your ability to match option strategies with investment objectives. The skills developed in this chapter will serve you well throughout your investing career.

Investing and trading with options is different from investing and trading with stocks for several reasons. First, the decision to initiate an option trade involves a consequence on the expiration date which depends on the underlying stock price (assuming the option position is not closed before expiration). The decision to buy a stock, however, has no such consequence. Second, option strategies involve many risk-reward trade-offs. Buying stocks involves only one. In fact, options open a range of investment alternatives, the positives and negatives of which will be discussed throughout this book. Third, the time horizon of using options is dictated by the expiration date, while stocks have no expiration. Fourth, option strategies have different break-even points than do stock strategies.

Profit and Risk Characteristics and Important Price Points to Identify

Strategy analysis begins with the basics. When completed, an expiration profit and loss diagram reveals many things about a strategy such as break-even points, maximum risk, and profit potential. Investors also need to know what stock position is created if the option is in-the-money at expiration. An in-the-money long call at expiration, for example, is assumed to be exercised and thus become a long stock position. These are important points to know because, looked at as a whole, they illustrate the investment trade-off a strategy offers. A trade-off involves benefits and risks, and an understanding of trade-offs will lead to strategy comparisons and, in turn, improves the decision-making process by clarifying investment choices.

Profit and Loss Diagrams—Basic Steps

A profit and loss diagram can be created in six basic steps.

Step 1 *Describe the opening transaction completely.*

Write down in words the transaction you want to diagram. For example, "buy a September 50 Call for 2" or "sell a May 75 Put at 4 1/4." Do not just write "buy a call" or "sell a put," since you will not have sufficient information to complete the diagram.

Step 2 *Start a grid.*

A profit and loss diagram is drawn on a grid which shows the profit or loss of an option strategy at the expiration date over a range of possible stock prices. The vertical grid line represents profit (+) or loss (−). The horizontal grid line represents a range of stock prices. When making a grid, start with the option strike price in the middle of the horizontal grid line and work out in each direction. Figure 2–1 shows a sample grid.

Step 3 *Select a stock price and calculate the option's value at expiration.*

At expiration, an option will be worth either the intrinsic value (the in-the-money amount) or zero. Intrinsic value is discussed in Chapter 1. For example, if the stock price is $56, the September 50 Call is worth 6 at expiration. If the stock price is $49, this call is worth zero. To start, choose a stock price within the range of prices on the grid and determine the value of the option.

Step 4 *Calculate the profit or loss.*

For an option that is purchased, calculate the profit or loss by subtracting the purchase price of the option from its value determined in Step 3. The 50 Call, purchased for 2, with an expiration value of 6, will show a profit of 4 (value of 6 minus the purchase price of 2). The same call with an expiration value of zero will show a loss of 2 (value of zero minus the purchase price of 2).

Figure 2–1 Sample Profit and Loss Grid

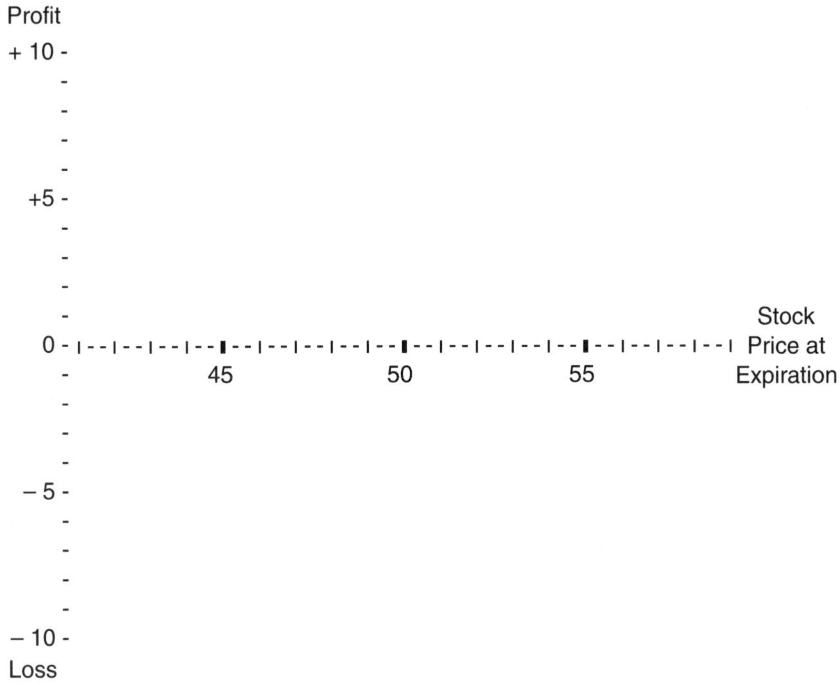

```
Profit
+ 10 -
     -
     -
     -
     -
+5 -
     -
     -
     -
     -
     -                                                                    Stock
 0 - |--|--|--|--|--|--|--|--|--|--|--|--|--|--|--|--|--|--|--| Price at
     -           45              50              55           Expiration
     -
     -
     -
-5 -
     -
     -
     -
     -
- 10 -
Loss
```

Table 2–1 Sample Table for a Two-Component Option Strategy

Stock Price at Expiration	Option Position #1 Profit/(Loss)	Option Position #2 Profit/(Loss)	Total Strategy Profit/(Loss)
$54			
$53			
$52			
$51			
$50			
$49			

For an option that is sold, subtract the value determined in Step 3 from the selling price. The 75 Put, sold at 4 1/4, with an expiration value of zero, yields a profit of 4 1/4. The same put with an expiration value of 7 will show a loss of 2 3/4.

Profit and loss calculations are easily made and clearly presented if a table such as Table 2–1 is used in conjunction with the grid. The left-most column indicates the range of stock prices which appear on the grid. Tables for simple option strategies contain only one column which indicates the profit or loss of the strategy at each stock price at expiration. Tables for more complicated strategies have columns for the profit or loss of each component of the strategy and a column for the strategy's total profit or loss. Table 2–1 is an example of a table used for a strategy with two components.

Step 5 *Chart the profit or loss.*

Place a dot on the grid above (if a profit) or below (if a loss) the selected stock price at a point even with the profit or loss calculated in Step 4. Figure 2–2 shows the placement of the $4 profit taken from Table 2–2. The 50 Call was purchased for 2 and had an expiration value of 6.

Step 6 *Repeat steps 3, 4 and 5 until the diagram is complete.*

Steps 3, 4 and 5 should be repeated over the range of stock prices on the grid. As dots are placed on the grid, a complete profit and loss diagram will emerge. The dots can be connected and will always form straight lines, although sometimes the lines will have different slopes.

Long and Short Stock Positions

The first diagrams of simple stock positions without any options are included here for two reasons. First, it is always good to start on familiar ground. Second, later in this chapter, stock positions will be combined with option positions to produce more complicated strategies.

Figure 2–3 illustrates the strategy of buying stock at $50. Table 2–3 contains the profit and loss results on a per-share basis. The potential results are straightforward: buying stock will result in a profit if the price rises and a loss if the price falls. The two dots on the line in Figure 2–3 correspond to two rows in Table 2–3, $53 and $46. A $3 profit results if the stock is sold at $53. A $4 loss is realized if the stock is sold at $46. The slope of the line in Figure 2–3 is 1×1—the profit or loss changes by $1 for every $1 change in the stock price.

Figure 2–4 illustrates the strategy of selling stock short at $50. Selling short will result in a profit if the stock price falls and a loss if the price rises.

Figure 2–2 Illustration of Charting a Profit or Loss

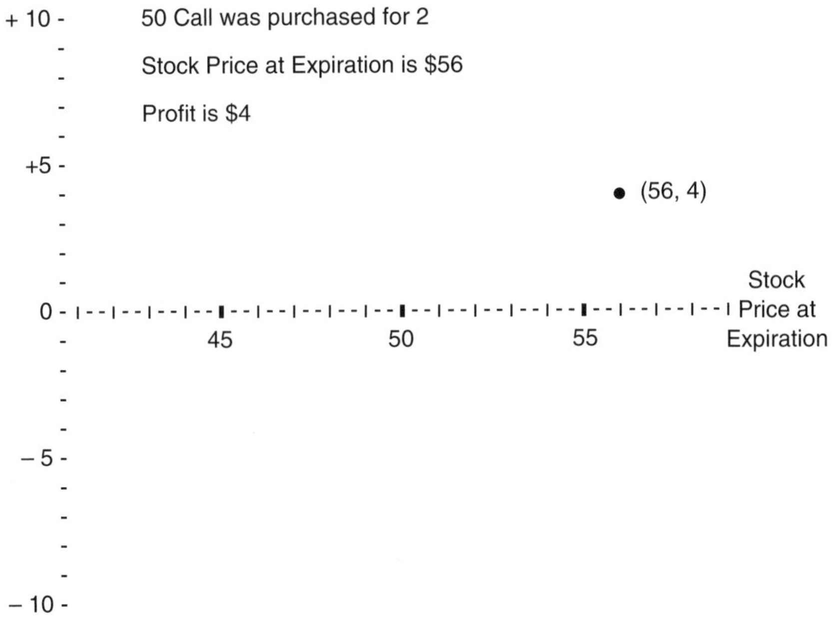

```
+ 10 -         50 Call was purchased for 2
     -
     -         Stock Price at Expiration is $56
     -
     -         Profit is $4
     -
 +5 -
     -                                                  ● (56, 4)
     -
     -
     -                                                          Stock
  0 - |--|--|--|--|--|--|--|--|--|--|--|--|--|--|--|--|--|--| Price at
     -          45             50            55        Expiration
     -
     -
     -
 - 5 -
     -
     -
     -
- 10 -
```

Table 2–2 Illustration of Profit Entered in Table

Stock Price at Expiration	Long 50 Call at 2 Profit/(Loss)
$58	
$57	
$56	+4
$55	
$54	

The line in Figure 2–4 has a –1 × 1 slope—the profit or loss changes by $1 in the opposite direction for every $1 stock price change. Table 2–4 contains the profit and loss results on a per-share basis based on stock prices within the range charted.

Figure 2–3 Long Stock at $50

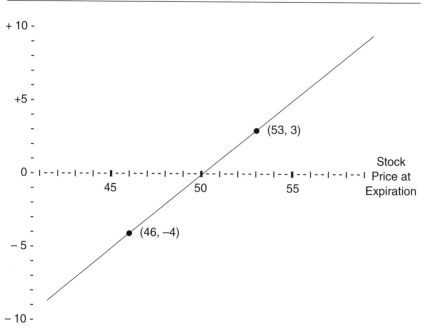

Table 2–3 Long Stock at $50—Profit and Loss Calculations

Stock Price at Expiration	Long Stock at $50 Profit / (Loss)
$55	+5
$54	+4
$53	+3
$52	+2
$51	+1
$50	0
$49	−1
$48	−2
$47	−3
$46	−4
$45	−5
$44	−6

Figure 2–4 Short Stock at $50

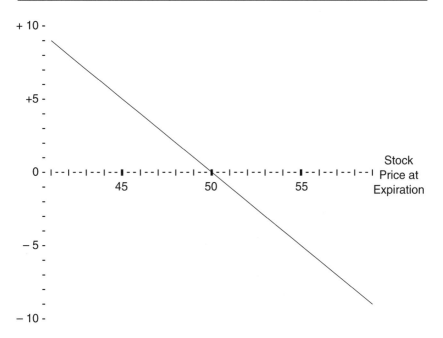

Table 2–4   Short Stock at $50—Profit and Loss Calculations

Stock Price at Expiration	Short Stock at $50 Profit / (Loss)
$55	−5
$54	−4
$53	−3
$52	−2
$51	−1
$50	0
$49	+1
$48	+2
$47	+3
$46	+4
$45	+5
$44	+6

Basic Option Strategies Diagrammed

We are now ready to tackle option strategies. Profit and loss diagrams for four basic option strategies will be presented in detail; then the important price points and strategy characteristics will be discussed. Unless otherwise stated, the stock price will be assumed to be $50 when the option position is established.

Strategy: Long Call

Example: Buy 50 Call at $3

1. Describe the opening transaction completely. Buy a 50 Call at $3.
2. Start a grid. Use the grid shown in Figure 2–1.
3. Select a stock price and calculate the option's value at expiration. With the stock at $50 at expiration, the 50 Call is worth zero.
4. Calculate the profit or loss. Loss of $3 ($0 expiration value minus $3 purchase price = $3 loss).
5. Chart the profit or loss. Figure 2–5A shows a dot indicating a $3 loss at $50.
6. Repeat steps 3, 4 and 5 until the profit and loss diagram is completed. Profit and loss results over a range of stock prices from $44 to $55 are presented in Table 2–5. Figure 2–5B shows a second dot indicating a $2 profit at $55, and Figure 2–5C shows additional dots after profit or loss outcomes are calculated at stock prices of $53, $49 and $48. Figure 2–5D shows the completed profit and loss diagram.

Observations about the Long Call

Break-even point: $53. This is calculated by adding the premium paid for the call to the strike price. In this case $50 + $3 = $53.

Maximum risk: This is limited to $3 (per share). No matter how much the stock price declines, purchasing the 50 Call can only result in losing the premium paid for the call.

Profit potential: This is theoretically unlimited. If the stock price rises dramatically, the option value will rise as well.

Figure 2–5 Long 50 Call at 3

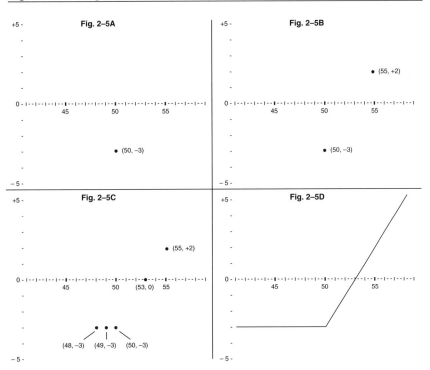

Table 2–5   Long 50 Call at 3—Profit and Loss Calculations

Stock Price at Expiration	Long 50 Call at 3 Profit/(Loss)	Stock Price at Expiration	Long 50 Call at 3 Profit/(Loss)
$55	+2	$49	−3
$54	+1	$48	−3
$53	0	$47	−3
$52	−1	$46	−3
$51	−2	$45	−3
$50	−3	$44	−3

Position created if option is in-the-money: The long call becomes long stock if the stock price is above the strike at expiration. (In expiration profit and loss diagrams, it is assumed all in-the-money long options are exercised.)

Investment trade-off: The positive aspect is that risk is limited to $3 per share. This is positive relative to owning stock, which has a theoretical risk of the stock price falling to $0 and the entire $50 investment being lost. There are two negative aspects: A break-even point of $53 compared to $50 for buying stock, and a limited time period for the call versus a long stock position which will not expire.

Desired price action: Bullish. A profit, at expiration, occurs only if the stock price rises above $53.

Strategy: Short Call

Example: Sell 50 Call at $3

1. Describe the opening transaction completely. Sell a 50 Call at $3.

2. Start a grid. Use the grid shown in Figure 2–1

3. Select a stock price and calculate the option's value at expiration. With the stock at $50 at expiration, the 50 Call is worth zero.

4. Calculate the profit or loss. Profit of $3 ($3 sale price minus $0 expiration value = $3 profit).

5. Chart the profit or loss. Figure 2-6A shows a dot indicating a $3 profit at $50.

6. Repeat steps 3, 4 and 5 until the profit and loss diagram is completed. Profit and loss results over a range of stock prices from $44 to $55 are presented in Table 2–6. Figure 2–6B shows a second dot indicating a $2 loss at $55, and Figure 2–6C shows additional dots after profit or loss outcomes are calculated at stock prices of $53, $49 and $48. Figure 2–6D shows the completed profit and loss diagram.

Observations about the Short Call

Break-even point: $53. This is calculated by adding the premium received for selling the call to the strike price. In this case $50 + $3 = $53.

Maximum risk: Theoretically, the risk is unlimited. As the stock price rises, the value of the 50 Call will rise, and the loss from the short call position will increase correspondingly.

Profit potential: This is limited to $3 per share. Regardless of how much the stock price falls, the option value at expiration can only drop to zero, thereby earning a profit of $3 per share or $300 per option.

Position created if option is in-the-money: The short call becomes short stock if the stock price is above the strike at expiration. (In expiration profit and loss diagrams, it is assumed all in-the-money short options are assigned.)

Investment trade-off: There are two positive aspects: First, the break-even point of $53 is higher than the break-even point of $50 for a short stock position. Second, the option has a limited life and will expire, but a short stock position could, in theory, exist for ever and cause a loss at any time. The negative aspect is that profit potential is limited to $3 per share. This is negative relative to selling stock short, which has the theoretical profit potential of the stock price falling to zero.

Desired price action: Neutral/Bearish. Profit potential in a neutral market is significant, because this aspect of some option strategies cannot be achieved by stocks alone.

Figure 2–6 Short 50 Call at 3

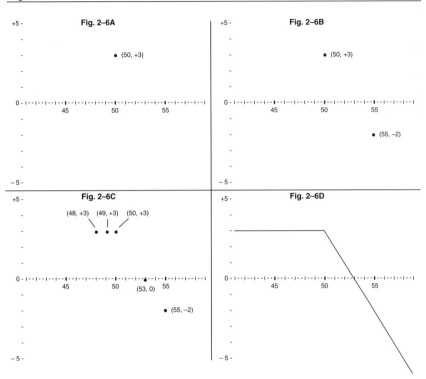

Table 2–6   Short 50 Call at 3—Profit and Loss Calculations

Stock Price at Expiration	Short 50 Call at 3 Profit/(Loss)	Stock Price at Expiration	Short 50 Call at 3 Profit/(Loss)
$55	−2	$49	+3
$54	−1	$48	+3
$53	0	$47	+3
$52	+1	$46	+3
$51	+2	$45	+3
$50	+3	$44	+3

Strategy: Long Put

Example: Buy 50 Put at $2

1. Describe the opening transaction completely. Buy a 50 Put at $2.

2. Start a grid. Use the grid shown in Figure 2–1.

3. Select a stock price and calculate the option's value at expiration. With the stock at $50 at expiration, the 50 Put is worth zero.

4. Calculate the profit or loss. Loss of $2 ($0 expiration value minus $2 purchase price = $2 loss).

5. Chart the profit or loss. Figure 2–7A shows a dot indicating a $2 loss at $50.

6. Repeat steps 3, 4 and 5 until the profit and loss diagram is completed. Profit and loss results over a range of stock prices from $44 to $55 are presented in Table 2–7. Figure 2–7B shows a second dot indicating a $2 profit at $46, and Figure 2–7C shows additional dots after profit or loss outcomes are calculated at stock prices of $53, $49 and $48. Figure 2–7D shows the completed profit and loss diagram.

Observations about the Long Put

Break-even point: $48. This is calculated by subtracting the premium paid for the put from the strike price. In this case $50 – $2 = $48

Maximum risk: This is limited to $2 (per share). No matter how high the stock price rises, purchasing the 50 Put can only lose the premium paid.

Profit potential: Theoretically, this is limited to $48, because the stock price cannot fall below zero.

Position created if option is in-the-money: The long put becomes short stock if the stock price is below the strike at expiration. (In expiration profit and loss diagrams, it is assumed all in-the-money long options are exercised.)

Investment trade-off: The positive aspect is that risk is limited to $2 per share. This is positive relative to shorting stock, which, theoretically, has unlimited risk. There are two negative aspects: a break-even point of $48 compared to $50 for short stock, and a limited time period for the put versus the short stock position which will not expire.

Desired price action: Bearish. A profit at expiration occurs only if the stock declines below $48.

Figure 2–7 Long 50 Put at 2

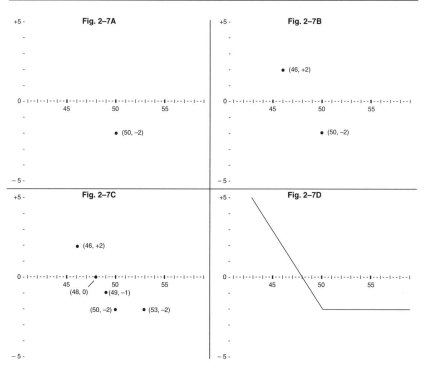

Table 2–7   Long 50 Put at 2—Profit and Loss Calculations

Stock Price at Expiration	Long 50 Put at 2 Profit / (Loss)	Stock Price at Expiration	Long 50 Put at 2 Profit / (Loss)
$55	−2	$49	−1
$54	−2	$48	0
$53	−2	$47	+1
$52	−2	$46	+2
$51	−2	$45	+3
$50	−2	$44	+4

Strategy: Short Put

Example: Sell 50 Put at $2

1. Describe the opening transaction completely. Sell a 50 Put at $2.
2. Start a grid. Use the grid shown in Figure 2–1.
3. Select a stock price and calculate the option's value at expiration. With the stock at $50 at expiration, the 50 Put is worth zero.
4. Calculate the profit or loss. Profit of $2 ($2 sales price minus $0 expiration value = $2 profit).
5. Chart the profit or loss. Figure 2–8A shows a dot indicating a $2 profit at $50.
6. Repeat steps 3, 4 and 5 until the profit and loss diagram is completed. Profit and loss results over a range of stock prices from $44 to $55 are presented in Table 2–8. Figure 2–8B shows a second dot indicating a $2 loss at $46, and Figure 2–8C shows additional dots after profit or loss outcomes are calculated at stock prices of $53, $49 and $48. Figure 2–8D shows the completed profit and loss diagram.

Observations about the Short Put

Break-even point: $48. This is calculated by subtracting the premium for selling the put from the strike price. In this case $50 – $2 = $48.

Maximum risk: Theoretically, the risk is limited to $48, because the stock price cannot fall below zero.

Profit potential: This is limited to $2 per share. Regardless of how much the stock price rises, the option value at expiration can only drop to zero, thereby earning a profit of $2 per share.

Position created if option is in-the-money: The short put becomes long stock if the stock price is below the strike at expiration. (In expiration profit and loss diagrams, it is assumed all short in-the-money options are assigned.)

Investment trade-off: There are two positives: a lower break-even point of $48 (relative to buying stock at $50), and a limited life of the option. The negative aspect is that profit is limited. This is negative relative to buying stock, which has an unlimited profit potential.

Desired price action: Neutral/Bullish. This is the second example of an option strategy which can make money in neutral markets. (The short call was the first example.)

Figure 2–8 Short 50 Put at 2

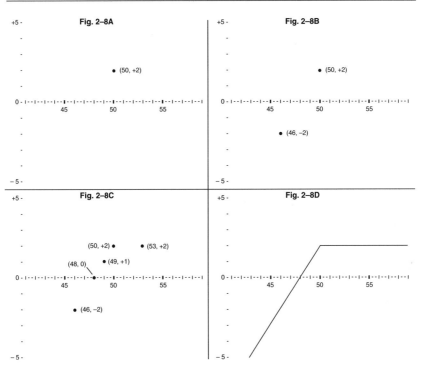

Table 2–8 Short 50 Put at 2—Profit and Loss Calculations

Stock Price at Expiration	Short 50 Put at 2 Profit/(Loss)	Stock Price at Expiration	Short 50 Put at 2 Profit/(Loss)
$55	+2	$49	+1
$54	+2	$48	0
$53	+2	$47	−1
$52	+2	$46	−2
$51	+2	$45	−3
$50	+2	$44	−4

Introduction to Multiple-Part Strategies

The ability to draw profit and loss diagrams of the six basic strategies just covered—long and short stock, long and short call and long and short put—is essential for moving forward. The next step is to combine two basic strategies to create more advanced strategies, thus increasing the number of alternatives and expanding the range of investment objectives which can be achieved.

Two strategies involving puts and calls will be presented first: the long straddle and short straddle. The third and fourth strategies involve stock and options: long stock plus long put, which is known as the protective put strategy, and long stock plus short call, which is known as covered writing. These four strategies will be diagrammed and analyzed in the same manner as the basic strategies just presented.

Strategy: Long Straddle

Example: Buy one 50 Call at $3 *and* buy one 50 Put at $2

1. Describe the opening transaction completely. Buy one 50 Call at $3 and buy one 50 Put at $2.

2. Start a grid. Preparation of a grid for a multiple part strategy is no different from a single-option strategy. Use the grid shown in Figure 2–1.

3. Select a stock price and calculate each option's value at expiration. With the stock price at $50 at expiration, both the 50 Call and the 50 Put are worth zero.

4. Calculate the profit or loss of each option and add the results together. Total loss of $5 (the call: $0 value minus $3 purchase price = $3 loss the put: $0 value minus $2 purchase price = $2 loss total: $3 loss on call plus $2 loss on put = $5 loss)

5. Chart the profit or loss. Figure 2–9A shows a dot indicating a $5 loss at $50.

6. Repeat steps 3, 4 and 5 until the profit and loss diagram is completed. Profit and loss results over a range of stock prices from $44 to $55 are presented in Table 2–9. Figure 2–9B shows a second dot indicating a $2 loss at $47, and Figure 2–9C shows additional dots after profit or loss outcomes are calculated at stock prices of $53, $49 and $48. Figure 2–9D shows the completed profit and loss diagram.

Figure 2–9 Long 50 Straddle at 5

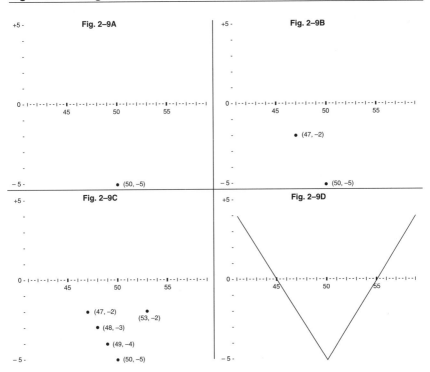

Table 2–9 Long 50 Straddle at 5—Profit and Loss Calculations

Stk Px at Exp	Long 50 Call Profit/ (Loss)	Long 50 Put Profit/ (Loss)	Total Profit/ (Loss)	Stk Px at Exp	Long 50 Call Profit/ (Loss)	Long 50 Put Profit/ (Loss)	Total Profit/ (Loss)
$55	+2	−2	0	$49	−3	−1	−4
$54	+1	−2	−1	$48	−3	0	−3
$53	0	−2	−2	$47	−3	+1	−2
$52	−1	−2	−3	$46	−3	+2	−1
$51	−2	−2	−4	$45	−3	+3	0
$50	−3	−2	−5	$44	−3	+4	+1

Observations about the Long Straddle

Break-even points: $45 *and* $55. This is the first example in which there are two break-even points. In this case the upper break-even point is equal to the strike price plus the total premiums paid; the lower break-even point is equal to the strike price minus the total premiums paid.

Maximum risk: Risk is limited to $5, the total premium paid. If the stock price exactly equals the strike price at expiration, both options will expire worthless.

Profit potential: This is unlimited. Profit is realized at expiration if the stock price is above $55 or below $45.

Position created if the option is in-the-money: Either long stock or short stock, depending on the stock price at expiration. If the stock price is above the strike price, the long call is exercised, and the position becomes long stock; if below the strike, the long put is exercised and the position becomes short stock.

Investment trade-off: The positive aspect is that profit can be realized with a stock price move in either direction; this is positive relative to purchasing only a call or a put. There are two negative aspects: the cost is two premiums, and the break-even points are further from the strike than with a single option strategy.

Desired price action: Large movement either up or down. This is called a "high volatility" strategy, because a large move is desired, but direction is not important.

Strategy: Short Straddle

Example: Sell one 50 Call at $3 *and* sell one 50 Put at $2

1. Describe the opening transaction completely. Sell one 50 Call at $3 and sell one 50 Put at $2.
2. Start a grid. Use the grid shown in Figure 2–1.
3. Select a stock price and calculate each option's value at expiration. With the stock price at $50 at expiration, both the 50 Call and the 50 Put are worth zero.
4. Calculate the profit or loss of each option and add the results together. Total profit of $5 (the call: $3 sales price minus $0 value = $3 profit the put: $2 sales price minus $0 value = $2 profit total: $3 profit on call plus $2 profit on put = $5 profit)
5. Chart the profit or loss. Figure 2–10A shows a dot indicating a $5 profit at $50.
6. Repeat steps 3, 4 and 5 until the profit and loss diagram is completed. Profit and loss results over a range of stock prices from $44 to $55 are presented in Table 2–10. Figure 2–10B shows a second dot indicating a $1 profit at $46, and Figure 2–10C shows additional dots after profit or loss outcomes are calculated at stock prices of $53, $49 and $48. Figure 2–10D shows the completed profit and loss diagram.

Observations about the Short Straddle

Break-even points: $45 and $55. The upper break-even point is equal to the strike price plus the total premiums received; the lower break-even point is equal to the strike price minus the total premiums.

Maximum risk: Risk is unlimited. A loss occurs at expiration if the stock price is above $55 or below $45.

Profit potential: This is limited to $5, the total premiums received.

Position created if option is in-the-money: Either long or short stock, depending on the stock price at expiration. If the stock price is below the strike price, the short put is assigned, and the position becomes long stock; if above the strike, the short call is assigned, and the position becomes short stock.

Investment trade-off: There are two positive aspects: the amount received is two premiums and the break-even points are further from the strike than with a single option strategy. The negative aspect is a loss which can be realized with a large move in either direction.

Desired price action: No movement. This is called a "low volatility" strategy, because a large move either up or down could cause a loss.

Figure 2–10 Short 50 Straddle at 5

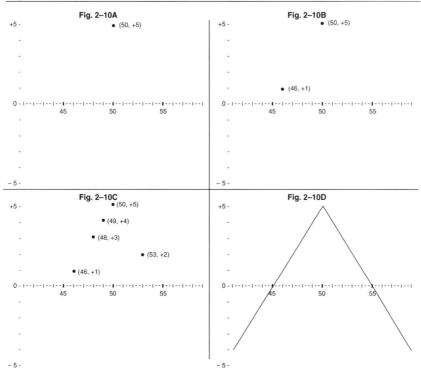

Table 2–10   Short 50 Straddle at 5—Profit and Loss Calculations

Stk Px at Exp	Short 50 Call Profit/ (Loss)	Short 50 Put Profit/ (Loss)	Total Profit/ (Loss)	Stk Px at Exp	Short 50 Call Profit/ (Loss)	Short 50 Put Profit/ (Loss)	Total Profit/ (Loss)
$55	−2	+2	0	$49	+3	+1	+4
$54	−1	+2	+1	$48	+3	0	+3
$53	0	+2	+2	$47	+3	−1	+2
$52	+1	+2	+3	$46	+3	−2	+1
$51	+2	+2	+4	$45	+3	−3	0
$50	+3	+2	+5	$44	+3	−4	−1

Strategy: Long Stock Plus Long Put (the Protective Put)

Example: Buy Stock at $50 *and* Buy 50 Put at $2

1. Describe the opening transaction completely. Buy stock at $50 and buy one 50 Put at $2.

2. Start a grid. Use the grid shown in Figure 2–1.

3. Select a stock price and calculate each component's value at expiration. With the stock price at $50 at expiration, the stock is worth $50 and the 50 Put is worth zero.

4. Calculate the profit or loss of each component and add the results together.
   Total loss of $2 (the stock: $50 value minus $50 purchase price = $0
   the put: $0 value minus $2 purchase price = $2 loss
   total: $0 result on stock plus $2 loss on put = $2 loss)

5. Chart the profit or loss. Figure 2–11A shows a dot indicating a $2 loss at $50.

6. Repeat steps 3, 4 and 5 until the profit and loss diagram is completed. Profit and loss results over a range of stock prices from $44 to $55 are presented in Table 2–11. Figure 2–11B shows a second dot indicating a $1 profit at $53, and Figure 2–11C shows additional dots after profit or loss outcomes are calculated at stock prices of $54, $49 and $48. Figure 2–11D shows the completed profit and loss diagram.

Observations about the Protective Put

Break-even point: $52. This is calculated by adding the premium paid for the put to the purchase price of the stock. In this case: $50 + $2 = $52.

Maximum risk: $2 per share. The most that can be lost in this example is the premium paid for the put. If the stock price is at or below the strike price, $50 in this example, the put is exercised and the stock is sold. The result is breaking even on the stock and a loss of $2 on the put.

Profit potential: This is unlimited. Profit is realized, at expiration, if the stock price is above $52.

Position created if option is in-the-money: No position. If the stock price is below the strike price at expiration, the put is exercised and the stock is sold.

Figure 2–11 Long Stock at $50 and Long 50 Put at 2

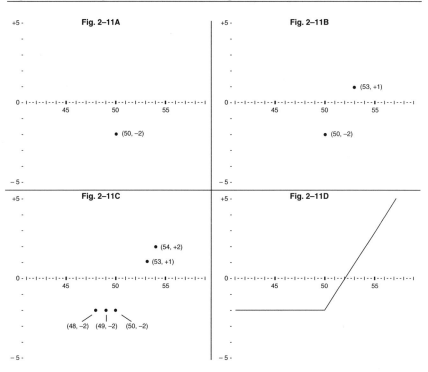

Table 2–11 Long Stock at $50 and Long 50 Put at 2
Profit and Loss Calculations

Stk Px at Exp	Long Stock Profit/ (Loss)	Long 50 Put Profit/ (Loss)	Total Profit/ (Loss)	Stk Px at Exp	Long Stock Profit/ (Loss)	Long 50 Put Profit/ (Loss)	Total Profit/ (Loss)
$55	+5	−2	+3	$49	−1	−1	−2
$54	+4	−2	+2	$48	−2	0	−2
$53	+3	−2	+1	$47	−3	+1	−2
$52	+2	−2	0	$46	−4	+2	−2
$51	+1	−2	−1	$45	−5	+3	−2
$50	0	−2	−2	$44	−6	+4	−2

Investment trade-off: The positive aspect is that risk is limited to $2 per share. This is positive relative to owning stock outright which has the theoretical risk of the stock price falling to zero. There are two negative aspects: a break-even point of $52 compared to $50 for the long stock, and a limited time period for the protection provided by the put.

Desired price action: Bullish. This strategy profits if the stock price rises above $52 at expiration.

Strategy: Long Stock Plus Short Call (the Covered Write)

Example: Buy Stock at $50 *and* sell 50 Call at $3

1. Describe the opening transaction completely. Buy stock at $50 and sell one 50 Call at $3.

2. Start a grid. Use the grid shown in Figure 2–1.

3. Select a stock price and calculate each component's value at expiration. With the stock at $50 at expiration, the stock is worth $50 and the 50 Call is worth zero.

4. Calculate the profit or loss of each component and add the results together.
Total profit of $3 (the stock: $50 value minus $50 purchase price = $0
the call: $3 sales price minus zero value = $3 profit
total: $0 result on stock plus $3 profit on call = $3 profit)

5. Chart the profit or loss. Figure 2–12A shows a dot indicating a $3 profit at $50

6. Repeat steps 3, 4 and 5 until the profit and loss diagram is completed. Profit and loss results over a range of stock prices from $44 to $55 are presented in Table 2–12. Figure 2–12B shows a second dot indicating a $1 profit at $48, and Figure 2–12C shows additional dots after profit or loss outcomes are calculated at stock prices of $53, $49, and $46. Figure 2–12D shows the completed profit and loss diagram.

Observations about the Covered Write

Break-even point: $47. This is calculated by subtracting the premium received for selling the call from the purchase price of the stock. In this case: $50 − $3 = $47.

Maximum risk: The risk is limited to $47, because the stock price cannot fall below zero.

Profit potential: This is limited to $3. If the stock price is above the strike price at expiration, the short call will be assigned and the stock sold. The maximum profit potential of covered writing is equal to the difference between the purchase price of the stock and the strike price of the call plus the call premium.

Figure 2–12 Long Stock at $50 and Short 50 Call at 3

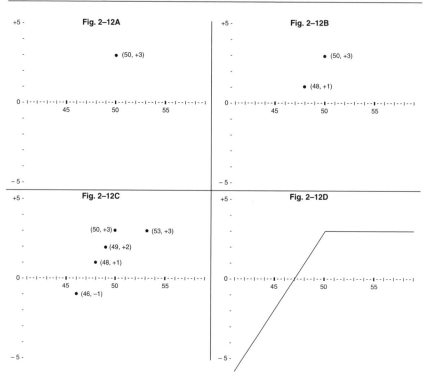

Table 2–12   Long Stock at $50 and Short 50 Call at 3
Profit and Loss Calculations

Stk Px at Exp	Long Stock Profit/ (Loss)	Short 50 Call Profit/ (Loss)	Total Profit/ (Loss)	Stk Px at Exp	Long Stock Profit/ (Loss)	Short 50 Call Profit/ (Loss)	Total Profit/ (Loss)
$55	+5	−2	+3	$49	−1	+3	+2
$54	+4	−1	+3	$48	−2	+3	+1
$53	+3	0	+3	$47	−3	+3	0
$52	+2	+1	+3	$46	−4	+3	−1
$51	+1	+2	+3	$45	−5	+3	−2
$50	0	+3	+3	$44	−6	+3	−3

Position created if option is in-the-money: No position. If the stock price is above the strike price at expiration, the short call will be assigned and the stock sold.

Investment trade-off: There are two positive aspects: a lower break-even price of $47 relative to long stock at $50, and a limited time period for the short call. The negative aspect is that profit potential is limited to $3 per share compared to owning stock outright which has an unlimited profit potential.

Desired price action: Neutral/bullish. This strategy profits if the stock price remains above $47.

Summary

The ability to draw expiration profit and loss diagrams is an important skill that enables the investor to understand the potential profits and risks of investing and trading with options. These diagrams are created by following a six-step process: (1) describing the opening transaction completely, (2) starting a grid, (3) selecting a stock price and calculating the value of each option at expiration, (4) calculating the profit or loss, (5) placing a dot on the grid above or below the selected stock price which corresponds to the profit or loss and, finally, (6) repeating steps 3, 4 and 5 over a range of stock prices until the profit and loss diagram is completed. The basic strategies are long and short stock, long and short call, and long and short put. These basic strategies can be combined to form more complicated strategies.

Once a profit and loss diagram has been completed, an investor should make these observations about the strategy: the break-even point at expiration, the maximum risk of the strategy which may be limited or unlimited, the profit potential which also may be limited or unlimited, the stock position created if the option is in-the-money at expiration, and, finally, the investment trade-off the strategy provides. The concept of a trade-off is that there is some relatively positive aspect and some other relatively negative aspect. Understanding trade-offs will lead to strategy comparisons and aid in the investment decision-making process.

Three

Why Options Have Value

Option Prices Are Related to Stock Prices

Because option prices are related to stock prices, this chapter will introduce some important concepts about stock prices before discussing option prices. Stock prices fluctuate, and thereby affect option prices. Consider an extremely simplified scenario in which a stock, currently trading at $50, has a 50% chance of rising to $55 and a 50% chance of falling to $45. Also, assume interest rates to be zero so that time becomes unimportant. Given these assumptions, what is the "expected stock price" and what is the "expected value" of the 50 Call option? This situation is depicted in Figure 3–1.

The expected stock price calculation is easy for most people. The "expected stock price" is the average of the two possible outcomes, which is $50. As presented in Figure 3–2, this result is calculated in two steps. First, the probability of each outcome is multiplied by the value of each outcome to arrive at an "expected value of each outcome." Second, the individual expected outcomes are added together to get the "total expected value" or, in this case, the "expected stock price."

Figure 3–1 Simplified Range of Outcomes

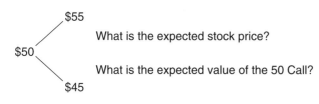

$55

What is the expected stock price?

$50

What is the expected value of the 50 Call?

$45

Figure 3–2 Expected Values

	Expected Stock Price	Expected Value of 50 Call
$55	.50 × 55 = 27.50	.50 × 5 = 2.50
$50		
$45	.50 × 45 = 22.50	.50 × 0 = 0
	= 50.00	= 2.50

The expected option value is calculated in a similar manner, but the result may be surprising to some readers. If the stock price rises to $55, the 50 Call will have a value of $5. If the stock falls to $45, the 50 Call will expire worthless and have a value of zero. Therefore, the 50 Call has a 50% chance of being worth $5 and a 50% chance of being worth zero. Consequently, as shown in Figure 3–2, the "expected value" of the 50 Call, given the above simplified assumptions, is $2.50 (.50 × 5.00 + .50 × 0).

The process just explained is similar to what insurance actuaries go through to determine the premium of an insurance policy. In its simplest form, if there were a 1% chance that any house might burn down, the insurance company would charge an annual insurance premium of 1% of value to all home owners—plus a mark-up to cover expenses and a profit margin. In fact, options on stocks are just like insurance policies! Consider the components that comprise an insurance policy premium: asset value, deductible, time, interest rates and risk.

The value of the insured asset directly affects the price of an insurance policy. All things being equal, the more expensive the asset being insured, the higher the premium. The amount of the deductible, however, inversely affects the policy premium; the larger the deductible, the lower the premium. Time affects insurance premiums directly: the longer the time, the greater the cost. Interest rates are a factor, because insurance companies invest the premiums received. In theory, premiums will decrease if interest rates rise, because the increased income will be returned to policy holders in the form of lower insurance rates. Interest rates, therefore, affect insurance premiums inversely. The last factor affecting insurance premiums is risk. Risk has a direct impact on insurance premiums: the higher the risk, the higher the premium.

The components of an option's value correspond directly to the factors which determine insurance premiums, and Table 3–1 summarizes the analogy between insurance premiums and option prices.

Stock Price (Asset Value) and Strike Price (Deductible)

Stock price corresponds to asset value. All things being equal, the more expensive an asset, the more expensive it is to insure. Similarly, the higher a stock's price, the higher the price of an option on that stock.

An option's strike price corresponds to the deductible of an insurance policy. Insurance policies with small or no deductibles are more expensive than policies with larger deductibles. An at-the-money option is like an insurance policy with

Options Are Like Insurance Policies

no deductible. An option with an out-of-the-money strike is like an insurance policy with a deductible: the first portion of loss is born by the insured party (in this case, the investor). When a loss exceeds the deductible, the insurance policy kicks in. In the case of options, the "coverage" or "protection" is the option's intrinsic value which increases as the stock price moves beyond the option's strike price.

Time (Time)

Time has a direct impact on option prices just as it has on insurance policies: the longer the period to expiration, the higher the option value.

Table 3–1 Components of Price—Options Compared to Insurance Policies

Insurance Policy	Option
Asset Value	Stock Price
Deductible	Strike Price
Time	Time
Interest Rates	Interest Rates and Dividends
Risk	Volatility
= Premium	= Premium

Interest Rates and Dividends (Interest Rates)

Interest rates are a factor in option prices because of the time value of money. If call options, for example, could be purchased below the value of interest on the cost of the underlying stock, it would be advantageous for stock investors to buy T-Bills and calls rather than the underlying stock. Consequently, the options market adjusts option prices as interest rates change.

Dividends also affect option prices, but the effect is somewhat difficult for option beginners to grasp. Dividends are, in essence, like an interest payment paid by the stock. Owning a stock which pays a dividend is more attractive than owning a stock which does not, all things being equal. Therefore, call options on dividend-paying stocks are less valuable than calls on non-dividend-paying stocks, all things being equal. The relationship is that as dividends rise, call values fall and put values rise. This concept will be easier to visualize when the computer program OP-EVAL™ is explained in Chapter 16.

Volatility (Risk)

"Risk" in the options market is called volatility. In the normal course of trading, stock prices fluctuate. The larger the price fluctuations, the riskier the stock, and, therefore, the more expensive the options on that particular stock.

Volatility is an important concept that deserves additional explanation. Fluctuation of stock prices can be measured in two ways: direction of price change and size of price change. Volatility is a measure of the size of price changes without concern about direction. In other words, volatility is concerned with how much prices move, not whether they move up or down. In mathematical formulas which calculate option prices, volatility is expressed as a percentage; e.g., 15% or 20%. This percentage is the annualized standard deviation of a stock's daily price movements. Although this definition is intimidating to non-mathematicians, volatility can be understood intuitively. The goal for most investors regarding volatility is to develop a subjective understanding and to incorporate that understanding into investment decisions.

Changing the Volatility

At this point it is useful to revisit the simple two-outcome scenario presented in Figures 3–1 and 3–2. Now, however, we will change the possible out-

Figure 3–3 Expected Values—Expanded Range

	Expected Stock Price	Expected Value of 50 Call
$60	.50 × 60 = 30.00	.50 × 10 = 5.00
$50		
$40	.50 × 40 = 20.00	.50 × 0 = 0
	= 50.00	= 5.00

comes to $60 and $40 and recalculate the expected stock price and the expected 50 Call value. This is done in Figure 3–3.

Figure 3–3 demonstrates that a wider range of outcomes increases the 50 Call value, but does not change the expected stock price. The wider range of outcomes is, in its simplest form, an increase in volatility. The securities markets, of course, are more sophisticated than this. The range of future stock prices is infinite, but the range can be analyzed with a statistical tool commonly known as the "bell-shaped curve." Option volatilities are stated in percentage terms: 10%, 20%, etc. These numbers describe the shape of a bell-shaped curve. Without delving into a detailed mathematical discussion, a lower volatility number means less movement which, in statistical terms, means most outcomes are expected relatively close to the mean. A higher volatility number suggests more outcomes occurring in a relatively wider range around the mean.

Although this is not a perfect analogy, the volatility component of an option's price is sometimes compared to the price/earnings ratio (p/e) of a stock. Why do some stocks trade at high p/e's and others at low p/e's? The typical answer is: "the market thinks high p/e stocks have higher growth potential." Why, then, do p/e's change? "Because the market changes its mind." In the options market, the volatility component of an option's price is the "market's opinion" about the likelihood of a big move—either up or down. When an option price has a low volatility component, this is said to reflect the "market's opinion" that a big move is relatively unlikely. When the volatility component is high, a big move, in the "market's opinion," is more likely.

But does the "market's opinion," as reflected in the volatility component of an option's price, guarantee a small movement or a big movement? Absolutely not! Not only can the market "change its opinion," the market can also be wrong! Referring to the p/e analogy, the market-determined p/e of a stock does not necessarily reflect accurately a company's earnings growth. Similarly, the volatility component of an option price does not indicate, definitively, whether the underlying stock will or will not make a large price change.

What Do Puts Insure?

Volatility is a subject that takes time to understand and feel comfortable with. Newcomers to options should be patient, and they should remind themselves not to be intimidated by more experienced options traders who understand it. By identifying what is not understood and by asking questions, anyone can grasp the concept of volatility.

Insurance Analogy Concluded

This chapter has compared the components of an option's value to the factors that determine insurance premiums. To conclude this insurance analogy, one might reasonably ask, "If options are insurance policies, what do they insure?" For put options, the answer is obvious: puts insure stock value. An obvious analogy is between buying a put option on a stock you own and buying an insurance policy on the house you own.

But what do calls insure? The answer is: cash. Call options insure cash deposits against missing a market rally. When investment assets are in Treasury bills (or other cash-like instruments) there is no risk of loss of capital. Rather, there is "risk" of missing a market rally. The investor who buys calls with a small portion of total capital and invests the rest in Treasury bills will participate in a price rise beyond the break-even point. The potential loss of the amount invested in calls is a limited amount of the total principal compared to having the total principal invested in the market.

When options are seen in this context—as insurance-like instruments—investors begin to think differently about options. Suddenly there are new horizons to explore. Of course, in the housing market, individuals can only buy insurance; whereas, in the stock market, individuals can just as easily sell insurance (sell options) or buy insurance (buy options). For individual stock investors, there are valid reasons for buying insurance and selling insurance. Which strategy is chosen depends on market opinion, investment objectives and risk tolerance. These issues will be discussed throughout the chapters that explain investment-oriented strategies.

What Do Calls Insure?

Table 3–2 How Changes in Components Effect Option Prices

Component	Effect on Call Price	Effect on Put Price
Stock Price	Direct	Inverse
Strike Price	Inverse	Direct
Time	Direct	Direct
Interest Rates	Direct	Inverse
Dividends	Inverse	Direct
Volatility	Direct	Direct

Direct effect means	as the component increases, and other factors remain unchanged, the option price will also increase.
Inverse effect means	as the component increases, and other factors remain unchanged, the option price will decrease.

Option Price Components Summarized

Table 3–2 lists the components of an option's price and summarizes how changes in the individual components change that price. Although this subject will be covered in greater depth in Chapter 4, How Option Prices Change, and in Chapter 16, which explains the computer program, at this point it is sufficient to know the conceptual relationships.

Summary

Option values can best be understood when compared to insurance: when there is a statistical possibility of an event occurring, the theoretical value of an insurance policy is the expected value of that event occurring. The components of option values directly correspond to the components of insurance premiums. For options, the stock price corresponds to the asset value in insurance. The option strike price corresponds to the deductible component in insurance—an at-the-money option is like a no-deductible policy; an out-of-the-money option is like a policy with a deductible. Time is a component of price for both options and insurance. Interest rates are a component of insurance premiums, and interest rates adjusted for dividends are a component of option prices. Finally, the factor called "risk" in insurance is called volatility in options.

Volatility is a measure of movement without regard to direction. While it is a statistical concept not easily grasped by non-mathematicians, volatility can be understood intuitively and incorporated, subjectively, into investment decisions.

When seen as insurance-like products, options open a new range of alternatives to investors. As will be explained in coming chapters, there are valid investment reasons for buying and selling insurance (options) on stocks.

Four

Option Price Behavior

I
nvestors, as opposed to traders, do not need to dwell on the information discussed in this chapter, because investment-oriented strategies, as will be explained in Section 2, generally focus on strategy results on the expiration date. Option price behavior prior to expiration is the realm of the short-term trader. Understanding how option prices change and developing realistic expectations about short-term option price behavior are important when trading options.

The value of an option, as explained in Chapter 3, depends on six factors: stock price, strike price, time to expiration, interest rates, dividends and volatility. In Chapter 3 these factors were explained, conceptually, in a static environment; but, of course in reality, these factors operate in a dynamic environment. This chapter will first discuss the effect of a change in each component, assuming others remain constant. Special emphasis will be placed on volatility, because it is such an important topic in any discussion of option price behavior. Subsequently, the discussion will cover option price changes when more than one component changes.

The following discussion gets fairly technical, and, again, it is not necessary for investors to comprehend every detail of this chapter. Short-term traders, however, do need to master this material. Newcomers to options may prefer to skim this chapter and come back to it when they are more familiar with the basic investing strategies presented in Section 2.

The Effect of Stock Price Change

With regard to the effect of stock price change, the general question is: if the underlying stock price rises by one unit and other factors remain constant, by how much will the theoretical value of an option change? To take a specific example, assume a stock price of $50, ninety days to expiration and a 50 Call theoretical value of 3.26. If the stock price is raised by $1, and the other factors are unchanged, the theoretical value of the 50 Call will change by 0.59 to 3.85. Table 4–1 illustrates option price changes and some other important aspects of option price behavior.

Table 4–1 contains theoretical values of a 50 Call at various stock prices and various days prior to expiration. The theoretical values were calculated using a mathematical formula known as the Black-Scholes Option Pricing Model. This formula involves advanced calculus; an explanation of the mathematics is beyond the scope of this book. Option values are presented in decimals rounded to the second place rather than in eighths and quarters for the sake of clarity in explaining several concepts. Table 4–1 contains eleven rows and seven columns. The rows indicate different stock prices; the columns indicate different days prior to expiration.

By looking up and down the columns and across the rows in Table 4–1, one observes how changes in stock price or time to expiration or both cause changes in the option's theoretical value. For example, with a stock price of $48 and 75 days to expiration (row 4, column 2), the theoretical value of the 50 Call is 1.96. If the stock price is raised by $1, the call value rises to 2.43. If the stock price is decreased by $1, the call value decreases to 1.55. In both cases, the call price moves less than the stock price. Looking anywhere on the table, this is always true. An option's theoretical value always changes less than one-for-one with a change in the stock price.

Table 4–1 Theoretical Values of 50 Call at Various Stock Prices and Days to Expiration (Interest Rates, 5%; Volatility, 30%; No Dividends)

	Stock Price	Col. 1 90 Days	Col. 2 75 Days	Col. 3 60 Days	Col. 4 45 Days	Col. 5 30 Days	Col. 6 15 Days	Col. 7 0 Days
Row 11	55	6.67	6.39	6.10	5.79	5.48	5.17	5.00
Row 10	54	5.90	5.61	5.30	4.97	4.61	4.24	4.00
Row 9	53	5.17	4.87	4.55	4.20	3.81	3.36	3.00
Row 8	52	4.48	4.18	3.85	3.48	3.06	2.56	2.00
Row 7	51	3.85	3.53	3.20	2.83	2.39	1.85	1.00
Row 6	50	3.26	2.95	2.62	2.25	1.82	1.26	0.00
Row 5	49	2.72	2.43	2.10	1.74	1.32	0.80	0.00
Row 4	48	2.24	1.96	1.65	1.31	0.93	0.47	0.00
Row 3	47	1.82	1.55	1.27	0.96	0.62	0.25	0.00
Row 2	46	1.45	1.20	0.95	0.68	0.40	0.12	0.00
Row 1	45	1.13	0.91	0.69	0.46	0.24	0.04	0.00

Furthermore, the ratio of option value change to stock price change varies. For example, when the stock price rises by $1 from $47 to $48 at 45 days, the call rises from 0.96 to 1.31 or approximately 35% of the stock price change. In another situation, when the stock rises from $52 to $53 at 60 days, the call rises from 3.85 to 4.55 or approximately 70% of the stock price change.

Figure 4–1 is a graph showing call option behavior relative to stock price behavior assuming ninety days to expiration. The option values in Figure 4–1 are taken from column 1 in Table 4–1. Figure 4-1 shows graphically that option prices change less than unit for unit with price changes in the underlying stock.

Delta

The ratio of option price change to stock price change is an important aspect of option price behavior, and it is referred to as the "delta" of an option. Specifically, the *delta* is the change in option theoretical value given a one unit change in price of the underlying stock assuming all other factors remain constant. Table 4–2 shows the delta of the 50 Call at different stock prices and at different times to expiration. The deltas in Table 4–2 correspond to the option values in Table 4–1. For example, the delta of .56 in col-

Figure 4–1 Theoretical Value of 50 Call 90 Days to Expiration

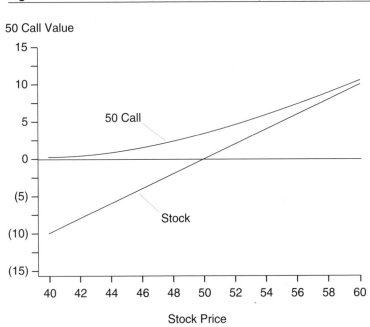

50 Call Value

**Table 4–2   Delta of 50 Call at Various Stock Prices and Days to Expiration
(Interest Rates, 5%; Volatility, 30%; No Dividends)**

	Stock Price	Col. 1 90 Days	Col. 2 75 Days	Col. 3 60 Days	Col. 4 45 Days	Col. 5 30 Days	Col. 6 15 Days	Col. 7 0 Days
Row 11	55	0.79	0.80	0.82	0.84	0.88	0.95	1.00
Row 10	54	0.75	0.76	0.78	0.80	0.84	0.94	1.00
Row 9	53	0.71	0.72	0.73	0.75	0.78	0.85	1.00
Row 8	52	0.66	0.67	0.67	0.68	0.71	0.76	1.00
Row 7	51	0.61	0.61	0.61	0.62	0.63	0.65	1.00
Row 6	50	0.56	0.56	0.55	0.54	0.53	0.52	0.00
Row 5	49	0.51	0.50	0.48	0.47	0.44	0.39	0.00
Row 4	48	0.45	0.44	0.42	0.39	0.35	0.27	0.00
Row 3	47	0.40	0.38	0.35	0.32	0.26	0.17	0.00
Row 2	46	0.34	0.32	0.29	0.25	0.19	0.09	0.00
Row 1	45	0.29	0.26	0.23	0.19	0.13	0.05	0.00

umn 1, row 6 of Table 4–2 (90 days, stock price $50) corresponds to the option price of 3.26 in the same square in Table 4–1. This means the 50 Call has a theoretical value of 3.26 and a delta of .56 given the stated inputs (stock price, $50; strike, $50; days to expiration, 90; interest rates, 5%; volatility, 30%; no dividends). The term "one unit" is used in the definition of delta rather than $1, because delta is the first derivative, or slope, of the curve in Figure 4–1 at one point. At each point on the curve the slope changes. Consequently, delta is dynamic; delta changes as the stock price changes. For example, with the delta of .56, if the underlying stock price rises by $1, the theoretical value of the 50 Call will increase from 3.26 to 3.85, which is slightly more than .56. The delta is an instantaneous measure of the rate of change in theoretical value, and delta changes as the price of the underlying changes.

Delta is used to gauge the "stock equivalency" of an option. One round lot of stock, 100 shares, is the benchmark. An option with a .56 delta will have a change in theoretical value approximately equivalent to 56 shares, all other factors being held constant, for a small price change in the stock. This is what happened in the example just cited. The stock price rose by $1 and the 50 Call rose by approximately .56—actually, .59. The 100 shares of stock rose $100 in value, and the 50 Call rose approximately $56 in value.

Call deltas are positive and range from 0.00 to +1.00. Out-of-the-money call options have deltas between 0.00 and +0.50; at-the-money call options have deltas of approximately +0.50; and in-the-money call options have deltas between +0.50 and +1.00. Put deltas are negative and range from −1.00 to 0.00. This means the delta of a put approaches −1.00 as a stock price falls. Out-of-the-money puts have deltas between −.50 and 0.00; at-the-money puts have deltas of approximately −.50; and in-the-money puts have deltas between −1.00 and −0.50. Tables 4–3 and 4–4 show theoretical values and deltas, respectively, of a 50 Put option at various stock prices and days to expiration.

Call Values Relative to Put Values

Many investors are confused about the relationship of call and put values. Newcomers to options may believe that calls and puts with the same strike and expiration should have the same price if the stock price equals the strike price. Actually, this is not true. Assuming no dividends, call prices will be greater than put prices because of an interest component. Evidence of this appears from a comparison of Tables 4–1 and 4–3. Row 6 in both tables

Table 4–3 Theoretical Values of 50 Put at Various Stock Prices and Days to Expiration (Interest Rates, 5%; Volatility, 30%; No Dividends)

		Col. 1	Col. 2	Col. 3	Col. 4	Col. 5	Col. 6	Col. 7
	Stock Price	90 Days	75 Days	60 Days	45 Days	30 Days	15 Days	0 Days
Row 11	55	1.07	0.89	0.70	0.49	0.28	0.07	0.00
Row 10	54	1.30	1.11	0.90	0.67	0.41	0.14	0.00
Row 9	53	1.57	1.37	1.15	0.90	0.61	0.26	0.00
Row 8	52	1.89	1.68	1.45	1.18	0.86	0.46	0.00
Row 7	51	2.25	2.04	1.80	1.53	1.20	0.75	0.00
Row 6	50	2.66	2.46	2.22	1.95	1.61	1.16	0.00
Row 5	49	3.13	2.93	2.70	2.44	2.12	1.70	1.00
Row 4	48	3.65	3.46	3.25	3.01	2.73	2.37	2.00
Row 3	47	4.22	4.05	3.87	3.66	3.42	3.15	3.00
Row 2	46	4.85	4.71	4.55	4.38	4.20	4.02	4.00
Row 1	45	5.54	5.42	5.29	5.16	5.04	5.00	5.00

**Table 4–4 Delta of 50 Put at Various Stock Prices and Days to Expiration
(Interest Rates, 5%; Volatility, 30%; No Dividends)**

		Col. 1	Col. 2	Col. 3	Col. 4	Col. 5	Col. 6	Col. 7
	Stock Price	90 Days	75 Days	60 Days	45 Days	30 Days	15 Days	0 Days
Row 11	55	−0.21	−0.20	−0.18	−0.16	−0.12	−0.05	0.00
Row 10	54	−0.25	−0.24	−0.22	−0.20	−0.16	−0.09	0.00
Row 9	53	−0.29	−0.28	−0.27	−0.25	−0.22	−0.15	0.00
Row 8	52	−0.34	−0.33	−0.33	−0.32	−0.29	−0.24	0.00
Row 7	51	−0.39	−0.39	−0.39	−0.38	−0.37	−0.35	0.00
Row 6	50	−0.44	−0.44	−0.45	−0.46	−0.46	−0.48	0.00
Row 5	49	−0.49	−0.50	−0.52	−0.53	−0.56	−0.61	−1.00
Row 4	48	−0.55	−0.56	−0.58	−0.61	−0.65	−0.73	−1.00
Row 3	47	−0.60	−0.62	−0.65	−0.68	−0.74	−0.83	−1.00
Row 2	46	−0.66	−0.68	−0.71	−0.75	−0.81	−0.91	−1.00
Row 1	45	−0.71	−0.74	−0.77	−0.81	−0.87	−0.95	−1.00

shows option values with the stock price at $50. At 90 days (column 1), the 50 Call has a value of $3.26 and the 50 Put has a value of $2.66. The call value is also greater than the put value in every square of row 6. The difference is attributed to an interest factor which is part of the call price, but which is not part of the put price.

The general concept of why call prices are greater than put prices is explained by a relationship known as put-call parity. It is beyond the scope of this book to explain this concept in depth, but put-call parity states that stock prices, call prices and put prices must have a certain relationship with each other or there will be arbitrage opportunities for professional traders to make nearly riskless profits. In fact, one strategy employed by professional floor traders is to look for "market inefficiencies"—where prices are out of line with each other—and take advantage of the arbitrage opportunity. Because of the fierce competition between professional traders, such arbitrage opportunities exist for only very short periods of time; and the "inefficiency" amounts to 1/8th or 1/16th of a point. For readers interested in exploring put-call parity in depth, books by Sheldon Natenberg and The Options Institute cover this topic very well.

The Relationship of Call Deltas and Put Deltas

Although call deltas are positive numbers and put deltas negative, one might suspect that, all other things being equal, the absolute value of call and put deltas would be equal. This also is not true. A comparison of Tables 4–2 and 4–4 reveal that the absolute value of call and put deltas, when added together, total 1.00. This phenomenon is another product of the put-call parity relationship. It is important for non-professional traders to know about this difference, because different deltas mean different price behavior. Understanding option price behavior and having realistic expectations about it are key elements of trading options.

An Explanation of Delta

Although an in-depth, mathematical explanation of delta is too complex to be included in this book, Figure 4–2 provides a brief conceptual explanation of this important aspect of option price behavior. The notion of two outcomes in each time period, introduced in Chapter 3, is the basis for an option pricing formula known as the binomial model. To develop delta, it is necessary to expand the example in Figure 3–1 to more than one time period. Figure 4–2A illustrates a four-period binomial example. In each period, it is assumed, the stock price has a 50–50 chance of rising or falling. As the number of time periods increases to four, the range of possible outcomes expands to a high of 104 and a low of 96. The final possible outcomes, however, do not have an equal probability of occurring. The highest-probability outcomes are near the center of the range. The probabilities for each final outcome are calculated by counting the number of paths the stock price could follow to that outcome. For example, there is only one path from 100 to 104, but there are 4 paths from 100 to 102. The total number of paths is 16, so there is one out of sixteen chances of ending at 104 and four out of sixteen chances of ending at 102.

In Figure 4–2A, the probability of each final outcome is shown along with the expected value calculations. The expected, or theoretical, value of the 100 Call is 0.75.

To demonstrate delta, assume the stock price rises $1 in the first period. After this move, the stock price is 101 and there are three periods remaining to expiration. The range of possible final outcomes has narrowed to a high of 104 and low of 98, and there are new probabilities for each remaining possible final outcome. The 100 Call has a new expected value of $1.25.

Figure 4–2 Demonstration of Delta

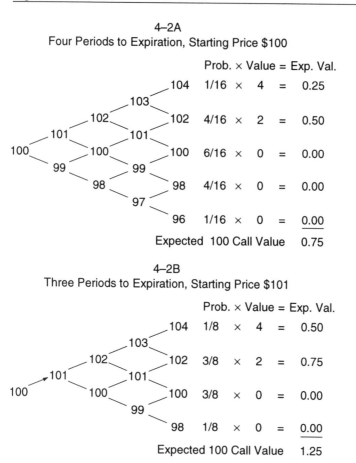

4–2A
Four Periods to Expiration, Starting Price $100

					Prob.	×	Value	=	Exp. Val.
				104	1/16	×	4	=	0.25
			103						
		102		102	4/16	×	2	=	0.50
	101		101						
100		100		100	6/16	×	0	=	0.00
	99		99						
		98		98	4/16	×	0	=	0.00
			97						
				96	1/16	×	0	=	0.00

Expected 100 Call Value   0.75

4–2B
Three Periods to Expiration, Starting Price $101

					Prob.	×	Value	=	Exp. Val.
				104	1/8	×	4	=	0.50
			103						
		102		102	3/8	×	2	=	0.75
	101		101						
100		100		100	3/8	×	0	=	0.00
			99						
				98	1/8	×	0	=	0.00

Expected 100 Call Value   1.25

This is presented in Figure 4–2B. In this case, the stock price has moved up by $1 and the 100 Call theoretical value has moved up by $0.50—equal to a delta of .50. This conclusion is consistent with the theoretical values presented in Tables 4–1 through 4–4.

The Effect of Time

It is well-known that options decrease in value with the passage of time (all other factors remaining constant). There are two ways of illustrating this graphically. Figure 4–3 shows option price behavior at three different times

**Figure 4–3 Theoretical Values of 50 Call
at 90 Days, 45 Days, 15 Days and Expiration**

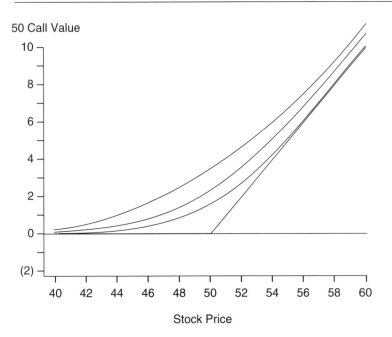

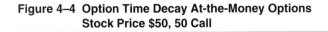

Stock Price

**Figure 4–4 Option Time Decay At-the-Money Options
Stock Price $50, 50 Call**

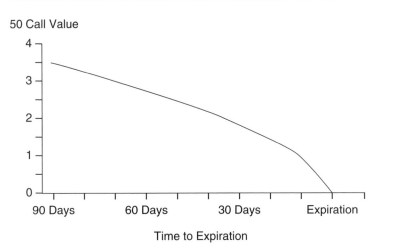

Time to Expiration

prior to expiration and at expiration. The values used to create the four lines in Figure 4–3 are taken from columns 1, 4, 6 and 7 in Table 4–1 which are 90 days from expiration, 45 days from expiration, 15 days from expiration and at expiration, respectively. Figure 4–3 shows how, as time passes, the graph of call option values approaches a shape similar to the expiration profit and loss diagram in Chapter 2, Figure 2–5.

Figure 4–4 illustrates how call prices change as time passes toward expiration assuming a constant stock price. Consider row 6, a stock price at $50. The 50 Call declines in value from 3.26 at 90 days to 2.95 at 75 days to 2.62 at 60 days, etc. The important observation is that time decay affects at-the-money options relatively little initially and relatively more as expiration approaches. Table 4–1 shows that when one-half of the time to expiration elapses, from 90 days to 45 days, approximately one-third of the 50 Call value erodes. A similar price/time relationship exists from 60 days to 30 days when the 50 Call declines from 2.62 to 1.82 and from 30 days to 15 days when the decline is from 1.82 to 1.26. Table 4–3 reveals a similar time decay rate for put options.

The name for time decay in options is theta. *Theta* is the change in option price given a one unit change in time. The term "one unit" is not specific; it could refer to one day, one week or some other time period. In the OP-EVAL™ option pricing program, the unit of time for theta is 7 days.

Time Decay Varies

Unfortunately for newcomers to options, the effect of time decay on option values is not so simple as it may first appear. While time decay for at-the-money options is low initially and increases per unit of time as expiration approaches, time decay for in-the-money and out-of-the-money options is different. Remember, it is only the time value portion of an option which decays. Consequently, with a stock price of $53, 90 days to expiration, and a 50 Call value of 5.17, time decay will affect only 2.17 of the value. Time decay during the first 15-day period is .30 and increases to .45 during the 30-to-15-day period. During the last 15 days prior to expiration, however, the option decreases in value by only .36. A similar rate of decay for the 50 Call occurs when the stock price is $47. The time decay is .27 from 90 to 75 days and .28 from 30 days to 15 days. But time decay is only .25 from 15 days to expiration. Figure 4–5 illustrates time decay for the 55 Call (out-of-the-money) and the 45 Call (in-the-money) when the stock price is $50. The passage of time has an identical effect on put options; at-the-money puts

**Figure 4–5 Option Time Decay In- and Out-of-the-Money Options
Stock Price $50, 50 Call and 45 Call**

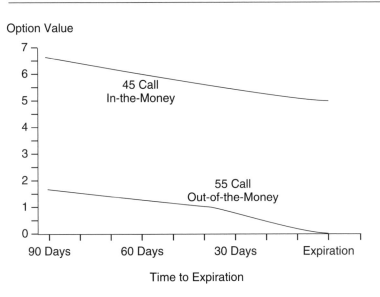

erode at an increasing rate, and in-the-money and out-of-the-money puts decrease least in the last period immediately prior to expiration.

A Demonstration of Time Decay

The binomial approach also illustrates the non-linear nature of time decay for at-the-money options. Figure 4–6 has six time periods and demonstrates the theoretical value of the 100 Call after time periods two, four and six. Although these time periods are equal in length, the theoretical value of the option does not change in equal amounts. This conclusion is consistent with the values presented in Tables 4–1 and 4–3.

The Effect of Interest Rates and Dividends

Interest rates and dividends are factors in the calculation of option theoretical values. Changes in these factors, however, have the least impact of all inputs. Figure 4–7 shows how changes in interest rates affect the theoretical value of a 50 Call, 90 days from expiration. The effect on call values is direct;

Figure 4–6 Demonstration of Option Time Decay

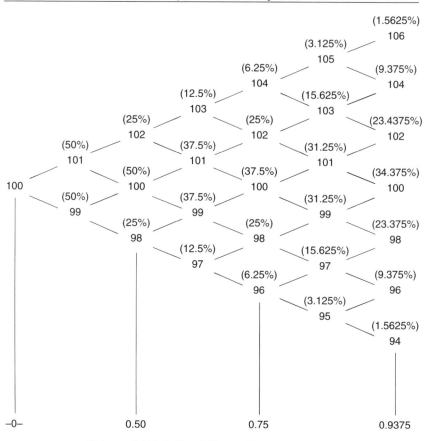

Values of 100 Call at Different Time Periods

as interest rates rise from 2% to 10% the 50 Call rises from 3.085 to 3.551. The effect on put values, however, is inverse; as interest rates rise from 2% to 10% the 50 Put falls from 2.841 to 2.390. This behavior is consistent with the put-call parity relationship referred to above.

The impact of dividends on option prices is opposite that of interest rates. With no dividends, the call value is greater than the put value by the cost of money (interest rate). With positive dividends, however, the cost of money is effectively reduced—the dividend proceeds can be used to pay the interest. Consequently, as dividends rise, the call value decreases and the put value rises. This is illustrated in Figure 4–8. The call and put values are equal when the dividend yield equals the interest rate.

Figure 4–7 Effect of Interest Rates on Option Prices
              50 Strike, 90 Days, No Dividends, Volatility 30%
              Interest Rates 2%–10%

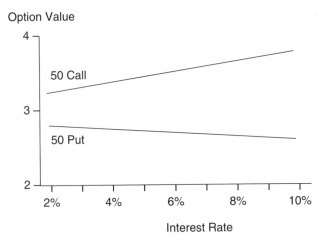

Option Value

50 Call

50 Put

Interest Rate

Figure 4–8 Effect of Dividends on Option Prices
              50 Strike, 90 Days, Interest Rates 5%,
              Volatility 30%, Dividends 0%–10%

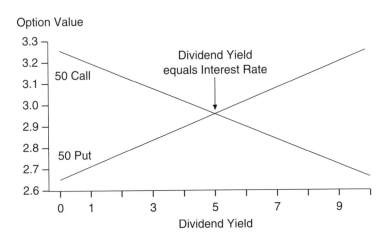

Option Value

Dividend Yield
equals Interest Rate

50 Call

50 Put

Dividend Yield

The Effect of Volatility

As described in Chapter 3, volatility is a measure of movement without regard to direction. The greater the volatility, the higher the option price. Volatility is stated in percentage terms. For example, the price action of a particular underlying security is said to "trade at 25% volatility," or an option theoretical value is said to be calculated "using a 30% volatility." Figure 4–9 illustrates how changes in volatility affect the value of a 50 Call assuming a $50 stock price and 90 days to expiration.

Because volatility is such an important topic in any discussion of options, the following observations are warranted. Although the explanation will get involved, do not lose track of the main goal. Traders must learn to understand volatility conceptually, as part of the subjective decision-making process. With practice and experience any option user can master the topic of volatility.

The direct relationship between volatility and option values illustrated in Figure 4–9 is only one of several important observations. Three more observations about volatility are: (1) volatility is a completely different concept than beta, (2) each stock has its own volatility characteristics and (3) the volatility characteristics of individual stocks can change and, in fact, do change frequently.

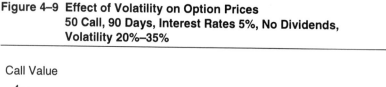

Figure 4–9 Effect of Volatility on Option Prices
50 Call, 90 Days, Interest Rates 5%, No Dividends,
Volatility 20%–35%

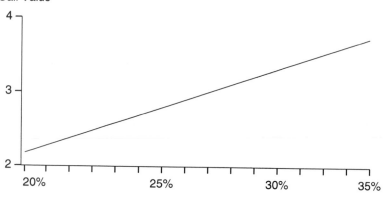

Volatility versus Beta

Volatility is a measure of the size of price movement without regard to direction. Volatility answers this question: can the price of a stock be expected to fluctuate a great deal or only a little over the next time period as a percentage of the base price (regardless of direction or correlation to the overall market)? Beta, in contrast, is a measure of correlation to the overall market. Beta answers this question: if the market is up by 1%, will this stock be up by 1%, more than 1% or less than 1%?

Any combination of beta and volatility is possible: high, high; high, low; low, high; or low, low. An example of low beta and high volatility might be a stock which is the subject of takeover rumors. As each new piece of information hits the market, this stock may move sharply (high volatility); all the while, the overall market is moving steadily in one direction. Consequently, this stock would have a low correlation to the market's overall trend (low beta).

An example of a high beta and high volatility stock might be a technology stock when technology stocks, as a group, are leading the overall market. A low beta, low volatility stock might be an interest-sensitive issue, such as a utility, that fails to rise during a broad market rally because interest rates are holding steady.

Each Stock Has Its Own Volatility Characteristics

It seems intuitive that each stock would have its own volatility characteristics, and yet there seems to be a belief that stocks in the same industry tend to have similar price action. Obviously, these notions are in conflict, so which is correct?

Within industry groups there can be a wide range of volatility characteristics. Using options, therefore, requires careful judgment about volatility, when making comparisons between stocks and their options. For example, Sandy, a San Francisco doctor, had extensively researched a medical technology company and became accustomed to a 90-day 50 Call trading at $4 when the underlying stock was trading at $50. Sandy then discovered a 90-day 50 Call on a new medical technology firm (also at $50) which was trading for $2, and automatically assumed this option was "cheap." Without doing any research on the new firm and its options, Sandy could be making an erroneous (and possibly expensive) assumption if the volatility characteristics of the two stocks are very different. A further discussion of using this concept in decision making is presented in Chapter 17.

Volatility Characteristics Can Change

An important point too frequently overlooked is the changing nature of volatility characteristics of individual stocks. The classic example is that of the old, stodgy company that becomes the subject of a takeover battle. Prior to the battle, the stock may have been priced at $40 and fluctuating $0.50 per day (a 1.25% daily price fluctuation). After the announcement of the original offer, which is followed by new offers and rebuffs, the stock could fluctuate $2 per day around a price of $60 (a 3.33% daily price fluctuation). Although this is a dramatic example, much less dramatic events can change the volatility characteristics of a stock. Any number of news events such as unexpected earnings, reorganizations, new product introductions or news about a competitor can affect a stock's price action. Just as the entire market goes through more volatile and less volatile periods, so too can individual stocks go through similar changes. Knowledge of past changes in a stock's volatility characteristics can be helpful when investing and trading with options. This information is available from option newsletters and data vendors.

Four Uses of the Word Volatility

Volatility is perhaps the most talked about and least understood topic in the options business. This is understandable, because volatility is a complicated, statistical concept. The non-directional aspect of the concept is especially confusing to many traders who spend most of their time trying to predict market direction. Adding to the confusion is that the term "volatility" is used in four different ways: historical volatility, future volatility, expected volatility and implied volatility.

Historical volatility is a measure of actual price movements in the past. Time periods studied vary from the most recent 10 days to 200 days. The actual volatility is calculated by statistical methods. There are two important observations to be made about historical volatility. First, the results of historical volatility calculations depend on the period chosen; different periods yield different results. Second, there is no guarantee that future volatility will be the same as historical volatility. Although historical information is a good place to start, there are many factors involved in volatility. Ultimately, predicting volatility is an art, not a science.

Future volatility is (1) unknown and (2) the determinant on an option's true theoretical value. This is what causes the most confusion for new option users. If an option's theoretical value depends upon something that is unknown, which it does, then how can the theoretical value be calculated?

Obviously, it cannot. However, the future volatility can be estimated, and a theoretical value calculation can be made using that estimate. Therefore, any number presented as "the theoretical value" of an option is actually only an estimate of the theoretical value.

Expected volatility is an individual's estimate of future volatility and used by that individual in theoretical value calculations. Frequently, traders use historical volatility in theoretical value calculations as the expected volatility. This is fine as long as the trader is aware of more information on the historical volatility such as the high and low for the year and recent changes. Such awareness aids traders in interpreting theoretical values and making strategy-selection decisions. Too often, however, traders are presented with "theoretical values" and advised not to pay more or sell for less. Such advice is often short-sighted and not properly set in a broader decision-making framework.

Implied volatility is the volatility number which justifies the market price of an option. In other words, it is the volatility number required, in order for an option pricing formula to calculate the current market price of an option. In Chapter 17 the process of determining implied volatility using the computer program OP-EVAL™ will be explained.

Summarizing the Differences

Distinguishing between these four uses of "volatility" may best be accomplished with an example. Consider a company whose stock has traded for the last 30 days at a volatility of 24%—as calculated by the statisticians. Recent reports about the company have been both good and bad: successful new product introductions on the one hand, but rumors abound of a pending "one-time" write-off because of a plant closing. Also an earnings report is due in three weeks. One well-known option strategist is advising clients to base option theoretical values on a volatility estimate of 30%, but the market is currently trading the options as if 35% volatility is expected.

In this example, each use of the word volatility can be matched with its proper adjective. The historical volatility of the stock price is 24%. Because of recent events and an imminent earnings report, however, the future volatility (which is unknown) is likely to be different. The expected volatility for one advisor is 30%, but the implied volatility in the market is 35%. Which is the "right" volatility number? Unfortunately, there is no "right" answer to this question, just the information. An option user must combine an interpretation of this information with a specific market forecast and choose a strategy that has, in the investor's opinion, a good chance of succeeding.

The preceding example is not intended to confuse newcomers to options. Rather, it is presented as a reminder that certain words in the options business often do not mean the same as in every day usage. Many options-related terms have very specific meanings, because the field is technical for full-time, professional traders. Individual investors, however, with longer term investment objectives need not be scared off by all the technical talk which can be intimidating. As will be explained in Section 2, Basic Investing Strategies, investors should concern themselves with whether an option and its price meets their objectives. It is not necessary for longer term investors to get involved with computers and detailed talk about volatility.

Dynamic Markets

The discussion to this point has assumed that one component of value changes while the rest stay constant. In the real world, of course, more than one component changes at a time. Market forecasts do not call for a stock to move up or down on just the same day while volatility remains unchanged. Rather, both stock prices and volatility commonly change over a period of time. All factors, stock price, time and volatility, will affect the option price. A trader's forecast must, therefore, take all three into account. Referring back to Table 4–1, if a prediction called for the stock price to rise from $47 at 90 days to $51 at 75 days, the call price might be expected to rise from 1.82 to 3.53, assuming interest rates and volatility do not change. If either or both of these change, the result will be a different option price.

Traders, therefore, must take into account the dynamic nature of markets. Tables of theoretical values, such as presented in this chapter, help traders to develop realistic expectations about option price behavior. The computer program which accompanies this book, of course, was used to create these tables. Using the program will be explained in Section 4. The benefit of the program is that, given a realistic expectation for option prices, traders can more easily select a strategy that matches the market forecast. With practice, any trader can master this.

Summary

Short-term option price behavior is the realm of the trader rather than the investor who, as will be explained in Section 2, focuses on strategy results at expiration. Option prices, prior to expiration, always move less than one-for-one with stock price changes. Delta is the name for expected option price change given a one unit stock price change. The passage of time causes option prices to decrease—all other things being equal. At-the-money options decrease with the passage of time in a non-linear manner, less initially and more as expiration nears. The time decay of in-the-money and out-of-the-money options is different, increasing time decay for a while and then less very close to expiration. Interest rates have a direct effect on call prices and an inverse effect on put prices. Dividends are the opposite of interest rates: dividends up, call prices down and put prices up.

Volatility has a direct impact on option prices, the higher the volatility, the higher both put and call prices. Volatility is a measure of movement without regard to direction. While it is a statistical concept not easily grasped by nonmathematicians, volatility can be understood intuitively and incorporated, subjectively, into trading decisions.

The term "volatility" is used four ways: historical, future, expected and implied. Historical volatility is the measure of actual price movements over a period of time in the past. Future volatility is unknown, and it is what option users are trying to predict. Expected volatility is a trader's estimate of future volatility; it is used in mathematical formulas to calculate theoretical option values. Implied volatility is the volatility number which justifies the current market price of an option.

Markets are dynamic, not static. A trader's forecast must, therefore, take into account changes in all factors which affect option prices.

SECTION 2

Basic Investing Strategies

Five

The Difference Between Investing and Trading Strategies

F inancial markets are comprised of three distinct types of participants: investors, speculators and market makers. Although each of these participants seeks to make profits, each uses the markets in different ways, with different strategies, different time horizons, different degrees of leverage and different ways of measuring results. A common misconception is that options can be used only to speculate. Nothing could be further from the truth! In fact, the primary theme of this book is that options have an important role in a long-term investing program. It is therefore important to distinguish the risk characteristics and objectives of investment strategies, those of speculative strategies and those employed by market makers.

Options Give Investors More Alternatives

Although whole chapters could be written on what distinguishes the three types of market participants, only a few significant differences need to be identified here. Investors generally have a longer time horizon; they measure results against market averages; they do not leverage their investment capital; and they buy at the offered price and sell at the bid price. Investors use option strategies which can insure or enhance

What Do Options Give Investors?

the performance of their stock portfolio. The message to be taken from Chapter 2 (profit and loss diagrams) is this: options provide investors with more alternatives—more risk profiles from which to choose. Without options, stock market investors have only three alternatives: buy stock, buy Treasury Bills or buy a combination of the two. The challenge of investing with options is to understand the investment objectives achieved by each strategy and to match the appropriate strategy with the market forecast. Unfortunately, the value of options as risk management and investment tools is undiscovered by many investors.

Unlike investors, speculators are oriented to shorter-term market risk; they believe in "high risk, high return;" and they frequently trade on margin. Also, speculators treat options as an independent trading activity not related to stock trading. The only similarity to investors is that speculators also buy at the offered price and sell at the bid price.

Market makers operate in a third way which is not easily understood by newcomers to options. Market makers attempt to earn the spread differential between the bid price and ask price. Primarily, they seek arbitrage opportunities, and by managing their positions, they attempt not to assume the risk of market direction. Market makers hope to make only a small amount on each trade, but they hope to do a high volume of trades. The subject of market making will not be discussed in this book. Interested readers should refer to the work of Sheldon Natenberg.

Investor and Trader Motivations Contrasted

An example which contrasts the motivations of the investor and the speculator is the strategy of selling put options. A speculator who sells a put is predicting a market rally. If the prediction is correct, either the put will be repurchased at a lower price or it will expire worthless and achieve the maximum profit potential. The speculator has no interest in buying the underlying stock and just wants to benefit from the expected short-term change in the option's price. The receipt of an assignment notice is viewed as a bad event by the speculator.

An investor's goal, in contrast, is to buy "good stocks" at "good prices." Therefore, when an investor sells a put, the investor hopes the put will be assigned and the stock will be purchased. That's right! Investors actually hope for assignment. This is a big difference. Exercise and assignment are viewed as good, or at least acceptable, events by investors.

If it is difficult to accept the notion that being assigned on a short put is a positive event, it might be that speculative thinking is very deeply ingrained. To understand thoroughly how options can be used to achieve investment objectives, it is necessary to get out of the "speculative mentality" when thinking about options.

Investors use options to protect or enhance a position in an underlying stock. An example of using options for protection is buying a put on stock owned; this strategy limits risk and allows participation in a price rise at the same time (less the cost of the put). An example of enhancement is selling a call when the underlying stock is owned and hoping for assignment. If the call is assigned, a more favorable selling price than the current stock price may be achieved. If the call expires worth-

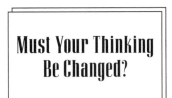

Must Your Thinking Be Changed?

less, income may be increased. Each of these strategies, of course, has a trade-off. Buying a put for protection has a cost; selling a call when the underlying stock is owned limits profit potential.

Investors Do Not Use Leverage

Leveraging investment capital is the sphere of the speculator. When purchasing stock, leverage is typically accomplished through the use of margin debt: borrowed money that enables $1 of capital to buy up to $2 of stock. The result is greater profit or greater loss from any price change. Investors, in comparison, pay cash in full when purchasing stocks and do not expose their holdings to the risks of leverage.

When Option Positions Are Not Leveraged

At expiration, if in-the-money option positions are exercised, stock transactions are created. If an option position exists on a share-for-share basis with the underlying stock, or if there is sufficient cash to pay for the stock position created, then that option strategy does not involve leverage.

Consider the case of John, an investor with $7,000 in a money-market account (or Treasury bills) who also owns a 70 Call on Power Industries for which he paid $500, or $5 per share. John has sufficient cash to pay for the stock if the call is exercised. Furthermore, John fully intends to exercise the call if it is in-the-money at expiration, because he wants to add Power stock to his long-term investment portfolio. This strategy, buy call plus T-Bill, as explained in Chapter 6, offers John the trade-off of limited risk in exchange for a higher effective purchase price if the call is exercised. To see that John's total position is not leveraged, consider what his position is if Power stock is at $60 at option expiration. John will not exercise his option and will lose only the $500 he paid for the call which is less than 10% of his investment capital and less than the $1,000 loss he would have realized had he paid $7,000 for 100 shares.

Now consider the case of Sharon who writes a call against 100 shares of Egan Enterprises which she owns in a cash account. Sharon's use of the call is known as covered writing. As discussed in Chapters 7 and 8, covered writing offers the trade-off of establishing a potentially higher selling price or potentially increasing income in return for limiting profit potential. If the stock is above the call's strike price at expiration, assignment of the call will result in Sharon selling her Egan stock and receiving cash. This strategy does not involve leverage. In fact, there is less risk for Sharon with the covered call strategy than with owning Egan stock outright, because the call premium she received reduced her cost basis.

As a third case, consider Debra, an owner of 1,000 shares of Peters Consulting which is currently trading at $30 per share. If Debra employs the protective put strategy discussed in Chapter 10, she will buy ten 30 Puts and thus limit the risk of her investment in Peters. Should the price of Peters decline, Debra will be able to exercise the puts and sell her stock at $30. This position is not leveraged, because the puts are purchased on a share-for-share basis with the owned stock.

"Basic Investment Strategies" Defined

The strategies described in this section are "basic" for at least two reasons. First, they are "stock oriented." They involve the underlying stock or have the goal of purchasing or selling the underlying stock at a "good price," which is a subjective determination of each investor. Second, these strategies do not involve leverage: either the underlying stock is owned or there is sufficient cash (or liquid assets) available to pay for the stock.

Summary

Financial markets involve the interaction of investors, speculators and market makers who buy and sell options for different reasons. Investors seek strategies which insure or enhance their stock holdings while speculators seek only short-term trading profits. Market makers set bid and offer prices based on arbitrage opportunities.

In its simplest form, speculating involves leverage and investing does not. Option strategies with an investment orientation meet one of two criteria: either (1) option positions exist on a share-for-share basis with the underlying stock, or (2) sufficient cash exists to fully pay for the stock position created by option exercise or assignment.

Chapters 6 through 10 discuss investment-oriented option strategies that enhance or insure stock positions. Chapter 6 discusses buying calls and T-Bills. Chapter 7 is a basic discussion of covered writing, and Chapter 8 discusses modified or adjusted covered write positions. Chapter 9 introduces a somewhat complicated but useful strategy known as "buy stock with ratio call spread." Chapter 10 explains how the protective put strategy works and when it might be employed.

Six

Buying Calls

Calls can be purchased for a variety of reasons. Short-term trading, or speculating is perhaps the most commonly known reason, and that strategy will be discussed in Chapter 17, but this chapter will explain investment-oriented reasons for purchasing calls. In the introduction of this book, an investor, as opposed to a speculator, was defined as being interested in the benefits of long-term stock ownership, and one investment use of options was described as facilitating the buying or selling of "good stocks" at "good prices." Call options, of course, involve the right to buy stock, and this chapter will explain using purchased calls in an effort to enhance the stock purchasing process.

In Chapter 3, options were compared to insurance policies. Essentially, because there is a probability that an event will occur, insurance policies have a value equal to the financial consequences of that event times the probability of that event occurring. Call options are insurance policies which insure investment capital held in short-term liquid investments against missing a stock price rise. An investor who owns a call will participate in a stock price rise above a certain price level. Below a certain price level, the call will expire; but the investment capital will not decrease in value. A call owner, of course, will not receive dividends, if any, paid by the underlying stock.

The question is: under what circumstances would an investor choose to own an insurance policy against a stock rising rather than own the stock itself? The answer, like the reasoning that goes into selecting any investment, is largely subjective, but this chapter will present some conceptual and historical examples. Although the examples may seem obvious, given twenty-twenty hindsight, they will be helpful in exploring the psychology of purchasing calls for investment purposes and will enable readers to examine their personal investing activities and identify similar situations.

85

Different Strategies Offer Different Trade-Offs

When facing the selection of an investment strategy, it would be nice to know "which one is best?" Focusing on this question, however, misses an important point about options. If knowledgeable participants are competing in the marketplace as described by the Efficient Market Theory (briefly mentioned in the Introduction), then all strategies, in some sense, should be equal. The difference between strategies is not that one is "better" than another; but that they offer a different set of trade-offs. The concept of a

Figure 6–1 Buy Call vs. Buy Stock—The Tradeoffs

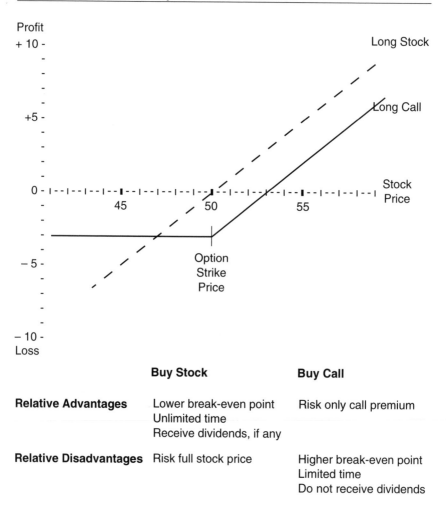

	Buy Stock	**Buy Call**
Relative Advantages	Lower break-even point Unlimited time Receive dividends, if any	Risk only call premium
Relative Disadvantages	Risk full stock price	Higher break-even point Limited time Do not receive dividends

trade-off is that each strategy has a relative advantage and a relative disadvantage compared to another strategy. Figure 6–1 compares the purchase of stock at $50 to the purchase of a 50 Call for 3. Purchasing stock at $50 breaks even at $50 (the positive), but risks $50 (the negative). The 50 Call, however, has a limited life and breaks even at $53 (the negatives), but risks only $3 (the positive).

Different Calls Offer Different Trade-Offs

As defined in Chapter 1, calls are categorized as in-the-money, at-the-money or out-of-the-money. Figure 6–2 illustrates the trade-offs each type of call offers. The assumptions are a stock price of $50 and three call options, the

Figure 6–2 Comparison of Three Long Calls

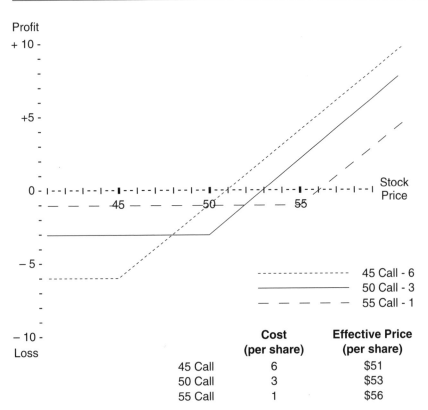

	Cost (per share)	Effective Price (per share)
45 Call	6	$51
50 Call	3	$53
55 Call	1	$56

45, 50 and 55 Calls priced at 6, 3 and 1, respectively. The calls differ in premium and effective purchase price. The premium, it will be recalled, is the total price of the option; and the "effective purchase price" is the price paid for the underlying stock which takes the option premium into consideration. The 45 Call, for example, has a premium of 6 and an effective buy price of $51. If the 45 Call is exercised, stock is effectively purchased at $51 per share (not including transaction costs).

What Are the 2 Steps in the Call Strategy?

The effective purchase price is calculated by adding the premium of the call to its strike price. If a call is exercised, the exerciser must pay the amount of the strike price in return for receiving the stock, but the total price—or effective price—includes the price paid for the call.

The 45 Call, in comparison to the 50 and 55 Calls, has a break-even point of $51—the positive—but risks $6 per share—the negative.

The 50 and 55 Calls offer different trade-offs relative to the 45 Call. The 50 Call has a premium (and risk) of $3 per share and an effective purchase price of $53. The premium is lower, but the effective purchase price is higher. The 55 Call has the lowest premium (and lowest risk)—$1 per share—and the highest effective purchase price ($56).

Consequently, none of the four strategies—buying stock or one of the three calls—is "better" in an absolute sense; each just offers a different set of trade-offs. The strategy with the lowest effective purchase price has the highest risk, and the lowest risk strategy has the highest effective purchase price.

Calls As Insurance

Susan, a marketing research analyst in Chicago, has been watching the stock of a soft drink bottler in Seattle (call it "SoftDrink") for some time and wants to buy the stock as a long-term investment. She is nervous, however, about a pending earnings report and rumors of a new product introduction. Susan believes this is the time to "take the plunge" and buy the stock, especially if the new product is successful, but she is concerned enough to want to limit her risk. Buying stock is a risk/reward profile every experienced investor knows: there is substantial profit potential and substantial risk. If Susan believes the stock could move up or down $10 as a result of pending developments, then the purchase of SoftDrink stock involves a $10 risk/reward profile.

What Is the Stock Risk/Reward?

How do call options change the situation? Read on.

For simplicity, assume that Susan has $5,300 to invest in SoftDrink stock and the 50 Call is trading for $300 ($3 per share). Again, if Susan believes the stock could move up or down $10 during the option's life, the 50 Call offers a different risk-reward profile than purchasing the stock outright. The risk of buying the call is $3 per share. The profit potential, Susan believes, is $7 per share if the stock rises $10. Because of the different risk/reward ratio, the call also offers a significantly different method of adding the stock to the investment portfolio.

The Call Option Alternative

The strategy involving the 50 Call involves two steps. Susan can first purchase the call for $300, and then deposit $5,000 in an interest-bearing account. If SoftDrink is above $50 on the option expiration date, Susan can purchase the stock by exercising the call and using the funds on deposit in the interest-bearing account. SoftDrink will have been purchased, effectively, for $53 and will be in Susan's investment portfolio. If SoftDrink is $60, she will have a $7 profit per share in the stock. Susan can then proceed to monitor this stock investment in the same manner as her other holdings. There is no reason necessarily to use options on this particular holding again.

What if SoftDrink has a disastrous earnings report or initial reaction to the new product is abysmal? If the stock price is below $50 at option expiration, Susan can let the call expire unexercised. Her maximum risk is the $3 per share paid for the call. At this point she can re-examine the decision to purchase the stock. If new information compels her to forget SoftDrink, Susan can feel relieved that she risked only $3 per share. Alternatively, if SoftDrink is judged to be a "better buy than ever," she can purchase the stock at the current market price.

In the SoftDrink example, the call option helped a long-term investor purchase a "good stock" and limit risk during the crucial, initial holding period. The trade-off was a higher effective purchase price—the negative—versus limited risk—the positive.

The Waiting Alternative

Another alternative for Susan would be to wait until after SoftDrink's "pending development" before purchasing any stock. In this case, there would be a $10 potential benefit versus a $10 opportunity loss. If no investment were made and the stock declined $10, Susan would be better off by $10 per share buying the stock at $40 versus $50. If the stock rose to $60, Susan would have missed the buying opportunity at $50 and be $10 per share worse off by paying $60. Regardless of whether stock is purchased prior to or after the "pending development," given the assumptions in this example, Susan faces a $10 potential benefit versus a $10 risk.

What Is the Call Risk/Reward?

Compared to the stock purchaser who faces a $10 risk/$10 reward ratio, the call buyer faces a $3 risk/$7 reward ratio. While this in itself is significant, it is not the only advantage of using the call.

In the real world, of course, there are more possible outcomes than the stock price moving up or down $10. First, the news event, if negative, could cause a larger drop in the stock price than $10. Second, a negative report could change the investor's fundamental view of the stock, leading the investor to not want to invest in this stock at all. In either of these cases, purchasing the call, while resulting in a loss, would be less costly than buying the stock.

Another possibility is that a rising stock price could cause a stock purchaser to believe that the opportunity "was missed" and lead to not investing at all. Only time would tell how this scenario would play out, but many investors have "stocks that got away." In this situation, the call might have changed the short-term risk-reward ratio in the investor's favor.

Calls versus Stop-Loss Sell Orders

Still another possibility is the frustrating "stop-loss scenario" in which a stock purchaser places a stop-loss sell order below the purchase price. The intent of this action is to limit risk. But in the worst-case scenario, the stock price dips to the stop-loss price which triggers the sell order, and then the stock price rises dramatically—a frustrating situation which many investors have experienced. The call option, while having a limited life and limited loss, does not have a limiting price. If the stock price dips and rallies during the option's life, the call purchaser still participates in the stock price rise above the option's break-even price. While this is a tremendous advantage that speaks in favor of options, this benefit is not free.

A Stop-Loss Order Is Dependent on What?

The call has a cost and a higher effective purchase price relative to purchasing the stock outright.

Remember, options offer different trade-offs, not alternatives that are "better" in an absolute sense. The higher effective purchase price is the cost paid in order to get the benefit of limited risk. A stock purchaser will profit more than a call purchaser if the price rises. A stock purchaser, however, has a higher risk potential than a call purchaser. Seen in this light, the call alternative demands somewhat different thinking than is typically required of stock investors.

Real World Examples

Let's move from the hypothetical to the actual by reviewing some historical situations in which options actually did help the long-term investor. In the two scenarios presented, the market view will be wrong one time and correct the other.

The first situation is July, 1992, when IBM dipped below $100 per share, its lowest price in 20 years. There was much controversy about whether IBM represented a good investment opportunity. Many investment advisors were touting IBM

A Call Option Is Dependent on What?

while others were keeping their distance. The dividend of 5% seemed attractive, and the company had announced several plans to turn itself around. Nevertheless, there was much competition, and the computer industry was turning away from mainframes, IBM's core business. Any investor considering IBM should have been aware of these conflicting opinions. If IBM's price dip below $100 was viewed as "risky, but a tremendous opportunity," then call options offered a way to take advantage of this opportunity and limit risk at the same time. On July 17, 1992, IBM closed at $95 and the January, 1993, 95 Call closed at $5 3/4. An investor with $9,500 to purchase 100 shares of IBM stock had the alternative of buying one 95 Call for $575 and leaving $8,925 in an interest-bearing account until the third Friday in January. The call offered the advantage of limiting risk to $575 minus any interest earned; the accompanying disadvantage was an effective purchase price of $100 3/4 per share, $5 3/4 above the then current market price of $95.

Those who followed IBM in 1992 know that the stock price fared poorly that year. By January 15, 1993, IBM's share price had dropped to $48 1/4 per share. For investors who purchased stock at $95 in July, 1992, and held, this represented a $46 3/4 loss per share. The investor who purchased the January, 1993, 95 Call instead was equally wrong in the outlook for IBM's share price but lost only $575 (less interest).

The second situation begins in August, 1993, when Xerox was the topic of investment debate. Its share price had more than doubled to $80 from its 1991 low of $39. For the previous six months, however, its price stayed in a narrow range around $70 to $75. Boosters of Xerox claimed this was inevitable, that the stock was "consolidating." The negative view was that the stock was overvalued in its highly competitive, mature industry. With Xerox's closing price of $75 on August 19, 1993, the January, 1994, 75 Call was offered at $4 3/8.

After August 19, 1993, Xerox's stock price traded below $70 before rising to $92 5/8 on January 21, 1994. A stock buyer at $75 may have been stopped out if inclined to use a stop-loss sell order as a loss-limiting technique. It may have looked bad for a while for the call buyer. But, from the first day, the maximum risk was known. And this is a situation which many investors can live with more easily than the anxieties of seeing some of an investment evaporate in 30 days and not knowing when, where or if the losses will stop. Investing is sometimes an anxiety provoking endeavor; one use of options is to reduce that anxiety when initiating new investment positions.

Using In-the-Money Calls

The previous examples illustrate how at-the-money calls can act as insurance policies which limit risk and insure against missing a price rise. In-the-money calls offer a different set of trade-offs. In-the-money calls, it will be remembered, cost more than at-the-money or out-of-the-money calls—the negative. In-the-money calls, however, offer a lower effective buy price than other options—the positive. When, then, would an investor want this choice? There are a number of situations.

Follow Tom, a car dealership owner in Houston, as he works through several investment strategies.

First, purchasing an in-the-money call is an alternative short-term risk management technique to placing a stop-loss sell order. Tom has been watching a chemical manufacturing stock, Chemco, that shows promise, although emerging environmental concerns can always cause dramatic changes in the company's fortunes. Chemco stock is trading at $50 and the 90-day 45 Call is available for 6. Tom could purchase Chemco for $50 and place a stop-loss sell order at $45, to act as a loss-limiting mechanism. Tom needs to realize, however, that a stop-loss order does not guarantee a maximum loss, because the market can trade through and below a stop-loss price for a number of reasons. One possibility is that a large volume of sell orders appear at the same time (perhaps the result of a rumor or a news item during market hours) and the stock trades down through and below $45 before buyers and sellers can find a new equilibrium between supply and demand. Another possibility is a "gap opening" below $45. Such a situation could occur when news released after the previous day's close causes an imbalance of sell orders on the next morning's opening. In situations like this, it is possible for a stock to open significantly lower than the previous day's closing price.

If Tom purchased a 90-day 45 Call for 6, instead of purchasing stock and using a stop-loss order, he could accomplish two things the stop-loss order cannot accomplish. First, if Tom does not exercise the call, his maximum loss is limited to $6 per share—the price of the call. Second, the call is not price-dependent as is the stop-loss order, which is triggered and immediately becomes a market sell order by a trade or offer at or below $45. Thus, Chemco could trade down to $45, trigger the stop-loss sell order, and then reverse direction and trade higher. Although the limited life of Tom's call is a negative, Chemco could trade at or below $45 during the call's life, but it would still be intact to participate in any price rise above $45 until its expiration date. When made aware of this time-dependent aspect of risk management that call options offer, many investors find it irresistible.

Planning for Future Cash Flows

A second situation in which an investor might choose an in-the-money call is when the cash to purchase stock is not immediately available but its receipt is anticipated. Assume Tom wants to purchase Chemco but needs his dealership's third quarter dividend to have the full purchase price, but the dividend will be declared and paid prior to an option's expiration. Investors regularly experience these situations, such as when a bond is about to mature, a year-end bonus is anticipated, or an investor is a regular saver and can anticipate when the needed amount will be available.

In Tom's situation, the lowest possible price is desired, and that leads to the in-the-money call. If Chemco is trading at $50 and a 90-day 45 Call is available for 6, then purchasing the call costs an extra $1 per share in terms of effective purchase price. During the period of the call ownership, of course, Tom will not receive dividends, if any, paid by the stock. Tom will, however, participate in any price rise in the stock above $51. Also, his risk is limited to $6 per share before the call is exercised. If his own fortunes decline and his dealership fails to pay the expected dividend, he will have shown great wisdom by limiting risk in using the option strategy.

Some investors, to whom this strategy is new, may have the initial reaction that paying $51 for a stock trading at $50 is the waste of a dollar per share. It was assumed, of course, that sufficient funds are not on hand immediately to purchase the stock at $50. Waiting until the money is available has its risks too. The stock may rally during the waiting period and reach a price greater than $51 per share. Of course, the price could also decline during the waiting period. Once again, the point is not that the call strategy is "better" in an absolute sense. Rather, the call offers a different set of trade-offs: buying now rather than waiting—the positive—but paying, effectively, $1 more per share—the negative.

An alternative to purchasing the in-the-money call is purchasing stock on margin. When stock is purchased on margin, an investor pays 50%, or more, initially and borrows the balance of the purchase price from the brokerage firm until the anticipated cash is received. Purchasing on margin is a viable alternative to purchasing an in-the-money call. The interest cost can be compared to the higher effective purchase price of the call. Buying on margin, however, assumes the immediate availability of at least 50% of the purchase price or other marginable securities which can act as collateral for the margin loans. The in-the-money call strategy, in the example above, required less than 15% of the stock price immediately.

Getting the "Best of Both"

A third situation in which in-the-money calls can be used is facilitating those difficult times when there are two stocks which have caught an investor's fancy, but there is insufficient capital to purchase both. Consider again Tom, who wants to purchase, but is wary of, Chemco. He also has his eyes on a grocery giant, Foodco, that has been attempting to make inroads into the Asian market. In this case Tom purchases Foodco stock and, at the same time, purchases an in-the-money call on Chemco. This gives him total exposure and total risk to Foodco and high exposure and limited risk to Chemco. Purchasing both stocks on margin would mean total exposure and total risk on both stocks.

With the in-the-money call on Chemco, Tom can participate in both stocks until a later date at or prior to the option expiration date when a final decision is made. If Foodco has performed better and is the preferred choice, then the Chemco call is sold (if it is in-the-money) or expires (if it is out-of-the-money) and that stock forgotten. If Chemco is the choice, then Foodco is sold. The proceeds from Foodco's sale can then be used to purchase Chemco when the call is exercised.

The risks of this third use of in-the-money calls should not be overlooked. If a 45 Call is purchased for $6 per share, then the investor who purchases one stock and this call on another stock is, in fact, taking an additional $6 risk (per share). A number of market scenarios could follow. Both stocks could rise in price and the purchased stock and the call could both show a profit. Both could fall and both show a loss. Or, one could rise and profit and the other fall and lose. There is no guarantee that the strategy described above will perform better than another strategy. The call option has, however, presented a new alternative which was not previously available.

A final point: this third strategy, attempting to get the best of both worlds, need not be limited to in-the-money calls. However, in-the-money calls offer the lowest effective buy price (if exercised) and the highest short-term price participation (if the stock price rises) relative to at-the-money or out-of-the-money calls. The trade-off is that in-the-money calls cost more than at-the-money or out-of-the-money calls.

Summary

This chapter introduced the idea that call options can be used like insurance policies to help investors buy stocks with limited risk during the life of the call. What options offer is a different set of trade-offs: limited risk in return for a higher effective buy price. Calls are a time-dependent risk management tool; they are not price-dependent like stop-loss orders. Finally, calls offer an alternative to buying stock on margin until the funds are available to pay for the stock in full.

Seven

Covered Writing

One of the most popular option strategies, covered writing, involves buying stock and selling calls on a share-for-share basis. This chapter will first look at the strategy as it is typically analyzed, then discuss why and when it might fit into an individual investor's portfolio. Typical objections to covered writing and some of the myths and misconceptions about it will be refuted and, since covered writing is different in many respects from a traditional "buy and hold" strategy, the psychological adjustment required of investors will be explored. Chapter 8 discusses "adjusted covered writes," which involve "rolling up," "rolling out," or a combination of the two, and the objectives of rolling.

Review of the Basics

Assume that Marc, an engineer in Boston, decides to engage in covered writing. He has been watching the price of a major airline. He likes the stock and would not mind holding it in his portfolio; on the other hand, he would also be happy with a small but tidy profit should the stock rise. He buys 100 shares of Flyco stock at $48 3/4 per share and sells one 60-day 50 Call for 1 5/8. An expiration profit and loss diagram is presented in Figure 7–1 and supporting calculations are in Table 7–1. For simplicity, transaction costs and the possibility of early assignment have been ignored. Early assignment may mean that a covered writer will not receive a dividend. Also, transaction costs can significantly influence the desirability of covered writing and, therefore, must be included in any real analysis.

Maximum Profit Potential

As illustrated in Figure 7–1, Marc's maximum profit potential is 2 7/8. If the price of Flyco is at or above the strike price of $50 at expiration, the call

Figure 7–1 Marc's Covered Write on Flyco—Buy Stock and Write Call

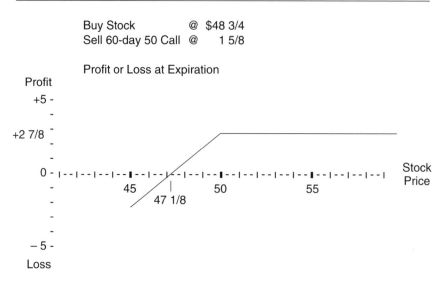

Buy Stock   @ $48 3/4
Sell 60-day 50 Call @   1 5/8

Profit or Loss at Expiration

Table 7–1 Marc's Covered Write on Flyco
Profit and Loss Calculations at Expiration

Stock Price at Expiration	Buy Stock @ $48 3/4 Profit or Loss	Sell 50 Call @ 1 5/8 Profit or Loss	Total Profit or Loss
$53	+4 1/4	−1 3/8	+2 7/8
$52	+3 1/4	− 3/8	+2 7/8
$51	+2 1/4	+ 5/8	+2 7/8
$50	+1 1/4	+1 5/8	+2 7/8
$49	+ 1/4	+1 5/8	+1 7/8
$48	− 3/4	+1 5/8	+ 7/8
$47	−1 3/4	+1 5/8	− 1/8
$46	−2 3/4	+1 5/8	−1 1/8
$45	−3 3/4	+1 5/8	−2 1/8

owner will exercise, and Marc, the call writer, will be assigned. Marc's stock will be sold at the strike price of $50, and the result for Marc is a profit of 2 7/8 per share. This profit is calculated by adding the option premium of 1

5/8 to the stock gain of 1 1/4. The stock gain is the difference between the $50 strike price of the call and $48 3/4 purchase price of the stock. Regardless of the stock price, if the covered writer is assigned, the stock is sold at the call strike price.

The Break-Even Stock Price at Expiration

An advantage of the covered writing strategy over purchasing stock outright is the lower break-even point. Covered writing breaks even, at expiration, at a stock price equal to the purchase price of the stock minus the amount received for selling the call. In Marc's case, the break-even stock price of $47 1/8 is calculated by subtracting the call premium of 1 5/8 from the stock purchase price of $48 3/4.

Selecting a Covered Write

Analyzing any investment requires the answer to this question: Is the potential profit worth the potential risk? When choosing a covered write, stock selection is the most important element. Compare Marc's risk to his profit potential: his profit potential is limited to 2 7/8 if the call is assigned, but his risk, theoretically, is $47 1/8—if the stock falls to zero. While not many stocks fall to zero, some stocks do suffer substantial price declines. Because of this risk, an investor must be thoroughly confident in the stock investment itself before entering this strategy.

Benchmark Measures of Profit

Although there are no absolute measures of profit, there are two benchmark measures for covered writing. With some experience, these measures can be included as part of the analysis in deciding whether a particular covered write is "worth it."

The "Static Rate of Return"

The first of two standard benchmark measures of a covered write's attractiveness is the static rate of return or the static return. The *static return* is the annualized percentage profit of a covered write, assuming the stock price is unchanged from the purchase price at option expiration, and the call expires unexercised. The static return calculation is made by dividing the "income" by the "net investment" and annualizing the result.

The "income" is the net call premium received plus dividends received. Net call premium is the total call premium less transaction costs (assumed here to be zero). For Marc, income is 1 5/8.

The "net investment" is the total price of the stock minus the net call premium received. The total price of the stock includes transaction costs. Since he purchased stock for $48 3/4 and sold the call for 1 5/8, Marc's net investment, on a per-share basis, is 47 1/8 (48 3/4 minus 1 5/8).

Dividing the income of 1 5/8 by the investment of 47 1/8 results in a profit of 0.034 or 3.40% for Marc *in 60 days.* To annualize the earnings, this amount is multiplied by the number of days per year and divided by the days to expiration. In this example, 0.034 is multiplied by 365 days per year and divided by 60 days. The result, .210 or 21.0%, is the static return. The assumption is the 3.40% earned in 60 days can be earned in every 60-day period for the rest of the year. There being slightly more than six 60-day periods in a 365-day year, the result is 6.08 times 3.40% or 21.0%. Of course, the assumption about repeating a given performance may not be realistic. Remember that this is a "benchmark" measure and achieving an excellent return one time does not guarantee future results. The static return calculations are summarized in Exhibit 7–1.

Exhibit 7–1 Marc's Static Rate of Return (Annual Rate)

Assumptions: Stock price is unchanged from purchase price at option expiration

                    Call expires unexercised

Marc's example: Stock Purchase Price: $48 3/4
                    50 Call Price: 1 5/8
                    Dividends: 0
                    Days to Expiration: 60

$$\text{Static Return} = \frac{\text{Income}}{\text{Investment}} \times \text{Annualization Factor}$$

$$= \frac{\text{Call Premium} + \text{Dividend}}{\text{Stock Purchase Price} - \text{Call Premium}} \times \frac{\text{Days per Year}}{\text{Days to Expiration}}$$

$$= \frac{1\ 5/8 + 0}{48\ 3/4 - 1\ 5/8} \times \frac{365}{60} = .210 = 21.0\%$$

The "If-Called Rate of Return"

The second standard benchmark measure is the if-called rate of return or the if-called return. The *if-called return* is the annualized percentage profit of a covered write, assuming the stock price rises to the strike price of the short call and is sold at that price on the option expiration date.

The if-called return is calculated in three steps. The "income" is added to the "gain." This sum is divided by the "net investment." The result is then annualized. The "income" is the same as for the static return: the net call premium plus dividends.

The "gain" is the difference between the option strike price and the stock purchase price. In Marc's example, the gain is 1 1/4, the difference between $50, the call strike, and $48 3/4, the purchase price.

The "net investment" is the same as for the static return, $47 1/8, which is the total stock price minus the net call premium received.

Adding the income of 1 5/8 to the gain of 1 1/4 and dividing that sum of 2 7/8 by the net investment of $47 1/8 results in a profit for Marc of 0.061 or 6.10% *in 60 days*. To annualize the earnings, this amount is multiplied by the number of days per year and divided by the days to expiration. In this example, 0.061 is multiplied by 365 days per year and divided by 60

Exhibit 7–2 Marc's If-Called Rate of Return (Annual Rate)

Assumptions: Stock price rises to or above strike price at option expiration

Call is assigned and stock is sold at the strike price

Marc's example: Stock Purchase Price: $48 3/4
50 Call Price: 1 5/8
Dividends: 0
Days to Expiration: 60

$$\text{If-Called Return} = \frac{\text{Income} + \text{Gain}}{\text{Investment}} \times \text{Annualization Factor}$$

$$= \frac{\text{Call Premium} + \text{Dividend} + (\text{Call Strike Price} - \text{Stock Purchase Price})}{\text{Stock Purchase Price} - \text{Call Premium}}$$

$$\times \frac{\text{Days per Year}}{\text{Days to Expiration}} = \frac{1\ 5/8 + 0 + (50 - 48\ 3/4)}{48\ 3/4 - 1\ 5/8} \times \frac{365}{60} = .371 = 37.1\%$$

days. The result is .371 or 37.1%, the annualized rate. The assumption is that the 60-day profit can be earned in every 60-day period for the rest of the year, which, as stated above, may be unrealistic. But this is only a "benchmark" calculation. The if-called return calculations are summarized in Exhibit 7–2.

Using the Static and If-Called Calculations

For newcomers to these calculations, the annualization process may raise some eyebrows. After all, it may be asked, how can one be sure of repeating this performance five more times in a row? A reasonable doubt, but it misses the point. Static and if-called return calculations are not absolute measures; they are objective calculations that can assist in investment analysis and selection. Even though selecting a covered write is as subjective as selecting any investment, these calculations provide a basis for comparison. By comparing several covered writing opportunities, an investor can get a feel for what the market is. The final choice is based on some objective information and some subjective information. The goal is a more informed decision.

When the Static Return Equals the If-Called Return

When a covered write involves an in-the-money call, the price of the underlying stock is above the strike price of the sold call. As an example, consider Sally, an income-oriented investor, who likes the shares of Qualityco, currently trading at $61 1/2. She is unhappy, however, with the $0.25 quarterly dividend which equates to an annual dividend yield of 1.6%. The annual dividend yield is calculated by adding the four quarterly dividends and dividing the total by the stock price. In Sally's case, $(0.25 \times 4) \div 61.5 = 0.016 = 1.6\%$.

The strategy of selling an in-the-money call, however, changes the income situation.

Assume Sally purchases 100 shares of Qualityco at $61 1/2 and sells a 90-day 60 Call for 4 1/4. The static return calculation assumes the stock price is unchanged at $61 1/2 at expiration. At this price at expiration, Sally's 60 Call would be assigned, and her stock would be sold at $60. Since the if-called return assumes the stock is called away, there is no difference, in Sally's case, between the static and if-called calculations.

Sally's "income" from the covered write has three parts: the option premium received, 4 1/4; the dividend received, 0.25 or 1/4; and the stock loss, –1 1/2, the difference between the purchase price of $61 1/2 and the selling price of $60. Sally's total income, therefore, is 3, not including transaction costs. Sally's "net investment" is the stock purchase price of $61 1/2 minus the call premium of $4 1/4, or $57 1/4. Given 90 days to expiration, the static return, not including transaction costs, is calculated as follows:

$$\text{Sally's Static Return} = (\text{income} \div \text{net investment})$$
$$\times (\text{days per year} \div \text{days to expiration})$$
$$= (3 \div 57\ 1/4) \times (365 \div 90) = 21.3\%$$

Sally's actual return will be lower because of transactions costs which include two stock commissions, one for buying at $61 1/2 and one for selling at $60.

While some investors are reluctant to sell in-the-money calls, no one should automatically reject "in-the-money covered writes." As will be discussed next, there are several considerations which should be included in the selection of a specific covered write.

Guidelines for Using Covered Writing

Covered writing is a "stock-oriented" strategy. This means a large part of the investment and risk is in the stock itself. Although the success or failure of all option strategies depends on the price behavior of the underlying stock, so-called stock-oriented option strategies are those in which an investor actually owns or has an interest in owning the underlying stock. This is different from short-term trading strategies with options where there is no interest in owning the underlying stock. Because of this stock orientation, Guideline Number One is: *an investor who employs covered writing must be comfortable owning the underlying stock.* In this regard, covered writing involves a stock selection process similar to buy and hold investing.

The strategy of covered writing, however, involves an aspect which ordinary stock investing lacks: the obligation to sell. While a typical investor purchasing a stock may not focus on a target selling price, the covered writer is obligated to sell at a price effectively equal to the call strike price plus the call premium. (The term "effective selling price" is defined in Chapter 1.) Guideline Number Two, therefore, is: *an investor who employs covered writing must be comfortable with selling the stock at the effective price dictated by the short call (strike plus premium).* This guideline has an important psychological implication for the investor. If an investor is satisfied selling the stock at the effective price of the short call, receiving an assignment is not only anxiety free, it is a positive event, because this means the "if-called return"— *the maximum possible profit*—has been earned.

Guideline Number Two leads to Guideline Number Three: *an investor who employs covered writing must calculate the static and if-called rates of return (including transaction costs) and enter the covered write only if those rates of return are deemed acceptable.* Although "acceptable" returns are impossible to define, covered writing returns can be compared to other returns such as the prevailing short-term risk-free rate of Treasury Bills, the average yield on the S&P 500 Index and the 30-year government bond rate. A desirable covered writing return, of course, should be higher than these, because covered writing involves the risk of stock ownership, the risk of which is substantially greater than owning Treasury Bills.

Although some investment professionals have touted a rule like "at least 2 to 3 times the three-month T-Bill rate after commissions," such rules can be misconstrued to place too much emphasis on the return calculations and not enough emphasis on stock selection and market forecasting. Since stock ownership is the largest element of risk in the covered writing strategy, it is important to place the most emphasis on this aspect.

Guideline Number Four relates to the return calculations themselves: *an investor who employs covered writing must interpret the return calculations very carefully.* This is necessary, because for very short time periods, the numbers can be misleading. For example, if a covered call on a $20 stock is sold one week prior to expiration and a premium of 1/4, after commissions, is received, this covered write may, theoretically, have a high annual rate of return, but how often and with what degree of investment confidence can such transactions be repeated? Such trades are often much more speculative than prudent. Consequently, an expansion of Guideline Number Four is Guideline Number Five: *an investor who employs covered writing should concentrate on time periods of sixty days or longer.* A ninety-day time frame is common, and investors should not be reluctant to look at 120 days or longer. Indeed, Harrison Roth, in his excellent book *LEAPS* (Irwin Professional Publishing, 1994), discusses the advantages of covered writing with long-term options.

The final guideline places emphasis on the real world factor of transaction costs. Guideline Number Six: *an investor who employs covered writing must include all transaction costs in the return calculations.* The static return calculation should include all costs related to the initial stock purchase (one commission) and the call sale (a second commission). The if-called return calculation should also include all costs of option assignment and sale of stock. Exhibit 7–3 is a work sheet for covered writing which includes all costs.

Exhibit 7–3 Covered Call Writing-Static Return and If-Called
                 Return Calculations

Stock / Price ———— Stock Cost ——————— Total Call Proceeds ———————

Call / Price ———— Stock Comm. ——————— Call Comm. ———————

Days to Exp. ———— If-Called Proceeds (Strike × shrs) ———————

Net Income = Net Call Proceeds + Dividends

Total Call Proceeds – Commissions =	Net Call Proceeds + Dividends =	Net Income
———— – ———— =	———— + ———— =	————

Net Investment = Total Stock Cost-Net Call Proceeds

Stock Cost + Commissions =	Total Stock Cost – Net Call Proceeds =	Net Investment
———— + ———— =	———— – ———— =	————

Gain (If-Called) = Net If-Called Proceeds-Net Investment

If-Called Proceeds – Commissions =	Net If-Called Proceeds – Net Investment =	Net Gain
———— – ———— =	———— – ———— =	————

Static Rate of Return (Annual Rate)

$$\frac{\text{Net Income}}{\text{Net Investment}} \times \frac{\text{Days per Year}}{\text{Days to Expiration}} = \text{Static Rate of Return}$$

$$\text{————} \times \frac{365}{\text{————}} = \text{————}$$

If-Called Rate of Return (Annual Rate)

$$\frac{\text{Net Income + Gain}}{\text{Net Investment}} \times \frac{\text{Days per Year}}{\text{Days to Expiration}} = \text{If-Called Rate of Return}$$

$$\text{————} \times \frac{365}{\text{————}} = \text{————}$$

Real World Considerations—Transactions Costs

An important point about commissions and other transaction costs is the concept of "quantity discounts." Virtually all brokerage firms have commission schedules which decrease on a per-share basis as the quantity of shares transacted increases. For example, it may cost substantially less to trade 300 shares on a per-share basis than to trade 100 shares. Similarly, the existence of minimum commission charges often means that three or four calls can be sold for nearly the same commission as one call. The implication of these factors for covered writers is economies of scale. In general, covered writing transactions must involve more than 100 shares since transaction costs are likely to lower the static and if-called returns to the point of making a covered write on 100 shares undesirable. Consequently, investors must determine whether or not they have sufficient capital to engage in covered writing.

Myths about Covered Writing

Covered writing is a popular option strategy. Virtually every broker and investor who has used options either knows about covered writing or has used this strategy. Even so, a number of myths and misconceptions about covered writing have developed and are worth discussing. With a more complete awareness of an investment strategy's strengths and weaknesses, an investor can achieve a certain psychological comfort. And what better way to increase awareness than to discuss the negative things people say?

Myth #1: "Being Assigned Is Bad."

When some investors initiate a covered write, they are not sure what they want to happen. On the one hand, there is the desire to have the stock price rise. On the other hand, there is the desire for it not to rise too far. These ambiguous feelings may stem from a sense of having given up control —a covered writer is obligated to sell at the whim of the call owner. Consequently, there is a feeling one might "lose" the stock or have it "taken away." Of course, if this same investor were to sell the stock at the effective price of the short call, such an action might be viewed as a proactive decision. It might be a "good sale," or "taking profits."

Covered writing is the only strategy in which a profit is sometimes described as a loss! Consider, for example, Herman, an academic in Phoenix, who regularly invests in stocks and follows the market carefully. He buys a pharmaceutical stock at $48 and sells it at $52. Seeing it rise the next week to $54, Herman is still pleased, saying, "At least I made money," or, "You never go broke taking a profit."

But Herman then decides to try his hand at options and starts with a covered write in which a high tech stock is purchased for $48 and the 50 Call is sold for 2. The stock price rises to $54 at expiration, and Herman's short call is assigned, of course, giving him an effective selling price of $52. His first reaction is one of dismay. His $4 profit became a "$2 loss"—the difference between 52 and 54! Herman says, "that option cost me $2," and "I had my stock taken away." For some reason, the $4 profit, a handsome if-called return, is forgotten.

Perhaps Herman's different reactions arise from the nature of making a proactive decision to sell versus having no control over when his short call is assigned. Whatever the reason, investors like Herman who employ covered writing, must make every effort to adapt psychologically to this investment strategy. No matter what the investment strategy, there is always "something better" that could have been done. One almost never buys at the exact bottom or sells at the exact top. "Selling early" is certainly not only caused by covered writing. All experienced investors have had some stocks they wish they had never sold.

Being assigned and selling stock is part of covered writing. On the positive side, it means the maximum possible return on that covered write has been earned. This is a good event! Adjusting to the reality of this psychologically is an important step in learning to use covered writing.

Myth #2: "Covered Writing Is a Good Strategy, because Most Options Expire Worthless."

This misconception is a commonly held belief, but it is illogical, and there are some facts which support the idea that this belief is illogical. If most options expired worthless, then there would be "excess returns" to be made from selling options. If this were true, then, in a competitive market place, opportunity-seeking capital would rush in to realize those "excess returns." To earn these supposed returns, many options would be sold, driving down option prices to the point where excess returns were no longer available. At such a point, it would no longer be true that "most options expire worthless."

The fact is, most options do not expire worthless. The Chicago Board Options Exchange (CBOE) publishes an annual statistics booklet which discloses the percentage of CBOE equity options in customer and firm accounts which are closed prior to expiration, exercised and expire worthless. The monthly numbers for 1993 and 1994 are presented in Table 7–2. These figures are percentages of the number of option contracts which were opened

Table 7–2   Equity Options-Liquidations, Exercises and Expirations (%)

1993	Closing Sells Total	Call	Put	Exercises Total	Call	Put	Long Expirations Total	Call	Put
JAN	56.1	47.8	58.9	9.9	11.3	9.4	34.0	40.9	31.7
FEB	47.2	47.9	46.9	11.2	18.4	8.1	41.6	33.7	44.9
MAR	55.8	48.7	58.8	9.0	11.3	8.1	35.2	40.0	33.2
APR	55.0	53.1	55.8	9.7	12.4	8.4	35.4	34.5	35.8
MAY	56.7	49.6	60.3	10.2	12.6	8.9	33.1	37.8	30.8
JUN	55.4	54.5	55.8	8.8	12.8	7.1	35.8	32.7	37.1
JUL	54.7	51.1	56.3	10.4	15.2	8.3	34.9	33.7	35.4
AUG	56.0	53.3	57.6	10.3	12.5	9.2	33.6	34.2	33.3
SEP	53.2	51.4	54.1	10.8	14.4	9.0	36.0	34.1	36.9
OCT	57.8	47.9	62.0	11.3	11.3	11.3	30.9	40.8	26.8
NOV	57.2	52.9	59.1	11.8	15.1	10.3	31.0	32.0	30.5
DEC	55.9	49.2	58.8	10.0	9.8	10.1	34.0	41.0	31.0
TOTAL	55.4	50.7	57.4	10.3	12.9	9.2	34.3	36.4	33.4

1994	Total	Call	Put	Total	Call	Put	Total	Call	Put
JAN	57.7	62.7	43.9	11.3	11.5	10.6	31.0	25.7	45.5
FEB	57.3	59.1	52.7	11.4	10.4	14.0	31.3	30.5	33.3
MAR	57.7	59.6	53.2	9.9	8.0	14.6	32.3	32.4	32.2
APR	53.3	49.8	62.8	9.1	5.5	18.8	37.6	44.7	18.3
MAY	58.3	58.3	58.2	9.6	7.8	13.4	32.2	33.9	28.4
JUN	54.5	54.2	55.3	11.9	10.8	14.7	33.5	35.0	30.0
JUL	30.3	31.0	28.3	14.6	12.4	20.5	55.1	56.6	51.3
AUG	52.8	56.7	44.4	12.2	12.5	11.5	35.1	30.9	44.0
SEP	50.9	54.2	42.3	14.2	15.9	9.8	34.8	29.9	48.0
OCT	54.7	56.7	50.1	11.4	10.5	13.4	33.9	32.8	36.6
NOV	52.6	53.2	51.3	11.4	9.4	16.6	36.0	37.5	32.2
DEC	47.35	45.6	51.6	13.5	9.21	24.0	39.2	45.2	24.4
TOTAL	53.1	54.3	50.2	11.5	10.2	14.9	35.4	35.5	34.9

Source: Chicago Board Options Exchange

during the contract life. One must be careful not to read too much into these numbers, because they do not include equity options in market maker accounts or index options, and they give no indication whether money was made or lost. The CBOE statistics indicate that approximately 35% of option contracts expire worthless.

Simply stated, investors should not write calls on stocks they believe will appreciate beyond the option break-even point.

Seen in its proper light, the covered write strategy offers a different set of trade-offs than outright purchase of stock. A stock purchase has a break-even price equal to the purchase price, makes nothing if the stock price does not rise and has unlimited profit potential. The covered write strategy, by comparison, has a lower break-even price, profits in an unchanged price environment but has limited profit potential. The two strategies, buying stock outright and covered writing, offer different trade-offs. No one knows in advance which will be better or even if either will be profitable, but competing forces in the market place determine the prices, and investors must select the strategy which, based on their judgment, is most likely to succeed and will best suit their risk preferences.

The options market simply presents investors with more alternatives, each of which is in some sense equal in the estimate of the combined market forces which determine prices. There are no "excess returns." Coming to grips with this notion will make it easier to move forward with the work of investing—researching investment opportunities and making decisions.

Myth #3: "Covered Writing Is a Bad Strategy, because It Forces Investors To Sell Winners and Keep Losers."

It is easy to see how this idea developed. When a stock price is above the strike of the short call on the expiration date, an assignment notice is received and the stock is sold. Thus the notion that "one sells winners." Similarly, if a stock falls in price, the call expires unexercised; and the "loser is kept." But who or what is responsible for "selling winners" and "keeping losers"—options or investors? Where is it written that a sold stock, whether sold by option assignment or conscious decision, cannot be repurchased? And where is it written that a stock which has declined in price cannot be sold outright if it is not called away by an option assignment?

In other words, why are the events described above the fault of options? Every investment must be managed if good results are expected. When stock prices start down, it is the investor's job to recognize the new trend and take appropriate action. Some investment professionals employ strict rules about stop-loss orders if a price declines by a certain percentage. Other experienced investors believe investing is too subjective to have one rule that fits all situations. Nevertheless, making decisions about selling stocks that are not performing or which have changed trend is the responsibility of every investor. Stock investments must be managed. Investors do not abdicate their management responsibilities when option strategies are employed.

Myth #4: "Commissions Make Covered Writing Impossible."

Commissions and other transaction costs are definitely important factors to be considered. Although there is a strong argument that transaction costs often make it prohibitive to purchase 100 shares and sell one call, transaction costs, as a general rule, decrease significantly as the number of shares increases. As mentioned earlier, most brokerage firms have a "break point" which means a point where a quantity discount kicks in. For example, many firms have a minimum commission which means that two, three or sometimes five options can be traded for nearly the same cost as one option. Obviously, trading two for the same cost as one means a lower price per share. And this difference can significantly impact the static and if-called return calculations. As stated earlier, investors must determine whether or not they have sufficient capital to engage in covered writing.

Myth #5: "Covered Writing Is Boring."

Any successful investor will agree that the task of identifying good investment opportunities is time consuming. Whether an investor does fundamental research independently, relies on investment letters, newspaper columns, or studies one of the many methods of technical analysis, getting good ideas takes time. Furthermore, once an investment idea has been selected and acted on, the role of patience increases; it does not decrease. Buying and holding stocks is a classic example. Once a stock has been purchased, it requires discipline and patience not to "take a quick profit" (or a quick loss!) if the investment was intended for the "long term."

Covered writing is similar. Entering a position for 60 to 120 days or longer may take more patience than short-term traders are accustomed to, but covered writing is a different kind of activity than short-term trading. It is prudent to commit a substantial amount of capital to covered writing, and covered write positions do not have to be monitored so frequently as short-term trades. If a covered writer is comfortable with the stock selection—as one must be—the position need not be reviewed any more often than longer-term holdings in a portfolio. At option expiration, either the short call expires, or an assignment notice is received (indicating the stock was sold). At this point another decision has to be made. If the stock is sold, the decision is between a wide range of alternatives including, but not limited to, repurchasing the same stock, buying another stock, entering into another covered write or leaving the funds in an interest-bearing account. If the call expires unexercised, the range of choices is equally wide starting with whether to hold or sell the stock. The call's expiration or being assigned does not make a decision for the investor: the smart investor consciously chooses the best investment given the current market environment.

Entering covered writes three or four times a year is much more active than buying and holding a stock. If an investor has two or three covered write positions at a time, then it is possible to stagger the expiration dates so that new decisions have to be made on a regular basis. This kind of activity is certainly not "boring." In fact, it adds variety and interest to the individual investor's management tactics.

Myth #6: "Covered Writing Underperforms"

Only a few studies have been conducted on the investment performance of a portfolio of stocks which consistently employed the covered writing strategy. One of the best studies is by James Yates of DYR Associates, Vienna, Virginia. In Yates' study, at-the-money calls are sold every 90 days on a portfolio of 99 stocks. The study was started at the inception of the option market in 1973 and the results through March 31, 1995 are presented in Figure 7–2.

At first glance covered writing appears to have underperformed the S&P 500 during the 21 years studied. However, a closer look reveals the following: covered writing outperformed the S&P 500 during the period 1973 through 1982 and underperformed during the period 1983 through 1993. In 1994, covered writing was the better performer.

Investment strategies designed to produce income, as opposed to growth, generally underperformed the S&P 500 Index during the 1980s; however, income-oriented investors probably still preferred (or needed) the income and would not have switched to growth strategies. Consequently, the fact that covered writing was not the best performer during one period does not diminish its importance in an investment portfolio. For income-oriented investors, the "proper role" of covered writing is undoubtedly larger than

Figure 7–2 Buy Stock—Write Call

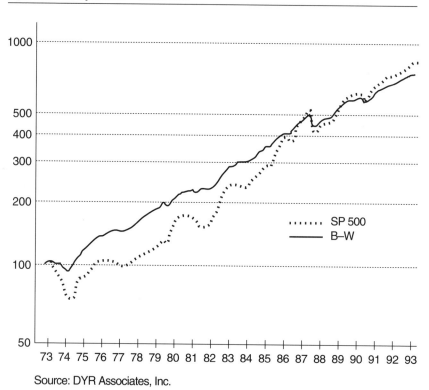

Source: DYR Associates, Inc.

in growth portfolios. If one believes, however, the current stock market environment is more like the stock market of the seventies, then more emphasis might be placed on this strategy in one's overall investing activities.

Summary

Covered writing is a conservative option strategy involving the purchase of stock and the selling of calls on a share-for-share basis. Selling a call when the underlying stock is owned pursues one of three investment objectives. In stable or sideways trading markets, the call expires worthless and the premium is kept. In rising markets, a selling price for the stock is established above the current stock price at the time the call is sold. In declining markets, the call premium acts as limited downside protection and lowers the break-even price on the owned stock.

Two traditional measures of covered writing positions are the static return, which assumes the stock price is unchanged at expiration, and the if-called return, which assumes the stock price is at or above the strike at expiration and the stock is sold at the strike price. These are benchmark measures to be used as part of the subjective decision-making process; they are not absolute measures. The stock purchase decision is the most important element of selecting a good covered write. Investors who employ the covered writing strategy must be willing to own the stock selected, and they must be willing to sell at the effective price dictated by the sold call. When properly understood, assignment of the short call, which requires the sale of the purchased stock, is not a "bad" event. Rather, assignment means that the maximum possible return from the covered write has been earned. If an investor determines the if-called return is satisfactory prior to establishing a covered write position, then assignment must be viewed as a "good" event.

There are a number of myths about covered writing which, upon reflection, are either illogical or incorrectly blame options for outcomes which are actually the result of an investor's failure to make conscious decisions. To employ covered writing, an investor must understand that the covered writing strategy is different from the traditional buy-and-hold strategy. When an investor comes to grips with the psychological differences required by covered writing, it is easier to find the proper place for this strategy within the sphere of an investor's activities.

Eight

Adjusted Covered Writes

Introduction

The decision to employ covered writing does not "lock in" an investor until the expiration date. When a market forecast proves inaccurate, when a forecast changes or when market conditions change, a covered writer may need to take action. Sometimes the appropriate action is to close a position and take a loss. Sometimes the profit potential and break-even point of a covered write position can be "adjusted" to match the revised forecast. Adjusting a covered write position is accomplished by a two-part trading action known as rolling.

This chapter discusses alternative courses of action available to covered writers when, for whatever reason, the market forecast has changed. Changing a market forecast, of course, is subjective and, for the purposes of the following examples, no attempt will be made to explain how the forecast was reached.

Rolling Defined

The typical "adjustment" to a covered write is to "roll" the short call. In the context of a covered write position, *rolling* means closing an existing short call position by purchasing it in the market and, at the same time, establishing another short call position by selling a call with a different strike and/or expiration. The result of this process is to change both the break-even point and the profit potential of the original covered write.

Rolling Up

Rolling up means repurchasing (or covering) an existing short call (to close the position) and selling a call with the same expiration but a higher strike. Rolling up raises both the maximum profit potential and the break-even point. Assume, for example, that 30 days ago Linda, a party planner in Chicago, entered a 90-day covered write on a large transportation stock, Railco. She purchased 100 shares of Railco at $64 and sold the 90-day 65 Call for 3. The stock pays no dividends, so Linda calculated the static and if-called returns to be 19.9% and 26.6%, respectively, not including transaction costs. In the last 30 days, Railco has done better than Linda expected. The price rose to $70 and has recently pulled back to $67. The 65 Call is now 4 1/2, and Linda's market forecast has changed. She originally thought Railco would trade around $65; now she thinks it will trade closer to $70. With the 70 Call trading at $2, and there being 60 days to expiration, Linda sees an opportunity to improve her profit potential.

Linda can "roll up" by repurchasing her short 65 Call for 4 1/2 (to close the position) and, simultaneously, selling the 70 Call for 2. The cost, or *net debit*, of this action is 2 1/2 (plus commissions), the difference between the purchase price of the 65 Call and the selling price of the 70 Call. Linda's changed profit potential is calculated in three steps. First, the new net purchase price is calculated by adding the net cost of the roll to the original net purchase price. Second, the new selling price is identified; this is simply the strike price of the new call, just as the original selling price was the strike price of the original call. Third, the new maximum profit potential is calculated by subtracting the new net purchase price from the new selling price.

Linda's original net purchase price was $61 per share (not including commissions). This is calculated by subtracting the price of the 65 Call (3) from the stock purchase price ($64). Her new net purchase price is $63 1/2 (not including commissions), the original net purchase price ($61) plus the net amount paid for the roll (2 1/2).

Linda's new selling price is $70, the strike price of the new call. The original selling price was $65, the strike price of the original call. It must be noted that the selling price is not equal to the call strike plus the call premium. In calculating the net purchase price, the call premium is subtracted from the purchase price of the stock. If the call premium were also added to the call strike price, then it would be counted twice.

Linda's original maximum profit potential was $4, the original strike price of $65 minus the original net purchase price of $61. Her new maximum profit potential is $6 1/2, the new strike price of $70 minus the new net purchase

Figure 8–1 Linda's Original and Adjusted Covered Write Positions

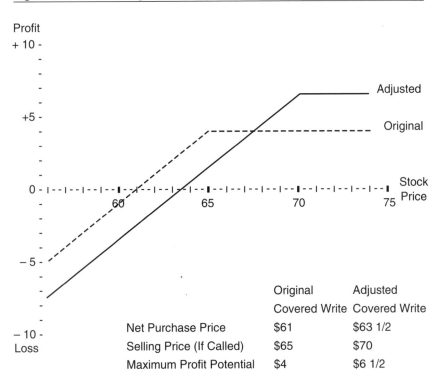

	Original Covered Write	Adjusted Covered Write
Net Purchase Price	$61	$63 1/2
Selling Price (If Called)	$65	$70
Maximum Profit Potential	$4	$6 1/2

price of $63 1/2. Again, for simplicity in explaining the concepts, none of these figures or calculations has included commissions. In real world examples, however, commissions are significant and must be included in all calculations. Figure 8–1 compares Linda's original position with her new one.

Which is better? There is no objective answer to this question! Linda's new situation has a higher profit potential, but it also has a higher break-even stock price. Her decision was a subjective one based on her revised forecast for Railco stock. Using the options market did not give Linda a "better" situation; it just gave her another alternative with different trade-offs.

Rolling Down

Rolling down means repurchasing (or covering) an existing short call (to close the position) and selling a call with the same expiration but a lower strike. Rolling down lowers both the maximum profit potential and the break-even point. In the following example, Bob, a traveling salesman who spends his spare time looking for "good covered writes," uses the rolling down technique to salvage a bad situation. Twenty-five days ago Bob bought stock in Surgeco, a large electrical equipment manufacturer, at $48 and sold the 75-day 50 Call for 1 1/2. Surgeco pays a .50 dividend two weeks before expiration, so Bob calculated the static return at 20.9% and the if-called return at 41.9% (not including commissions). Surgeco, however, is now trading at $45, and the 50 Call is now 1/4. Bob realizes this was a bad trade and is now forecasting that Surgeco will continue to trade near $45 until expiration in 50 days. Bob could take a net loss of $1 3/4 per share by selling the stock at $45 (–$3) and buying back the 50 Call at 1/4 (+1 1/4). Instead, given his new forecast, Bob has identified an opportunity which, in his opinion, is likely to do better. He decides to roll down to the 45 Call which is trading at 2 1/4.

Bob can roll down by repurchasing his 50 Call for 1/4 and selling the 45 Call for 2 1/4. The amount received, or *net credit*, of this action is 2 (less commissions), the difference between the selling price of the 45 Call and the

Figure 8–2 Bob's Original and Adjusted Covered Write Positions

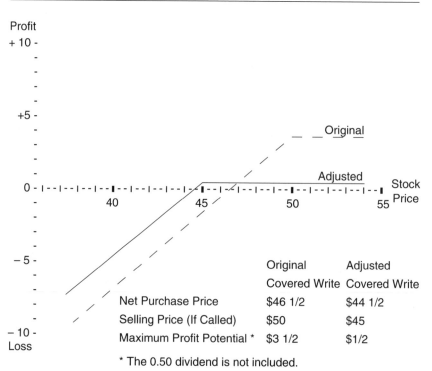

	Original Covered Write	Adjusted Covered Write
Net Purchase Price	$46 1/2	$44 1/2
Selling Price (If Called)	$50	$45
Maximum Profit Potential *	$3 1/2	$1/2

* The 0.50 dividend is not included.

purchase price of the 50 Call. Bob's changed profit potential is calculated in three steps, similar to the calculations made for Linda.

Bob's original net purchase price was $46 1/2 per share (not including commissions). Subtracting the net credit of 2 received for rolling down, the new net purchase price is $44 1/2.

Bob's original selling price, if assigned, was $50, the strike price of the original call. The new selling price is $45, the strike price of the new call. Consequently, with a net purchase price of $44 1/2 and a selling price of $45, Bob's new maximum profit potential is 1/2, not including commissions or the 0.50 dividend. Figure 8–2 compares Bob's original position with his new one.

While Bob's original position was much better than his new position, unfortunately, Bob is not choosing between these two. He is choosing between taking a $1 3/4 loss at current prices or rolling down and hoping to make 1/2 if the stock price remains at or above $45. Readers must remember that rolling is *not* necessarily preferable to taking the loss. Which strategy turns out to be better depends on actual stock price action and, as every investor knows, forecasting stock prices is an art, not a science. Consequently, only time will tell whether Bob made the "right" choice. But whatever the outcome, the option market gave Bob a viable alternative which does not exist in the stock market alone.

Rolling Out

Rolling out means repurchasing (or covering) an existing short call (to close the position) and selling a call with the same strike but a later expiration. Rolling out increases the maximum profit potential, lowers the break-even point and extends the time period. In this example, Joe, an attorney with the government in southern Illinois who gets good investment advice from a friend in Chicago, has had a very successful covered writing experience. Eighty days ago he entered a 90-day covered write on the stock of Grainco, a large animal feed distributor. Joe purchased stock at $96 and sold the December 100 Call for 3 1/8. The stock paid a .75 dividend last week, so the static return was 17% and the if-called return was 35% (before commissions). Grainco has traded in a narrow range since this covered write was initiated and is now trading at $97. December expiration is ten days away, and the December 100 Call is now 1/4. Joe is happy with this covered write and forecasts the stock will continue to trade between $95 and $100. The March 100 Call, 108 days to expiration, is trading at 3 5/8. Joe sees an opportunity, given his forecast, to extend this attractive income-oriented investment.

Joe can roll out by repurchasing the December 100 Call for 1/4 and selling the March 100 Call for 3 5/8. The net credit of this action is 3 3/8 (less commissions). Joe's adjusted profit potential is calculated in three steps. His original net purchase price was $92 7/8 per share (not including commissions). His new net purchase price is $89 1/2, the $92 7/8 original net purchase price less the 3 3/8 credit received for rolling out. His original maximum profit potential was $7 1/8, not including the 0.75 dividend or commissions. His new maximum profit potential is $10 1/2, not including next quarter's dividend or commissions, *but this is for a longer time period.*

Making New Static and If-Called Calculations

Because of the longer time period, the decision to roll out should not be based on the market forecast alone, but should also include new static and if-called return calculations. To make these calculations, Joe must assume he is making a *fresh start*, buying the stock at $97 and selling the 108-day March 100 Call for 3 3/8. Note that the figure used for the price of the March 100 Call is the net credit received (less commissions which are not included for simplicity). In Joe's case the December 100 Call is repurchased (or covered) for 1/4 and the March 100 Call is sold for 3 5/8, for a net credit of 3 3/8. An additional positive factor is the absence of a commission for purchasing the stock, since it is already owned, although an extra commis-

---

Exhibit 8–1 Joe's Adjusted Covered Write Position

New Static Rate of Return Calculation

> Current Stock Price: $97
> 100 Call - Net Received: 3 3/8 (3 5/8 – 1/4)
> Dividends: .75
> Days to Expiration: 108

$$\text{New Static Return} = \frac{\text{New Income}}{\text{New Investment}} \times \text{Annualization Factor}$$

$$= \frac{\text{Net Call Premium} + \text{Dividend}}{\text{Current Stock Price} - \text{Net Call Premium}} \times \frac{\text{Days per Year}}{\text{Days to Expiration}}$$

$$= \frac{3\ 3/8 + 3/4}{97 - 3\ 3/8} \times \frac{365}{108} = .149 = 14.9\%$$

Exhibit 8–2 Joe's Adjusted Covered Write Position

New If-Called Rate of Return Calculation

> Current Stock Price: $97
> 100 Call - Net Received: 3 3/8 (3 5/8 – 1/4)
> Dividends: .75
> Days to Expiration: 108

$$\text{New If-Called Return} = \frac{\text{New Income + New Gain}}{\text{New Investment}} \times \text{Annualization Factor}$$

$$= \frac{\text{Net Call Premium + Dividend + (Call Strike Price – Current Stock Price)}}{\text{Current Stock Price – Net Call Premium}}$$

$$\times \frac{\text{Days per Year}}{\text{Days to Expiration}}$$

$$= \frac{3\ 3/8 + 3/4 + (100 - 97)}{97 - 3\ 3/8} \times \frac{365}{108} = .257 = 25.7\%$$

sion will be paid for repurchasing the December 100 Call. Joe's static return for the covered write extended to March is calculated in Exhibit 8–1. The if-called return will, of course, include a sell commission for the stock. The if-called return for Joe's extended covered write is calculated in Exhibit 8–2.

Now all the pieces are in place and Joe can make a decision with complete information. His market forecast is that Grainco will trade between $95 and $100 for the next 108 days. The static return of 14.9% and the if-called return of 25.7% (before commissions) are in line with the previous covered write returns which he finds acceptable. Furthermore, Joe is willing to sell his Grainco stock and realize the if-called return if assignment occurs. Joe, being satisfied with the return calculations and courageously believing in his market forecast, instructs his broker to buy the December 100 Call and sell the March 100 Call.

Common Mistakes in Rolling

The only real reason to adjust a covered write position, or any investment position for that matter, is a changed market forecast. Linda felt her stock would trade closer to $70 than $65 and decided to increase her profit potential. Bob believed Surgeco would stay above $45 and he adjusted his covered write in an effort to recoup his loss. Joe extended the time horizon of his original forecast and rolled out to the March option because it offered a desirable return, given his perception of the risk.

Because rolling involves transaction costs and has implications for returns, a covered writer must make a conscious decision to adjust a covered write and not roll just for the sake of rolling. Some of the reasons for *not rolling* are the following: Do not roll for fear of "losing the stock" or "paying extra commissions due to assignment." Do not roll for fear of "early exercise." Do not roll "to get my money back." Each of these will be explained in turn.

Rolling to "Avoid Losing the Stock"

The last chapter warned the covered writer to be ready and willing to sell the underlying stock at the price dictated by the short call. If assignment occurs, therefore, an investor is not "losing the stock" but realizing the maximum profit, the if-called return. The covered writer is seeing the logical consequence of a conscious decision. Some investors must struggle with this when first engaging in covered writing.

Rolling to "Avoid Paying Extra Commissions Due to Assignment"

The initial analysis of static and if-called returns must include an accurate estimate of commissions, including a commission for selling stock in the if-called scenario. If those returns are deemed satisfactory, then being assigned and selling the stock does not incur extra commissions. Those costs were included in the original return calculations.

Rolling to "Avoid Early Exercise"

Equity options in the U.S. are American style, which means the option owner has the right to exercise at any time prior to expiration. If a call option is deep in-the-money and/or expiration is very close, then it may be exercised just prior to a dividend payment. Consequently, covered writers may be required to sell stock and, as a result, will not be eligible to receive the dividend. While there is no way to avoid this situation, there is a way to anticipate it and to determine whether it is an "acceptable" event.

All that needs to be done is an additional return calculation. For lack of a better name, this return is dubbed the "called-at-dividend return," the assumption being that the call is assigned immediately prior to the ex-dividend date and the stock is sold at the strike price of the short call. There are two differences between this return and the if-called return. There is no dividend in the "income," and the number of days is lower. If the "called-at-dividend" return is deemed acceptable, then being assigned early and not receiving the dividend is acceptable.

An unacceptable called-at-dividend return does not, however, automatically disqualify a covered write. This is just another subjective element of the investment-selection decision. The investor must consciously make a decision about the likelihood of the scenario occurring. If an out-of-the-money or at-the-money call is being considered, there is less chance of early assignment than if an in-the-money call is being considered.

Rolling "To Get My Money Back"

A covered write position will lose money if the stock price is below the breakeven price at expiration. If the price drops below this point prior to expiration, it is only natural for an investor to feel anxiety. In the example of rolling down presented above, Bob faced this situation and decided to roll down to the 45 Call. It was clearly stated that Bob's forecast called for the stock to trade at or above $45 until expiration in 50 days. There are no hard and fast rules about what to do in such a situation, but an investor's action should be consistent with the market forecast. Hope will not cause a declining stock price to stop declining. Sometimes it is best to close out a position and take a loss. This is just as true in covered writing as it is in other investment situations.

Summary

Rolling up, rolling down or rolling out involve the repurchase (to close) of a short call and the simultaneous sale of another call at a different strike and/or later expiration. Rolling will change the maximum profit potential and break-even point of the original position. When rolling out to a later expiration, new static and if-called return calculations should be made as if the investor were starting over. In these calculations, use the net credit received for the roll as the price of the sold call. Any decision to roll should be based on a consciously made market forecast and not for fear of losing the stock, paying extra commissions or being assigned early.

Nine

Buy Stock with Ratio Call Spread

The strategy discussed in this chapter has a cumbersome name. It is, however, an important strategy to master. This chapter will first explain the mechanics of the strategy, and then some applications will be presented.

Strategy Mechanics

Although the name "Buy Stock with Ratio Call Spread" is cumbersome, it has one advantage: it is descriptive! To implement this strategy, an investor buys stock and, at the same time, buys one at-the-money call for each 100 shares purchased and sells two out-of-the-money calls. The option position is called a ratio spread, because it involves a different number of long and short options, a one by two ratio in this case.

> **What Is a Ratio Call Spread?**

Figure 9–1 and Table 9–1 illustrate this strategy on a per-share basis assuming the purchase of stock at $50, the purchase of one 50 Call at 3 and the sale of two 55 Calls at 1 1/2 each. For the sake of simplicity, commissions and other transaction costs are not included. In the real world, however, these factors have a significant impact on this strategy, and they will be discussed later in this chapter.

Some Observations

First, note that there are no uncovered short calls. One short call is covered by the long stock; the other is covered by the owned 50 Call. Second, this strategy is stock-oriented and does not involve leverage if the stock price declines; losses from a price decline are equal to owning the stock outright. Leverage, however, is involved if the stock price rises. Figure 9–1 and Table 9–1 illustrate how the profits of this strategy are $2 per share for each $1 price rise between $50 and $55 at expiration. With the stock price at $51 at expiration, for example, the total position will profit by $2 per share, not including commissions, even though

Only "Covered" Options Are Involved

the stock has only risen by $1. The limited profit potential of this strategy is the third important observation. With the stock price above $55 at expiration, the maximum profit potential of $10 per share is realized.

The Mechanics at Expiration

Exercise of the long 50 Call and/or assignment of the two short 55 Calls depend on the underlying stock price. There are three possible outcomes in the example presented above. The stock price might be (1) at or below $50, (2) above $50 and at or below $55 or (3) above $55. Each possibility will be examined.

If the stock price is at or below $50 at expiration, all options expire worthless. The amount of the loss depends entirely on the stock position since the option position, in this example, was established for zero cash outlay, not including transaction costs. At expiration, this example of the strategy will lose $1 per share for each $1 decline in the stock price below $50. At a stock price of $48, the result is a $2 loss per share as illustrated by Table 9–1.

If the stock price is above $50 and at or below $55 at expiration, the profit in this example is twice the stock profit. With the stock at $53, for example, the profit of 6 is comprised of a $3 profit from the stock price rise, a break-even result on the 50 Call and a profit of 3 from the two short 55 Calls, which expire worthless and profit by 1 1/2 each. The total profit of 6 in this example is twice the stock profit of 3.

The existence of the in-the-money 50 Call has both positive and negative consequences which the investor must anticipate. On the positive side, the value of the 50 Call caused the profit in this example to double that of stock ownership.

Below the Lower Strike: Long Stock

The negative is the issue of exercise and related costs. Since the 50 Call is in-the-money, its exercise will create a long position of a second

Figure 9–1 Buy Stock with Ratio Call Spread

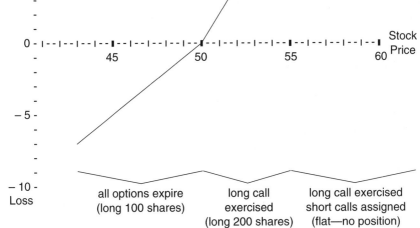

Profit
+ 10 -
    -
    -
    -
    -
    -
+5 -
    -
    -
    -
    -
0 -
    -
    -
    -
    -
− 5 -
    -
    -
    -
    -
− 10 -
Loss

Buy Stock   @ $50
Buy 1 50 Call   @ 3
Sell 2 55 Calls @ 1 1/2 each

Profit or Loss at Expiration (per share)

45   50   55   60

Stock Price

all options expire
(long 100 shares)

long call
exercised
(long 200 shares)

long call exercised
short calls assigned
(flat—no position)

Table 9–1 Buy Stock With Ratio Call Spread—Profit or Loss Per Share

Stock Price at Expiration	Long Stock @ $50	Long 1 50 Call @ 3	Short 2 55 Calls @ 1 1/2 ea.	Total P/(L) at Expiration
$57	+7	+4	−1	+10
$56	+6	+3	+1	+10
$55	+5	+2	+3	+10
$54	+4	+1	+3	+8
$53	+3	0	+3	+6
$52	+2	−1	+3	+4
$51	+1	−2	+3	+2
$50	0	−3	+3	0
$49	−1	−3	+3	−1
$48	−2	−3	+3	−2

100 shares. It must be decided whether to accept and pay for these shares (including transaction costs) or to sell them immediately (and incur additional transaction costs). Either situation adds transaction costs.

Between the Strikes: Long Stock & Long Call

Exercising the call and selling the stock involves additional risks for the investor to consider. There may be a timing difference between the stock purchase and its sale. If the call is exercised on expiration Friday and the stock is sold Monday, there is risk that the stock price may change adversely. Also, the over-the-weekend stock ownership must be financed. Although stock can be sold on a "next day basis" to avoid the financing, this involves additional transaction costs. These concerns must be thought through in advance of the expiration date when action is required.

Another risk to be considered is the price behavior of the options prior to the expiration date. Chapter 4 discussed how option prices change with the price of the underlying stock, with the passage of time and with changes in volatility, interest rates and dividends. If the option position is closed prior to expiration, it is possible that a loss may result.

The third outcome is a stock price above $55 at expiration. Figure 9–1 and Table 9–1 show a profit of $10 per share, not including transaction costs. At any stock price above $55, the long 50 Call is exercised, and the short 55 Calls are assigned. This means a second 100 shares will be purchased by the call exercise and all 200 shares will be sold by the assignment. These transaction costs must be considered before initiating this strategy.

With a stock price above $55, in this example, there is also the possibility of early assignment of one or both short calls. If one call is assigned early, the owned stock is sold; and this may mean a dividend is not received. If both calls are assigned early, then a short stock position is created; and this may result in an obligation to pay a dividend. Furthermore, it may not be possible to fulfill this obligation by exercising the long call. Although this sounds complicated, even intimidating, to inexperienced option users, these intricacies are part of investing with options and can be learned by anyone who examines each step in the exercise

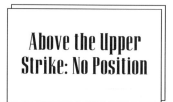

Above the Upper Strike: No Position

and assignment process and thinks through the timing at which each step might occur.

Motivations for This Strategy

An investor should not ask, "is buy stock with ratio call spread better than buying stock outright?" Option strategies, remember, are not better in an absolute sense; they just offer a different set of trade-offs.

Figure 9–2 and Table 9–2 compare three strategies: buying stock outright, the covered write and buy stock with ratio call spread. The prices are the same as for the example above: Stock Price, $50; 90-day 50 Call, 3; and 90-day 55 Call, 1 1/2.

> 3 Strategies:
> 3 Sets of Trade-Offs

The positives and negatives of each are apparent from Figure 9–2 and can be summed up as follows: buying stock has the positive of unlimited profit potential and the negative of $50 per share of risk. The positives of the covered call are the lower risk of $47 and a $3 profit in a "do-nothing" market. The negative of the covered write is the limit on profit potential of $3 per share. Buy stock with ratio call spread offers a third combination. The positives are twice the profits of owning stock between $50 to $55 with no additional risk. The negative is a limit on profit to $10 per share. Figure 9–2 does not include transaction costs which are an important consideration.

It is not a question of "Which is better?" Rather, it is a question of "What is the investor's forecast?" A sideways forecast favors the covered write. Forecasting a price rise above $60 favors buying stock outright, and forecasting a modest price rise, between $52 and $58, favors buy stock with ratio call spread. When an investor thoroughly understands what each strategy offers, an informed selection can be made.

How Realistic Are the Prices in This Example?

The first example in this chapter works perfectly. The stock price is exactly $50, and price of the 50 Call is exactly twice the price of the 55 Call, so the ratio call spread is established for no cash outlay (not including commissions). Is this example made up for the purpose of this book, or do such opportunities actually exist in the real world?

In fact, the relationship of the at-the-money call price being approximately twice that of the next higher strike call exists quite frequently when the time to expiration is four to six months and the stock price is above $50.

Figure 9–2 Comparison of Three Strategies

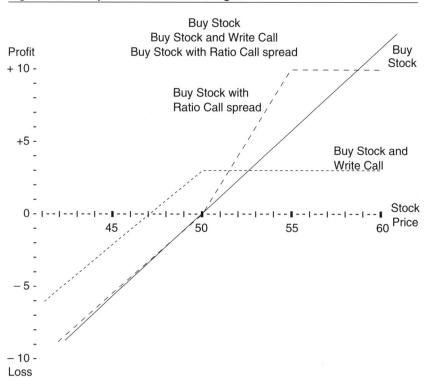

A brief review of option prices on a particular day revealed these actual bid and offer prices on well-known large capitalization stocks:

	Stock Offer Price	At-the-Money Call Offer Price	Out-of-the-Money Call Bid Price	Days to Expiration
Stock #1	73	75 Call—3 3/4	80 Call—1 3/4	138
Stock #2	49 1/2	50 Call—3 1/2	55 Call—1 1/2	138
Stock #3	80 1/4	80 Call—4 3/4	85 Call—2 3/8	138
Stock #4	60 1/2	60 Call—5 1/8	65 Call—2 5/8	159

Using Real World Prices

Assume that Terry expects the price of Stock #1 to be $80 at expiration and investigates the buy stock with ratio call spread strategy. Using the prices list-

**Table 9–2   Buy Stock, Buy Stock and Write Call, and
            Buy Stock with Ratio Call Spread**

Stock Price at Expiration	Long Stock @ $50	Long Stock @ $50 and Short 50 Call @ 3	Long Stock @ $50 and Long 1 50 Call @ 3 and Short 2 55 Calls @ 1 1/2 ea.
$62	+12	+3	+10
$61	+11	+3	+10
$60	+10	+3	+10
$59	+9	+3	+10
$58	+8	+3	+10
$57	+7	+3	+10
$56	+6	+3	+10
$55	+5	+3	+10
$54	+4	+3	+8
$53	+3	+3	+6
$52	+2	+3	+4
$51	+1	+3	+2
$50	0	+3	0
$49	−1	+2	−1
$48	−2	+1	−2
$47	−3	0	−3
$46	−4	−1	−4
$45	−5	−2	−5

ed above, Terry cannot establish the option position for zero cash outlay. If he buys one 75 Call at 3 3/4 and sells two 80 Calls for 1 3/4 each, Terry has paid a net of 1/4, not including transaction costs, to establish the option position.

Figure 9–3 and Table 9–3 present an analysis Terry might use prior to engaging in this strategy. For simplicity, transaction costs are not included, and Terry is assumed to have confidence in his market forecast and be willing to assume the risk of owning Stock #1 at $73 per share.

With a stock price below $75 at expiration, Terry's position is no different than owning stock outright at a price of $73 1/4. Between $75 and $80 at expiration, however, the option strategy increases Terry's profits, and at or above $80, the maximum profit of 11 3/4 is achieved—7 from the stock price rise from $73 to $80 and 4 3/4 from the option position. If the stock

Figure 9–3 Example with Real Prices—138 Days to Expiration

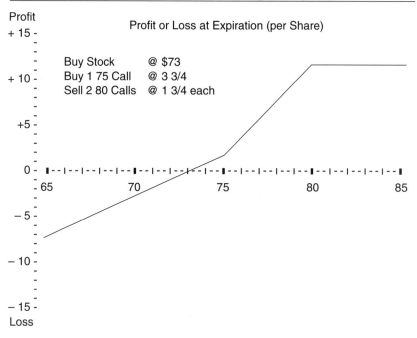

Profit

+ 15 -

Profit or Loss at Expiration (per Share)

+ 10 -
Buy Stock   @ $73
Buy 1 75 Call   @ 3 3/4
Sell 2 80 Calls   @ 1 3/4 each

+5 -

0 -

- 65   70   75   80   85

− 5 -

− 10 -

− 15 -
Loss

Table 9–3   Example with Real Prices—Profit or Loss Per Share

Stock Price at Expiration	Long Stock @ $73	Long 1 75 Call @ 3 3/4	Short 2 80 Calls @ 1 3/4 ea.	Total P/(L) at Expiration
$82	+9	+3 1/4	− 1/2	+11 3/4
$81	+8	+2 1/4	+1 1/2	+11 3/4
$80	+7	+1 1/4	+3 1/2	+11 3/4
$79	+6	+ 1/4	+3 1/2	+9 3/4
$78	+5	− 3/4	+3 1/2	+7 3/4
$77	+4	−1 3/4	+3 1/2	+5 3/4
$76	+3	−2 3/4	+3 1/2	+3 3/4
$75	+2	−3 3/4	+3 1/2	+1 3/4
$74	+1	−3 3/4	+3 1/2	+ 3/4
$73	0	−3 3/4	+3 1/2	− 1/4
$72	−1	−3 3/4	+3 1/2	−1 1/4

price is between $75 and $80 as expiration nears, Terry must plan whether (1) to sell the call or exercise it and (2) hold or sell the stock.

Another Application—The Stock Repair

The examples presented above assume the stock and option positions are initiated simultaneously. We now consider the situation of Sue who purchased 100 shares of Bellco at $65 last year. Sue had expected this doorbell manufacturer to do well in an expanding economy with increasing home construction. Unfortunately, the price of Bellco declined to its current price of $55. Ugh!! Sue has a loser! What to do?

In any investment decision, the most important element is the market forecast. If Sue predicts a continued adverse price move, the rational action is to take a loss (i.e., sell the stock). For the purposes of this example, however, assume that Sue is more optimistic and forecasts a price rise to $60 at option expiration.

"Doubling Up"

Given this situation, a $10 unrealized loss and a forecast for a $5 price rise, Sue might consider the old, standby strategy of "doubling up," or "dollar cost averaging," as buying a second 100 shares is frequently called. Purchasing a second 100 shares at $55 creates a 200 share position with an average cost of $60 per share. Consequently, if Sue's expectation of a price rise to $60 occurs, her loss is recouped. There are, however, at least two disadvantages to "doubling up." First, an additional capital investment is required. Second, the risk is doubled; if the stock price declines, contrary to Sue's forecast, then her losses mount at $2 per share for each $1 decline in the stock price.

Instead of automatically buying more stock, Sue could consider the advantages and disadvantages of the ratio call spread. Figure 9–4 and Table 9–4 illustrate how the strategy of purchasing one 55 Call for 4 and selling two 60 Calls at 2 each offers a new alternative. First, the break-even stock price of $60 is achieved. This is the same price as if Sue purchased a second 100 shares. Second, no additional capital investment (other than transaction costs) is required. Third, the risk is not doubled if the stock price declines, as Sue's outright stock ownership never exceeds 100 shares.

Figure 9–4 and Table 9–4 also illustrate the negative trade-off of using the ratio spread: breaking even is the best result possible—it doesn't get any better. Above $60, the result will be no position.

Figure 9–4 The Stock Repair Strategy

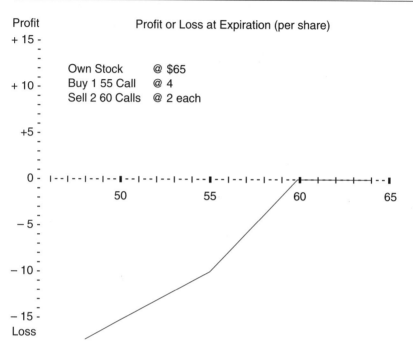

Table 9–4 The Stock Repair Strategy—Profit or Loss Per Share

Stock Price at Expiration	Own Stock @ $65	Long 1 55 Call @ 4	Short 2 60 Calls @ 2 ea.	Total P/(L) at Expiration
$64	−1	+5	−4	0
$63	−2	+4	−2	0
$62	−3	+3	0	0
$61	−4	+2	+2	0
$60	−5	+1	+4	0
$59	−6	0	+4	−2
$58	−7	−1	+4	−4
$57	−8	−2	+4	−6
$56	−9	−3	+4	−8
$55	−10	−4	+4	−10
$54	−11	−4	+4	−11
$53	−12	−4	+4	−12

Which is "better"—doubling up or using the ratio spread? Once again, there is no "better." Each strategy offers a different set of trade-offs. Doubling up lowers the break-even price and allows unlimited profit potential in return for increased investment and doubling of risk. The ratio call spread, in contrast, lowers the break-even price without increasing risk and without increased investment, in this example, but gives up participation in a price rise above $60. Neither is "better." The selection depends on an investor's forecast, risk tolerance and available capital.

Not a Trading Strategy

The figures and tables in this chapter have illustrated the "buy stock with ratio call spread" strategy at expiration. Although the OP-EVAL™ options pricing program can create tables (see Chapter 16) to illustrate how this strategy behaves prior to expiration, it is too cumbersome for the purposes of this book to do so here. Suffice it to say that short-term price behavior of this strategy makes it an undesirable trading vehicle. Even if transaction costs are ignored—which they should not be when analyzing real situations—the combined position of long stock, long one call and short two calls does not change sufficiently with two or three point moves in the stock price in short time periods to justify entering and exiting the position with any frequency. When this strategy is established, an investor must be committed to holding the position until expiration. Market conditions cause investors to change their forecasts, and a dramatically changed forecast is the exception. Nevertheless, this strategy should not be entered into with the intention of "trading in and out."

Summary

Buy stock with ratio call spread is a stock-oriented strategy which offers a different set of trade-offs than either covered writing or buying stock outright. In essence, this strategy adds low-cost leverage over a limited price range in the underlying stock. If the option positions can be established at the right prices, risk is not increased beyond owning the underlying stock. The negative is that upside participation is limited.

Because there are three options involved, commissions and other transactions costs can dramatically affect the desirability of this strategy. Generally, this strategy must be established in conjunction with the purchase or ownership of 200 shares or more so that per-share transaction costs are reduced. Finally, before employing this strategy, an investor must become thoroughly familiar with the mechanics at expiration. The purchase and/or sale of stock (resulting from exercise and/or assignment) has implications for transaction costs, the resulting investment position and the possible financing requirement of additional shares.

Buy stock with ratio call spread can be used as an initial strategy to add leverage without increasing risk, or it can be used as a "stock repair" strategy to lower the break-even point of a losing stock position. Regardless of how this strategy is used, this is not a "trading strategy."

Ten

The Protective Put

The Protective Put Strategy Defined

The protective put strategy is simply a two-part strategy in which stock and put options, on a share-for-share basis, are purchased simultaneously. The put option acts like an insurance policy on the stock. Any time an investor is bullish, but worried about short-term price action, the protective put strategy offers a way to purchase stock and limit risk at the same time.

> **Insure Stocks As You Insure Your Home**

This chapter will present in detail a situation in which an investor might employ the protective put strategy. In the following example, a profit and loss diagram will be created, and the expiration mechanics will be explained. This strategy will also be compared to another risk-limiting technique, the stop-loss order. At the end of this chapter, the concept of put-call parity will be introduced, because the risk profile of the protective put strategy is identical to the risk profile of another option strategy, and it is important to discuss why this occurs.

The Cautious Investor

Consider Kim, an experienced investor with a keen sense for opportunity and an equally keen desire to limit risk. Kim has been following Healthco, a medical supply company. The stock hit an all-time high of $75 two years ago but fell out of favor after a series of poor earnings reports. Its price declined to $32 1/2 six months ago and, since then, has traded in a narrow range around its current price of $36. The quarterly reports have discussed cost

137

cutting and new marketing efforts, and the sales figures have been favorable. Kim predicts the earnings report, due in two weeks, will surpass expectations and cause the stock price to rise. Kim realizes, of course, her assessment could be wrong and an unfavorable report could send the stock to new lows.

Kim wants to buy Healthco stock in order to take advantage of her bullish opinion, but she wants to limit risk, in case her forecast is incorrect. When purchasing 100 shares of Healthco at $36 per share, the strategy of simultaneously purchasing one 60-day 35 Put for 1 offers Kim an opportunity to accomplish her objectives. This strategy, known as the protective put strategy, is suited to Kim's situation, because it allows Kim to participate if the price rises and it limits her risk if the price declines.

Figure 10–1 is an expiration profit and loss diagram of Kim's position. The hyphenated line is the long stock. The dotted line is the long put. And the solid line is the combined position. Table 10–1 shows how the calculations are made. The top line of Table 10–1, for example, illustrates the outcome at $40. The purchased stock has increased in value by $4 per share, and the purchased put expires worthless, losing $1 per share. The combined position therefore earns $3 per share, not including commissions. In another example, a stock price of $32, the purchased stock loses $4 per share, the put earns a profit of $2, and the combined position loses $2 per share, not including commissions.

Expiration Mechanics

The purchased put gives Kim the right to sell her Healthco stock at the strike price, in this case $35 per share, at any time until the expiration date. If the stock is trading below $35 on the last day prior to expiration, the put will be trading at, or very near, its intrinsic value. In such a situation, Kim has two alternatives: first, she can exercise the put and, as a result, sell her Healthco stock at $35 per share. She will then be left no position. She will, of course, have $3,500 in cash (less commissions) from selling her 100 shares. She can then look for the next investment opportunity. As indicated in Figure 10–1 and Table 10–1, Kim will have a $2 per share loss with the stock price at $35 or below at expiration.

Alternatively, if Kim were favorably disposed to holding the stock at its current price, she could choose to sell the put in the open market and collect, in cash, the put's intrinsic value (less commissions). If Kim chooses this course of action, her position will be owning the originally purchased 100 shares of Healthco stock plus the cash proceeds from selling the put. Her

Figure 10–1 The Protective Put Strategy

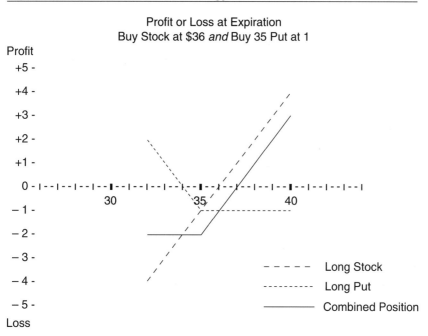

Profit or Loss at Expiration
Buy Stock at $36 *and* Buy 35 Put at 1

- - - - - Long Stock

---------- Long Put

———— Combined Position

Table 10–1 The Protective Put Strategy
Calculation of Profit or Loss at Expiration

Stock Price at Expiration	Long Stock @ $36 P/(L)	Long 35 Put @ 1 P/(L)	Combined Position P/(L)
$40	+4	−1	+3
$39	+3	−1	+2
$38	+2	−1	+1
$37	+1	−1	0
$36	0	−1	−1
$35	−1	−1	−2
$34	−2	0	−2
$33	−3	+1	−2
$32	−4	+2	−2

total holdings, stock plus cash, will be approximately the same $3,500 as if she chose to exercise the put. But, as explained above, Kim's loss will be $2 per share with a stock price of $35 or lower at expiration.

Protective Puts *Do* Limit Losses

Which is the best course of action? The answer to this question is a subjective decision which only Kim can make based on her forecast for Healthco stock.

If the price of Healthco is at or above $35 at expiration, Kim also has two choices. The 35 Put will expire worthless, but Kim can still review her decision to own the stock. If no new information has caused her to change her forecast, then Kim can continue to hold. She may in fact include it among her long-term holdings and never employ an option strategy on her Healthco stock again. Alternatively, if for any reason she has changed her opinion about the stock, Kim can sell it in the open market and look for another investment opportunity.

Motivations for the Protective Put Strategy

Any time an investor is "bullish but worried," the protective put strategy can be employed. Kim's case of a pending earnings report is not the only example of such situations. An investor could have a bullish opinion on a particular stock but a negative opinion on the market in general. Another appropriate time for purchasing a protective put to limit risk is when "trying to pick the bottom" on a particular stock. Some investors like to limit risk on all new positions and use protective puts, because they cannot follow those positions closely enough to be sure of selling if a particular loss level results.

Any time an investor views an investment opportunity as a "good price, but a risky time," the protective put strategy is one method of managing risk. Buying stock outright at such a time could prove costly if a sharp price decline occurs. *Not* buying, however, could mean missing a profitable opportunity.

Although stock purchasers face such choices frequently, the protective put strategy offers an alternative of dealing with the situation with its own set of positives and negatives, an alternative which does not exist without options. As Figure 10–1 illustrates, the protective put strategy limits risk, its advantage relative to buying stock outright. The strategy's disadvantage is a higher break-even price, $37 versus $36 for purchasing stock alone. Which alternative is "better"—simply buying stock or buying both the stock and the put? Again, there are no objective answers to such a question. In Kim's situation, she must evaluate her stock price forecast in conjunction with her tolerance for risk.

The Psychology of Insurance

Many investors find the logic of the protective put strategy difficult to accept. After all, if an investor is bullish, why purchase insurance? Why buy something you hope will expire worthless? When one stops to think about it, this is actually something people do all the time! Think about home insurance, car insurance, health insurance. No honest person wants a home to burn in order to collect insurance proceeds. No one wants to get into a car accident. Everyone wants these insurance policies to expire worthless! But these same people rest easy knowing that they are "protected."

Protective Puts Are
Time Dependent

The protective put strategy applies the same logic. Investors buy protective puts so they can rest easy; they hope the stock rises in price and their insurance policies, the puts, expire worthless. One difference, of course, is that no one is forcing an investor to buy insurance, whereas lenders and state laws compel home and car owners to buy insurance. Investors are also subject to "Monday morning quarterback-type thinking." If the stock rallies after investors buy both stock and puts, they kick themselves for having bought the puts. If the stock declines, even though the put limits the loss, they kick themselves for having bought the stock. This is a quandary for new investors, but experienced investors realize that making a certain percentage of losing investments is inevitable. Many experienced investors believe that the discipline of limiting an initial loss provided by the protective put is well worth the cost.

The Protective Put versus a "Stop-Loss" Order

Some investors may ask, "Why spend money on the put; why not just use a stop-loss order?" A stop-loss sell order is an order to sell at the market price, contingent on a stock trading at or being offered at a specified price which is below the current market price. For example, an investor who owns 100 shares of a stock trading at $45 might place a stop-loss order at $42. If the stock trades at or is offered at $42, the stop-loss order becomes an order to sell at the market and the shares are sold at the best available price. The motivation behind stop-loss orders is a desire to limit risk. Stop-loss orders do not assume a limited loss, because it is impossible to say, for certain, at what price the stock will be sold. Stock prices do not have to change in an orderly price sequence between trades. They can "gap" between trades, an occurrence most common at the start of trading each morning, since there is no guarantee that prices today will open where they closed yesterday. Stock prices can also "gap" during trading hours when a news item is released or an announcement from the company is made.

> ## Stop-Loss Orders Are Price-Dependent

The protective put strategy, however, does limit the loss of holding a stock during the put's life. Regardless of how much lower a "gap" trade might be, the owner of a protective put can exercise that put and sell the stock at the option strike price thus limiting the potential loss.

The most significant difference between the protective put and the stop-loss sell order is the nature of the limiting factor. A stop-loss sell order is price dependent; a protective put is time dependent. Within the life of the put, it is possible for the stock price to trade down to or below the specified stop-loss price level and then rebound higher, much to the dismay of the investor who placed the stop-loss order. The negative scenario for the protective put investor is the stock price decline occurring after the put expires worthless.

For these reasons, it cannot be said that a protective put is "better" than a stop-loss order. Protective puts just offer a different set of trade-offs: a limit on loss is the positive; limited life and cost are the negatives. A stop-loss sell order, in contrast, does not guarantee a maximum risk, the negative; but its positives are an unlimited life and it costs nothing.

Put-Call Parity Introduced

Figure 10–2 compares the profit and loss diagram for the protective put strategy introduced in this chapter and the call plus Treasury bill strategy presented in Chapter 6. The components and combined position of both strategies are illustrated. The combined positions appear identical. Many newcomers to options are confused by this and similar situations, and it is, therefore, important to discuss why strategies with different components have similar risk profiles.

The concept of put-call parity is that the prices of calls, puts and stock are related by interest rates. If the prices are not "in line" with each other, then arbitrage opportunities will exist. An in-depth explanation of put-call

**Figure 10–2 The Protective Put versus Buy Call Plus T-Bill
Expiration Profit and Loss Diagrams**

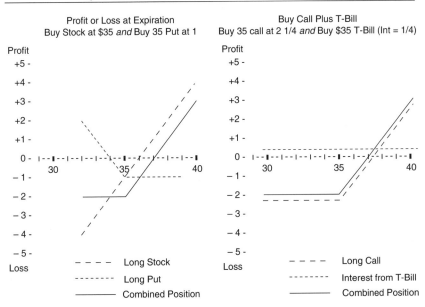

parity is beyond the scope of this book, but the following comments are warranted because they reinforce an understanding of the mechanics of option strategies at expiration.

Essentially, put-call parity means that calls, puts and stock can be added together in different combinations to create identical risk profiles, or profit and loss diagrams. The "protective put" strategy and the "buy call plus Treasury Bill" strategy are two strategies which are identical, assuming no commissions, because of the put-call parity concept. Figure 10–2 shows that the two strategies have the same risk profile. Table 10–2 shows how the two strategies result in positions which are identical or of equal market value at expiration.

In both strategies, if the stock price is above the strike at expiration, the resulting position is long stock. In the case of call plus T-Bill, the in-the-money call is exercised, and the purchased stock is paid for with the proceeds from the maturing T-Bill. In the case of the protective put, the put expires worthless when the stock price is above the strike, and the investor is left with the stock position originally purchased.

If the stock price is below the strike price at expiration, both strategies result in no stock position, only cash. The call plus T-Bill investor is left with cash from the maturing T-Bill when the out-of-the-money call expires

Table 10–2   Position at Expiration—Protective Put versus Buy Call + T-Bill

Buy Call + T-Bill	Stock Price at Expiration	Protective Put
LONG STOCK Call exercised and stock is purchased with proceeds from T-Bill	Stock Price Above Strike Price	LONG STOCK Put expires and long stock position is unaffected
CASH VALUE EQUALS STRIKE PRICE Call expires Investor may or may not choose to purchase stock with proceeds from T-Bill	Stock Price At Strike Price	STOCK VALUE EQUALS STRIKE PRICE Put expires Investor may or may not choose to sell stock
NO POSITION Call expires Investor may or may not choose to purchase stock with proceeds from T-Bill	Stock Price Below Strike Price	NO POSITION Put exercised, stock sold Investor may or may not choose to repurchase stock

worthless. The protective put investor is left with cash when the in-the-money put is exercised and the stock is sold.

In the third possible outcome, when the stock price is exactly at the strike price at expiration, the call plus T-Bill investor is left with the value of the strike price in cash when the call expires and can decide to keep the cash or convert it to stock (by buying stock). The protective put investor with the stock price exactly at the strike price at expiration, has stock equal in value to the strike price and can decide to keep stock or convert it to cash (by selling the stock). Consequently, with the stock price exactly at the strike price, both investors have exactly the same market value and can choose either stock or cash.

The conclusion to be drawn from Figure 10–2, Table 10–2 and the preceding discussion is that the call plus T-Bill investor has the same risk profile and ends up, at expiration, with the same outcome as the protective put investor. This is the result of the put-call parity concept.

The Real World Choice

Knowing that the positions of call plus T-Bill and stock plus put are equivalent, theoretically, the question becomes: What are the advantages and disadvantages of each in the real world? When speculative strategies versus investment strategies were defined in Chapter 5, the important criteria was the amount of equity capital available to pay for a position in the underlying stock. A clear advantage of the protective put strategy is that the stock is purchased, so the capital is obviously available. The protective put strategy can, therefore, be easily defined as "investment oriented."

Buying a call, by itself, does not involve the underlying stock. To make this strategy investment oriented, it is therefore necessary to set aside sufficient cash to pay for the underlying stock. This requires discipline at the very least and segregation of funds at the most. Consequently, it is not always easy to tell whether calls are purchased speculatively or as a short-term risk management technique for entering the underlying stock unless cash, or liquid investments, readily available to pay for the stock, can be identified.

The disadvantage of the protective put strategy is extra up-front transaction costs: one commission to purchase stock and one to purchase the put. There is also the possibility of a third commission for selling the stock if the put is exercised. Buying a call plus a Treasury Bill involves related commissions which are typically less than stock commissions. However, there will be a stock commission if the call is exercised. In the theoretical world, where commissions are ignored and discipline to maintain cash reserves is assumed, these two strategies are identical. In the real world, an investor must choose between extra commissions and maintaining discipline.

Summary

The protective put strategy offers investors an advantage relative to outright purchase of stock, because it combines the purchase of stock with limited risk for a limited time. The disadvantage of this strategy relative to the outright purchase of stock is the higher break-even point at expiration. While implementation of this strategy is subjective, it is appropriate when a stock purchaser is thinking "this is a good price, but a risky time."

The protective put strategy offers a different set of trade-offs than stop-loss orders. A stop-loss order involves no up-front payment; it is price dependent and has no time limit, but it does not assure a limited loss. The protective put, in contrast, has a limited life and requires an up-front payment, including commissions, all of which might be lost if the put expires worthless. The protective put, however, places a limited loss on owning the stock during its life.

Because of the put-call parity concept, the protective put strategy and buy call plus T-Bill are theoretically equivalent. There are real world differences, however, involving transaction costs and disciplined cash management.

SECTION 3

Advanced Investing Strategies

Eleven

Introduction to Margin Account Strategies

Risk in Relation to Account Equity

There are many ways to define risk. Investing in stocks is "risky" in one sense, but some ways of investing are more "risky" than others. When an investment strategy is established in a cash account, the maximum theoretical risk is known and fully funded. For example, if an investor buys stock or options in a cash account, the risk of total loss is paid in advance. If total loss occurs, the investor is not called upon for any additional payment.

Some margin account strategies are different because they involve obligations beyond the account equity. If an adverse price move occurs, then the margin account investor may be called upon to deposit additional equity or to close the position. While some margin account strategies involve this potential risk, some do not. Therefore, the need for a margin account does not necessarily mean that a strategy involves excessive risk.

Why Margin Accounts Were Created

Both cash accounts and margin accounts place certain requirements on investors, and each type of account offers a range of services. The primary distinction between the two types of accounts is the *risk to the brokerage firm*. Cash accounts allow only transactions which are fully paid for up front by the customer. The risk in a *cash account* is never greater than the account equity, and there is *virtually no risk to the brokerage firm*.

Margin accounts, in contrast, allow many transactions including those which require borrowing. The risk of positions held in margin accounts is potentially larger than the account equity, and *the brokerage firm has potential risk.* Because of this potential risk to the brokerage firm, customers are required to sign an agreement which gives the brokerage firm certain rights including the right to liquidate positions if certain equity levels are not maintained.

Buying Stock: Cash versus Margin

Consider the cases of Geoff, a cash buyer of stock, and Debra, a margin buyer. Both Geoff and Debra have $5,000 of capital. Geoff buys 100 shares of a $50 stock for $5,000. Debra buys 200 shares, the second 100 shares being financed with borrowing "on margin."

Figure 11–1 and Table 11–1 illustrate Geoff's cash purchase of stock. The assumption is that Geoff has used his $5,000 to purchase the 100 shares at $50 per share. Geoff's maximum, theoretical risk is $5,000, and no matter how much the stock price declines, the brokerage firm will never call upon Geoff for additional equity.

Figure 11–2 and Table 11–2 illustrate Debra's margin purchase of stock. The maximum, theoretical risk of her position is $10,000, if the price of the 200 shares purchased for $50 each declines to zero. Since Debra has only $5,000 of capital, the brokerage firm has the potential risk of losing the $5,000 loan made to Debra. The brokerage firm will therefore monitor Debra's position more closely than it monitors Geoff's position. Furthermore, if an adverse price move occurs, the brokerage firm will call upon Debra to deposit additional equity or sell her shares.

There are two differences between the lines in Figure 11–1 and Figure 11–2. First, the slopes are different. Figure 11–1 is Geoff's standard stock investment line with a 1 × 1 slope—$1 of profit or loss per share for each $1 rise or fall in the stock price. Figure 11–2, in contrast, has a steeper slope, 2 × 1—$2 of profit or loss per share for each $1 change in stock price.

The second difference is the point of intersection on the horizontal axis. The line in Figure 11–1 intersects the horizontal axis at $50, the original purchase price. For simplicity, transaction costs have been omitted. The line in Figure 11–2, however, intersects the horizontal axis at $50 1/2. Debra's leveraged strategy breaks even above $50, because the stock price must rise by enough to cover the interest costs which depend on the length of time the position is margined and the interest rate (which can fluctuate in the real world). Note that Table 11–2 contains an extra column for Debra's interest expense.

Figure 11–1   Geoff's Cash Purchase of Stock
               Capital, $5,000; Buy 100 Shares at $50 per Share

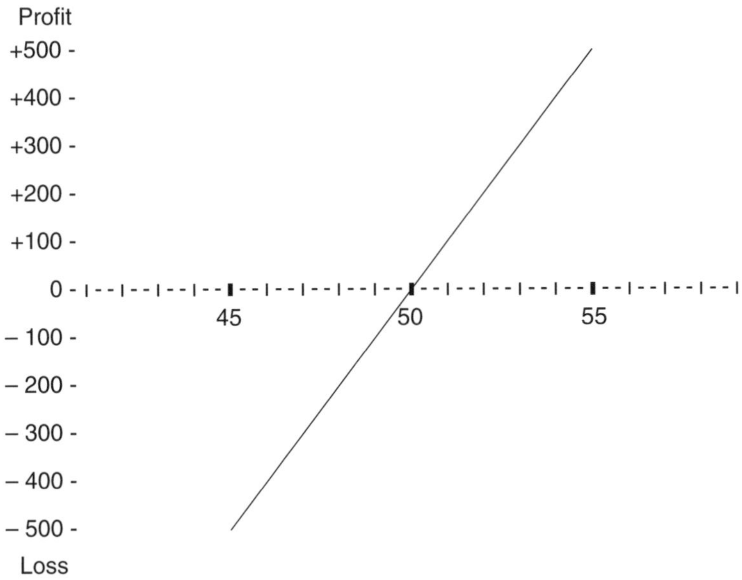

Table 11–1   Geoff's Cash Purchase of Stock.
              Capital, $5,000; Buy 100 Shares at $50 per Share

Stock Price at Sale	Long 100 Shares @ $50 Profit/(Loss)
$55	+500
$54	+400
$53	+300
$52	+200
$51	+100
$50	0
$49	−100
$48	−200
$47	−300
$46	−400
$45	−500

Figure 11–2 Debra's Margin Purchase of Stock
          Capital, $5,000; Buy 200 Shares at $50 per Share
          (Finance the Second 100 Shares with Borrowing)

```
Profit
+500 -
+400 -                                    /
+300 -                                   /
+200 -                                  /
+100 -                                 /
    0 - |--|--|--|--|--|--|--|--|--|--|--|/-|--|--|--|--|--|--|--|--|--|
  - 100 -      45                50 /            55
  - 200 -                         /
  - 300 -                        /
  - 400 -                       /
  - 500 -                      /
Loss
```

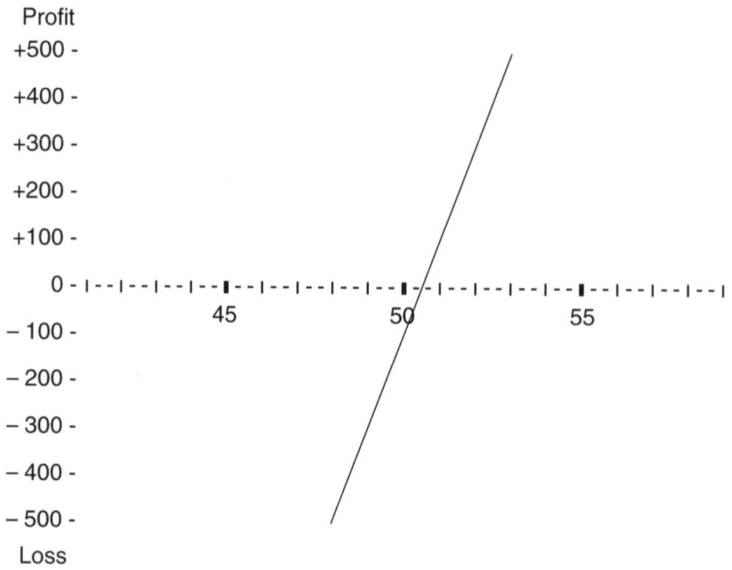

Table 11–2 Debra's Margin Purchase of Stock
          Capital $5,000; Buy 200 Shares at $50 per Share
          (Finance the Second 100 Shares with Borrowing)

Stock Price at Time of Sale	Long 200 Shares @ $50 Profit/(Loss)	Interest Expense*	Total Profit/(Loss)
$55	+1,000	−100	+900
$54	+800	−100	+700
$53	+600	−100	+500
$52	+400	−100	+300
$51	+200	−100	+100
$50	0	−100	−100
$49	−200	−100	−300
$48	−400	−100	−500
$47	−600	−100	−700
$46	−800	−100	−900
$45	−1,000	−100	−1,100

*Interest Expense at 8% (annual rate) = $100 (.08 × $5,000 × 90/360)

Other Marginable Transactions

Margin accounts are perhaps best known for money lending services and so-called buying of stock on margin. In addition, there are other transactions which do not initially require financing but must be established in a margin account. Selling stock short is one example. When stock is sold short, an investor is required to make a "margin deposit" which is a good faith deposit against meeting transaction costs and the risk of loss. Margin deposits vary depending on the level of risk of the transaction.

Selling (or writing) an uncovered option is another type of transaction which is typically established in a margin account. Since short options represent contingent obligations, their margin requirement is usually less than that required for purchasing stock or selling short. The contingent obligation of a short option becomes real if assignment occurs.

The risk of selling uncovered call options is, theoretically, unlimited. An uncovered short call is a call sold, or written, when the investor does not own the underlying stock or its equivalent. If assignment occurs, stock must be delivered, and the brokerage firm will borrow and deliver shares and thereby create a short stock position in the investor's margin account. If insufficient equity exists to support the short stock position, the firm might call for additional margin or cover (repurchase) the short stock in the open market, and the investor must absorb transaction costs and potential losses. If the account equity is low enough, and the stock price rise large enough, it is possible for the account equity to drop below zero.

A sold, or written, put is another option position which many brokerage firms require be established in a margin account. A short put, remember, represents a contingent obligation to buy the underlying stock. If assignment occurs, the obligation becomes real and stock must be purchased. If there is insufficient equity to support the long stock position—even with margin loans—then the firm might call for additional margin or liquidate (sell) the shares, and the investor must absorb transaction costs and any losses. If the account equity is low enough, and the stock price decline large enough, it is possible for the account equity to drop below zero.

Monitoring the Risk of Uncovered Options

Chapters 12 through 14 discuss strategies which involve short options and/or margin borrowing. The level of risk will be described by the ratio of account equity to maximum, theoretical position risk. The greater the account equity, the lower the percentage risk. The risk of some short option positions is the same as the risk of owning stock. Some short option positions involve the same risk as buying stock on margin. Other short option positions involve greater risk.

Conclusions about Leverage

In the simplest terms, non-leveraged strategies have 1 × 1 sloping lines—$1 of profit or loss for a $1 rise or fall in stock price. These, by definition, are investment strategies. Speculative strategies, in contrast, involve leverage. Speculative strategies have lines with steeper slopes—more than $1 of profit or loss for a $1 rise or fall in stock price.

When margin accounts are used, leverage may or may not be involved, depending on the amount of equity supporting a position. Geoff, in the example above, could have purchased his 100 shares in a margin account; but, by paying the full $5,000 in cash, he avoided the use of leverage. Debra, however, chose to take on $5,000 of margin loans which leveraged her investment capital.

The Strategies in This Section

This section will discuss option strategies which must be established in margin accounts and present some practical advice in identifying which strategies involve relatively higher degrees of risk and which involve relatively lower risk. Some of the strategies will involve sold, or written, puts. The account equity assumption will be clearly stated, and the risk, relative to purchasing stock for cash, will also be stated.

Chapter 12 explains "Covered Writing on Margin," a leveraged variation of standard covered writing with the addition of margin loans. Chapter 13 explains "Writing Puts," a strategy which will be seen to have many similarities to covered writing. Chapter 14, presents many instances when investors might use a strategy known as "Buy Stock and Write Straddle."

Twelve

Covered Writing on Margin

Introduction

Covered writing on margin involves writing covered calls on stock that is purchased on margin. The goal of this strategy is to realize a profit from the additional shares in the covered write that will not only pay the borrowing costs but will also compensate the margined covered writer for the increased risk. Because of the leverage gained from the margin loans, this strategy is speculative, and must, therefore, be monitored closely.

This chapter will first explain how the leverage component increases both the profit potential and the risk relative to cash account covered writing. Second, the necessary calculation adjustments will be explained, and, finally, the psychological differences for covered writers on margin will be discussed.

The Effect of Leverage

Figure 12–1 and Table 12–1 compare cash account covered writing to covered writing on margin. For simplicity, commissions and other transaction costs are not included. Assume an account equity of $5,000, a stock price of $50 and a 90-day 50 Call price of 3. In the cash account covered writing example, illustrated by the hyphenated line, 100 shares are purchased and one 50 Call is sold. In the covered writing on margin example, shown as the solid line, 200 shares are purchased (100 shares are financed with margin loans) and two 50 Calls are sold. Assume the interest expense for the second 100 shares is $100, 2% on $5,000 for 90 days, or 8% annually.

155

**Figure 12–1 Cash Account Covered Writing versus
                      Covered Writing on Margin**

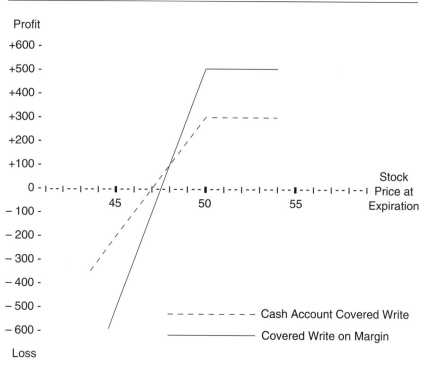

Different Trade-Offs

A comparison of the solid and hyphenated lines in Figure 12–1 reveals that cash account covered writing and covered writing on margin offer different trade-offs. The positive aspect of covered writing on margin is a higher profit potential; the negative aspect is greater risk. The greater risk of covered writing on margin is represented in Figure 12–1 by the steeper slope of the downward sloping line. If two units of stock are purchased with one unit of capital and one unit of borrowing, the slope of the downward sloping line is 2×1—$2 per share is lost for each $1 decline in the stock price. The greater profit potential, with the stock price at or above $50 at expiration, occurs because the call price is greater than the interest expense on the margin loans.

The difference between the $300 received for writing the second 50 Call and the $100 interest expense is the additional maximum profit potential. This higher profit potential is the reward for assuming increased risk if the stock price declines.

**Table 12–1   Cash Account Covered Writing versus
                Covered Writing on Margin**

	Cash Account Covered Write			Covered Write on Margin			
Stock Price at Exp	Long 100 Shares at $50 P/(L)	Short 1 50 Call at 3 P/(L)	Total P/(L)	Long 200 Shares at $50 P/(L)	Short 2 50 Calls at 3 each P/(L)	Interest Expense 8% (ann.) for 90 Days ($100)	Total P/(L)
$54	+400	−100	+300	+800	−200	−100	+500
$53	+300	0	+300	+600	0	−100	+500
$52	+200	+100	+300	+400	+200	−100	+500
$51	+100	+200	+300	+200	+400	−100	+500
$50	0	+300	+300	0	+600	−100	+500
$49	−100	+300	+200	−200	+600	−100	+300
$48	−200	+300	+100	−400	+600	−100	+100
$47	−300	+300	0	−600	+600	−100	−100
$46	−400	+300	−100	−800	+600	−100	−300
$45	−500	+300	−200	−1000	+600	−100	−500

Higher Break-Even Point

Figure 12–1 and Table 12–1 also illustrate that covered writing on margin has a higher expiration break-even stock price than cash account covered writing. In this example, the break-even price of $47 1/2 is easy to calculate. The interest cost of $100 equals 50 cents or 1/2 per share for each of the 200 shares purchased. Consequently, the stock price must rise 1/2 after ninety days to cover this interest cost.

Margin Loans (and Leverage) Can Be Varied

The maximum margin loan as a percentage of purchased stock is established by Federal regulations. Although this has remained steady at 50% for several years, the Federal Reserve has changed the percentage in the past. Investors should be aware that this percentage can be changed at any time, because this is a risk affecting any strategy involving margin loans. A decrease in the maximum margin loan percentage could prompt margin calls to fully margined investors, which might trigger forced sales and unexpected transaction costs if an investor were unable to deposit the required equity.

There is no rule, however, that margin borrowers must borrow the maximum percentage! Investors for whom the concept of margin borrowing is new are well advised to start conservatively. The extent to which margin loans are employed directly affects the slope of the solid line in Figure 12–1 and, therefore, the risk. As margin borrowings are decreased to zero, the slope of the downward sloping line shifts to 45 degrees or 1×1, the same slope and risk assumed by cash account covered writers.

Calculating Returns

The cash account covered writing return formulas must be adjusted to include the interest expense on the margin loans. The "net income," when reduced by the interest expense, becomes: Call Premium (less commissions) Plus Dividends Minus Interest Expense. The "net investment" must take into account the margin loans and becomes: Stock Cost (plus commissions) Minus Call Premium (less commissions) Minus Margin Loans.

An Example

Consider Jean, an editor, who has a hobby of making aggressive stock trades. She has confidence in her ability to pick stocks, and she frequently trades on margin. In this example we assume Jean pays 9% (annual rate) on her margin loans.

Jean is considering a short-term purchase of Large Media, Inc., a stock trading at $38. Jean thinks it will rise above $40 at expiration in 67 days, and she would be pleased to sell it at $41 1/2. She can buy 400 shares of Large Media, borrow half of the $15,200 total purchase price and only be responsible for depositing $7,600 cash, not including commissions. If she also sells 4 67-day 40 Calls at 1 1/2 each, she will receive $600 (4 × $150) which can be used toward her $7,600 required deposit.

The short calls, remember, obligate Jean to sell her 400 shares at $40, or, effectively, $41 1/2 if the call premium is taken into consideration. Jean, of course, will suffer the loss of owning 400 shares if the price falls below the break-even point. No matter what happens to the stock price, Jean must repay $7,600 to her brokerage firm with interest.

Intrigued by this opportunity, Jean decides to analyze the situation further. Her first steps are to calculate static and if-called rates of return, draw an expiration profit and loss diagram and determine the break-even stock price at expiration.

Covered Writing on Margin—Static Rate of Return

The static return for cash account covered writing is:

$$\frac{\text{Net Income}}{\text{Net Investment}} \times \frac{\text{Days per Year}}{\text{Days to Expiration}}$$

or:

$$\frac{\text{Net Call Premium + Dividends}}{\text{Total Stock Cost − Net Call Premium}} \times \frac{\text{Days per Year}}{\text{Days to Expiration}}$$

The static return for covered writing on margin is:

$$\frac{\text{Net Call Premium + Dividends − Interest}}{\text{Total Stock Cost − Net Call Premium − Loans}} \times \frac{\text{Days per Year}}{\text{Days to Expiration}}$$

In Jean's case, the net investment is \$7,000: the total cost of 400 shares, \$15,200 (\$38 × 400), less the call premium received, \$600 (4 × \$150), less the margin loans, \$7,600 (.50 × \$15,200). The "income" is the call premium, \$600, plus the dividends, zero in this example, minus the interest expense, \$125, which is calculated as follows:

$$\text{Principal} \times \text{Interest Rate} \times (\text{Days to Expiration} \div \text{Days per Year})$$

or:

$$\$7,600 \times .09 \times (67 \div 365) \approx \$125.55 \approx \$125$$

Using these numbers in the static return calculation, Jean gets:

Static return of covered writing on margin equals

$$\frac{600 + 0 − 125}{15,200 − 600 − 7,600} \times \frac{365}{67} = 36\%$$

This compares favorably to the static return on cash account covered writing which would be

$$\frac{600 + 0}{15,200 − 600} \times \frac{365}{67} = 22\%$$

Covered Writing on Margin—If-Called Rate of Return

The if-called return for cash account covered writing is:

$$\frac{\text{Net Income} + \text{Gain}}{\text{Net Investment}} \times \frac{\text{Days per Year}}{\text{Days to Expiration}}$$

or:

$$\frac{\text{Net Call Premium} + \text{Dividends} + \text{Gain}}{\text{Total Stock Cost} - \text{Net Call Premium}} \times \frac{\text{Days per Year}}{\text{Days to Expiration}}$$

The if-called return for covered writing on margin is:

$$\frac{\text{Net Call Premium} + \text{Dividends} - \text{Interest} + \text{Gain}}{\text{Total Stock Cost} - \text{Net Call Premium} - \text{Loans}} \times \frac{\text{Days per Year}}{\text{Days to Expiration}}$$

In Jean's case, the gain on 400 shares from $38 to $40 is $800. Using this number in the if-called return calculation, she gets:

If-called return of covered writing on margin equals

$$\frac{600 + 0 - 125 + 800}{15,200 - 600 - 7,600} \times \frac{365}{67} = 99\%$$

This compares favorably to the if-called return on cash account covered writing which would be

$$\frac{600 + 0 + 800}{15,200 - 600} \times \frac{365}{67} = 52\%$$

To get a complete picture, Jean now draws the expiration profit and loss diagram presented in Figure 12–2, the calculations for which are in Table 12–2.

From the figure and table, Jean can determine that the expiration break-even stock price is approximately $36 3/4.

Assessing the Risk Factor

Having all available information in front of her, Jean can now decide what to do. Unfortunately, there are no objective rules which will tell Jean if the margined covered write on Large Media is a good strategy. After the analysis presented above, Jean must make a subjective decision. Some of the questions

Figure 12–2 Jean's Margined Covered Write on Large Media

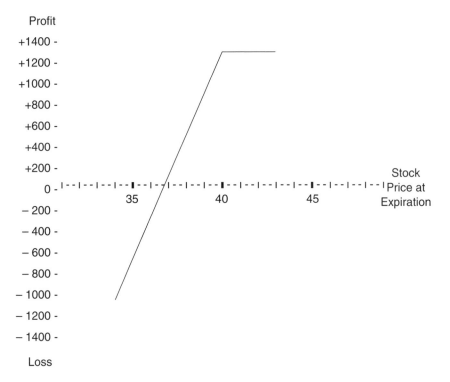

Table 12–2   Jean's Margined Covered Write on Large Media

Stock Price at Exp	Long 400 Shares at $38 P/(L)	Short 4 40 Calls at 1 1/2 each P/(L)	Interest Expense 8% (ann.) for 50 Days ($125)	Total P/(L)
$43	+2,000	−600	−125	+1,275
$42	+1,600	−200	−125	+1,275
$41	+1,200	+200	−125	+1,275
$40	+800	+600	−125	+1,275
$39	+400	+600	−125	+875
$38	0	+600	−125	+475
$37	−400	+600	−125	+75
$36	−800	+600	−125	−325
$35	−1,200	+600	−125	−725
$34	−1,600	+600	−125	−1,125

Jean might ask herself when confronting this decision are the following: How certain am I of my market prediction that Large Media will be above $40 at expiration? Am I comfortable taking on $7,600 in margin debt? Can I withstand the loss of an unexpectedly large stock price decline? Do I have the time to monitor this position during the next 67 days? Will I have the discipline to "cut my losses" if this position starts to move against me?

Only Jean can answer these questions. She will be better equipped to answer these questions if she has experience with regular covered writing and margin trading. Although options change some of the specifics, options do not change significantly the psychological elements of shorter-term trading on margin and the attendant risk factors.

The Psychological Factor

Covered writing on margin, just like any leveraged investment strategy, increases the stakes. Higher risk is assumed in the hopes of earning a higher profit potential. The leverage element also increases the probability that a strategy will be closed out prior to the option expiration date. Consequently, how the option price behaves can affect the outcome. First, as explained in Chapter 4, time decay of option prices is not linear under normal circumstances. Therefore, if a covered write position is closed prior to expiration, one cannot expect the call price to have decreased in value by an amount in proportion to the passage of time. Also, if volatility or interest rates increase, the option price may not erode as originally expected or at all. Also, the bid-ask spread may widen if liquidity conditions change. These factors, combined with the added risk of leverage, may make covered writing on margin psychologically unacceptable for some traders. Only after a thorough analysis of the calculations presented above and of one's own willingness to take on increased risk can an investor decide if this strategy is suitable.

Summary

Covered writing on margin is a leveraged form of covered writing in which margin borrowings finance the purchased stock up to 50% or the current maximum percentage allowed by Regulation T. It is not required to borrow the maximum allowed, and beginners in using margin debt are well advised to start conservatively by borrowing significantly less than the maximum allowed.

The concept behind covered writing on margin is that the additional call premium received covers the interest expense and offers a higher profit potential which compensates an investor for assuming higher risk. Profit and loss diagrams illustrate the trade-off that covered writing on margin offers: higher profit potential for increased risk. Covered writing on margin is speculative and short-term oriented and, therefore, requires increased monitoring. Only the person who employs this strategy can decide whether it fits desired risk parameters and whether the investor is disciplined enough to act appropriately if the market forecast proves to be incorrect.

Thirteen

Writing Puts

Introduction

The purpose of this chapter is to present a full and balanced picture of writing puts. After briefly reviewing the strategy mechanics, this chapter will explain how put writing can be used in an effort to accomplish investment objectives. The subject of put-call parity will emerge again, and put writing will be compared to another option strategy. Finally, the focus will shift to risk and an explanation of why selling puts is too often viewed as involving unacceptable risk.

Profit and Loss Diagram and Strategy Mechanics

The maximum, theoretical risk of writing a put equals purchasing 100 shares of stock at a price equal to the strike price minus the premium received. Figure 13–1 illustrates a profit and loss diagram at expiration of a short 50 Put sold for $200, or $2 per share. If the stock price is $50 or higher at expiration, the put expires and the $2 per share maximum profit is realized. If the price is below $50 at expiration, the short put is assigned, and the put writer purchases 100 shares at an effective price of $48 per share. If the stock price is below $48 at expiration, this strategy results in a loss.

Investment Uses of Short Puts

One objective of conservative investors stated in the Introduction is to "buy good stocks at good prices." What constitutes a "good stock" and a "good price" are subjective considerations. A common practice, however, is placing a limit-price buy order with the specified price below the current market

Figure 13–1 Short Put at Expiration
Profit and Loss Diagram for a Short 50 Put Sold for 2

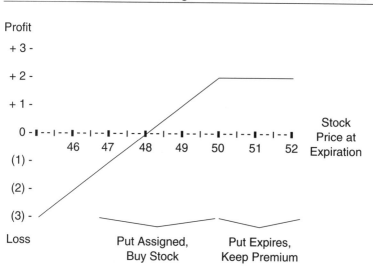

price. Investors who employ this technique have decided that this stock is a "good stock" and that this price is a "good price." In these situations, the question becomes, "can writing puts help conservative investors?" The answer is a resounding "yes!" Here's how.

The Stock Buyer with a Neutral Market View

Consider Alex, a young investor, who wants to buy Spider Industries, currently trading at $36. Alex, however, is in no rush to buy Spider since he forecasts the price will dip in the near term. In this example, assume the 35 Put with 75 days to expiration is trading at 1 1/4 and that Alex has $3,375 in a money market account which he wants to use to purchase Spider stock. For simplicity, commissions and margin account minimum balance requirements are not included.

Rather than place an order to buy Spider at $33 3/4, Alex's strategy is to sell the 75-day 35 Put at 1 1/4 and hope the stock price is below $35 at expiration. Alex's brokerage firm will require him to make a minimum deposit of cash or marginable securities in his margin account to help protect the firm in the event stock purchased as a result of assignment of the short put must be sold at a loss. Among the reasons a firm may find it necessary to liquidate the stock are that an investor fails to deposit the margin required, or the firm determines a stock has become too risky for margin loans. Alex may keep the balance of his $3,375 in a money market account.

Is Assignment a Big Risk?

If his forecast is accurate, the short put will be assigned, and Alex will buy 100 shares of Spider at an effective price of $33 3/4, the $35 strike less the 1 1/4 put premium received. If the stock price remains above $35, the put will expire worthless, but Alex will keep the premium.

Has Alex taken an unreasonable risk by selling the put? No!

The maximum risk of Alex's short put is the same as buying 100 shares at $33 3/4, and this is something Alex is willing to do. His alternative, remember, was to place a limit-price buy order at $33 3/4. Relative to the limit-price buy order, if the stock price is between $33 3/4 and $35 at expiration, the short put will be assigned and Alex still gets to buy Spider stock at an effective price of $33 3/4. Furthermore, if Spider's price is above $35 at expiration, Alex will keep the 1 1/4 put premium, thus increasing his income. The limit-price buy order offers no such benefit.

The Stock Buyer with a Neutral-to-Bullish Market View

Amy is a long-term investor seeking to add Mathco, a scientific research company, to her portfolio. Amy, however, is only neutral or slightly bullish on Mathco for the next 90 days. With this market forecast, Amy feels she can do better than buying Mathco at its current price of $68 by selling a 90-day 70 put for 4. If this put is assigned, Amy's effective purchase price is $66 (plus transaction costs), the $70 strike minus the $4-per-share put premium. Amy's maximum theoretical risk is equal to purchasing stock at $66, and her maximum profit potential from the short put is $4 per share. Amy, hoping for assignment so she can buy the stock, is forecasting that Mathco will stay below $70 for 90 days and rise after that.

When Does Amy Want Mathco to Rally?

The "Average-In" Stock Buyer

Felecia is considering the purchase of 200 shares of Serviceco, an auto repair franchiser, which is currently trading at $62. Felecia is neutral to bearish on Serviceco for the next two months, and, ideally, she would like to buy 200 shares at $60. But she does not want to miss a rally, so she is considering buying 100 shares now and entering a limit-price buy order for another 100 shares at $58. If that limit-price buy order is filled, her average purchase price for the 200 shares will be the desired $60 per share.

As an alternative, Felecia could buy 100 shares at the current price of $62 and, simultaneously, sell a 55-day 60 put for 2. If assigned, that short put would result in an effective buy price of $58 per share for the second 100 shares. The average price for Felecia's 200 shares would be the desired $60. If Serviceco is above $60 at expiration, the 60 Put expires and Felecia keeps the $2-per-share put premium. If she chooses to buy 100 shares of Serviceco at the market price at that time, the put premium will, effectively, reduce her purchase price by $2 per share.

Selling the "Right" Put

As with other strategies, the "right" option depends on the market forecast. A stock buyer who is totally neutral and willing to buy stock slightly below the current market price might be most inclined to sell an at-the-money put. A stock buyer who is willing to buy only at a much lower price might prefer an out-of-the-money put. A third stock buyer, with a neutral-to-bullish forecast, might be inclined to sell an in-the-money put. As long as there is time premium in the put price when it is sold, assignment means that stock is purchased at a lower effective price than paying the current market price.

Short Put versus Limit-Price Buy Order Below the Current Market Price

The concept of "trade-off" appears once again, because neither the short put nor the limit-price buy order is "better" in an absolute sense. In Felecia's case, both strategies have a maximum theoretical risk of buying the second 100 shares at $58. The short put has the relative advantages of buying stock if the price is between $58 and $60 at expiration and earning the $2 per-share premium if the price is above

Short Puts Are *Time & Price Dependent*

$60 at expiration. The limit-price buy order does not purchase stock unless the stock trades at $58 in sufficient quantity to fill Felicia's order and whatever orders may have been ahead of her at that price. Also, the limit-price buy order earns nothing if the price is higher and the order is not filled. The limit-price buy order, however, is price dependent, rather than time dependent like the short put. This means that if the price of Serviceco trades below $58 and rallies above $60 prior to expiration, then the limit-price buy order would buy stock at $58 and earn the corresponding profit, which could be substantial, whereas the short put, at most, could earn its maximum profit of the premium received. Table 13–1 summarizes the differences between short puts and limit-price buy orders.

A Comparison to Covered Writing

Many readers will have observed that the profit and loss diagrams for the short put (Figure 13–1) and covered writing (Figure 7–1) are similar. This observation is correct and occurs because of the put-call parity concept introduced in Chapter 9. One put-call-parity-related concept is that puts and calls with the same strike price and expiration date can be combined with the underlying stock to create theoretically identical profit and loss diagrams. Covered call writing and put writing, when cash is available to buy the underlying stock, are two strategies which, in theory, are identical.

To emphasize the presence of sufficient cash to purchase the underlying stock, this strategy will be referred to as *"cash-secured"* put writing.

Table 13–1   Short Put versus Limit-Price Buy Order

Stock Price at Expiration	Short Put	Limit-Price Buy Order (Limit Price Is Below Current Market Price)	Which Is "Better"?
Above Strike	Put Expires Keep Premium	Nothing Happens	Short Put
Between Strike and Strike Minus Premium	Put Assigned Buy Stock	Nothing Happens	Short Put
Below Strike Minus Premium	Put Assigned Buy Stock	Buy Stock	Equal

Whatever the stock price is at expiration, the covered call writer and cash-secured put writer will end up with the same position. If the stock is above the strike price at expiration, the covered writer will be assigned, will sell stock and will be left with the cash proceeds from the stock sale. The put writer will also end up with cash, since the sold put expires worthless.

If the stock price is below the strike price at expiration, the covered call writer will see the short call expire worthless and be left owning stock. The cash-secured put writer will also be left owning stock, because the short put will be assigned, and stock will be purchased.

If the stock is exactly at the strike, both the covered call writer and the cash-secured put writer will have cash or stock in an amount equal to the strike and can buy or sell stock to end up with the preferred position.

Consequently, these strategies are identical, ignoring commissions and assuming the two investors manage their capital in the same manner, i.e., that the covered call writer pays cash for the stock, and the put writer has readily available cash to purchase the stock.

Calculating Returns for Cash-Secured Put Writers

In the first case presented above, Alex is a cash-secured put writer. If Alex's 35 Put expires worthless, Alex's income is increased. Alex's income can be calculated as an annual percentage of his capital of $3,375 using the following formula:

$$\text{Annual Rate of Return} = \frac{\text{Income}}{\text{Investment}} \times \frac{\text{Days per Year}}{\text{Days to Expiration}}$$

In this formula, "income" for *cash-secured* put writing consists of the net put premium plus the interest earned, if any, on the margin account deposit and on the money market account balance. The "investment" is Alex's capital of $3,375, which, in this example, is assumed to earn 5% interest (annual rate), or approximately $35, for 75 days. If the put expires worthless, Alex's total annualized rate of return, not including commissions, is:

$$
\begin{aligned}
\text{Annual Rate of Return} &= \{(\text{interest} + \text{put premium}) \div \$3,375\} \, \{365 \div 75\} \\
&= \{(35 + 125) \div \$3,375\} \times \{365 \div 75\} \\
&= 23\%
\end{aligned}
$$

The 23% annualized rate of return is 18% greater than the assumed 5% annual rate of interest, but this return is earned only if the put expires worthless. One must not forget that the short put position is an obligation to purchase stock at an effective price of $33 3/4 in Alex's example. If the stock price is below $33 3/4 at expiration, this strategy will result in a loss.

Risk

The maximum, theoretical risk of writing a put equals purchasing 100 shares of stock at the strike price less the put premium received. The risk assumed by stock purchasers, it will be recalled from Chapter 11, varies depending on whether stock is purchased for cash or on margin. Theoretically, the cash purchaser of stock risks 100% of the capital invested. The margin purchaser, however, risks more, because the margin purchaser is theoretically risking all invested capital plus the amount of the margin loan. Graphically, as illustrated in Chapter 11, Figure 11–2, the level of a strategy's risk is represented by the slope of the line in the profit and loss diagram.

These concepts of risk apply directly to the strategy of writing puts. To demonstrate how the amount of capital supporting a position changes the level of risk, Figure 13–2 and Table 13–2 illustrate put writing under three different leverage assumptions. In all three cases, *$4,800 of capital is assumed.* For simplicity, potential interest income and commissions are ignored.

Line 1 in Figure 13–2 assumes one 50 Put is sold at 2, Line 2 assumes two 50 Puts are sold at 2 each, and Line 3 assumes three puts are sold. The slope of each line is different, because the amount of risk is different. Table 13–2 has columns which present the profit or loss calculations and which correspond to the lines in Figure 13–2.

The risk of writing puts, quite simply, depends on an investor's *willingness and ability* to purchase the underlying stock. In Figure 13–2, the slope of Line 1 is 1 × 1, equal to cash purchase of stock. The maximum, theoretical risk of Line 1 is $4,800, 100% of the assumed capital, if the stock falls to zero.

The slope of Line 2 is 2 × 1, equal to a fully margined purchase of stock. The maximum, theoretical risk of Line 2 is $9,600, 200% of assumed capital, if the stock price falls to zero.

The slope of Line 3 is 3 × 1, steeper than a fully margined purchase of stock. The maximum, theoretical risk of Line 3 is $14,400, 300% of assumed capital, if the stock price falls to zero. Assignment of the *three* short puts *cannot* be met with the same amount of capital required to buy 100 shares for cash or 200 shares on margin. Consequently, if assignment of the three short puts occurs, at least some of the stock would be immediately sold because the assumed capital of $4,800 is insufficient to support 300 shares.

Margin Accounts and Short Puts

Many brokerage firms require short put positions to be carried in a margin account, even if the full purchase price of the underlying stock is readily available in cash. This is required because cash is easy to transfer, and there

Figure 13–2 Profit and Loss for Short 1, 2, and 3 Puts

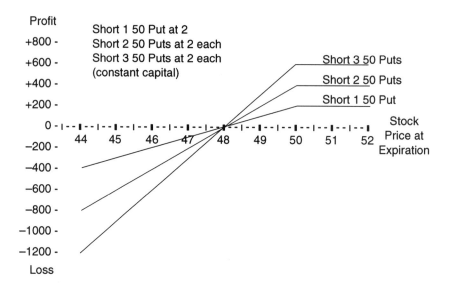

Table 13–2 Profit and Loss Calculations for Short 1, 2, and 3 Puts

Stock Price at Expiration	Short 1 50 Put @ 2 Profit or Loss	Short 2 50 Puts @ 2 ea. Profit or Loss	Short 3 50 Puts @ 2 ea. Profit or Loss
$52	+200	+400	+600
$51	+200	+400	+600
$50	+200	+400	+600
$49	+100	+200	+300
$48	0	0	0
$47	−100	−200	−300
$46	−200	−400	−600
$45	−300	−600	−900
$44	−400	−800	−1,200
$43	−500	−1,000	−1,500

are technical problems of matching cash availability with potential assignment risk. Brokerage firms also have minimum margin requirements. If a put writer desires to maintain more than the minimum margin requirement, the put writer, not the brokerage firm, needs to monitor the account or the ready availability of sufficient cash.

Brokerage firms also require that investors meet established minimum financial requirements before they are allowed to trade in margin accounts and even stricter requirements before they are allowed to write put options. These requirements include minimum net worth and minimum account balance criteria. There are also account application and risk disclosure forms to be read carefully and signed. Investors, therefore, must be fully informed about and fulfill a firm's requirements before engaging in the put writing strategies discussed in this chapter. This is also true for each and every option strategy discussed in this book.

Summary

The maximum theoretical risk of writing puts is equal to purchasing stock at a price equal to the strike price minus the put premium received. As long as there is time premium in the put price at the time of its sale, assignment results in a lower effective purchase price than buying stock at the current market price. Stock buyers can use this strategy as an alternative to a limit-price buy order. A short put performs better than a limit-price buy order if the stock price, at expiration, is above the strike or between the strike and a price equal to strike minus premium. If the stock price is below strike minus premium, then the two strategies are equal; both purchase stock at effectively the same price. Limit-price orders are price dependent, while short puts are time and price dependent.

Theoretically, according to the concept of put-call parity, writing cash-secured puts and cash-account covered call writing are identical strategies. Calculating the returns of put writing involves adding the interest earned on the available cash to the put premium and analyzing the sum as an annualized percentage of the available cash.

The risk level of short puts depends on the way capital is managed. Cash-secured put writing is equal in risk to buying stock at the price implied by the short put. Selling two puts for one unit of capital equals the risk of buying stock on margin. Selling three or more puts increases risk even more and means that, if assignment occurs, at least some shares must be sold for lack of equity capital to support the stock position.

Fourteen

Buy Stock and Write Straddle

Strategy Description

The strategy, as its name implies, involves three parts: the purchase of stock, the sale of a call and the sale of a put. The put and call have the same strike price and expiration. Writing both a call and a put means the investor is taking on two obligations: the obligation of selling the owned stock (if the call is assigned) and the obligation of buying more stock (if the put is assigned). This three-part strategy is likely to involve more transaction costs than typical "buy and hold" strategies; and although they are not included in the examples in this chapter, transaction costs and margin requirements can significantly affect the desirability of this strategy and must be taken into consideration before using real options on real stocks.

Since calls are sold on a share-for-share basis against owned stock, the short call in this strategy is covered. Whether or not leverage is involved, however, depends on (1) there being no margin loans and (2) the presence of sufficient cash (or other liquid assets) to pay for purchased stock if the short put is assigned.

Profit and Loss Diagram

For this example, assume $10,000 of capital, interest rates of 4% (annual rate), 90 days to expiration, a stock price of $50, a 50 Call price of 3 and a 50 Put price of 2 1/2. To establish this strategy, an investor buys 100 shares at $50 (total $5,000), sells one 90-day 50 Call for $300 ($3 per share), sells one 90-day 50 Put for $250 ($2 1/2 per share) and invests $5,000 at 4% for 90 days (interest equals $50). For simplicity, commissions and potential interest on the option premiums are ignored.

175

Figure 14–1 is an expiration profit and loss diagram of buy stock and write straddle. The supporting calculations are presented in Table 14–1.

Figure 14–1 Buy Stock and Write Straddle

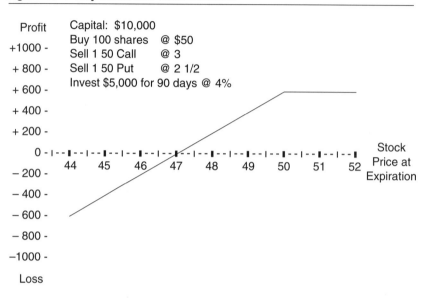

Table 14–1 Buy Stock and Write Straddle—Profit and Loss Calculations

Stock Price at Expiration	Long 100 Shares @ $50 P/(L)	Short 1 50 Call @ 3 P/(L)	Short 1 50 Put @ 2 1/2 P/(L)	Invest $5,000 @ 4% for 90 Days (Interest = $50)	Total P/(L)
$54	+$400	–$100	+$250	+$50	+$600
$53	+$300	0	+$250	+$50	+$600
$52	+$200	+$100	+$250	+$50	+$600
$51	+$100	+$200	+$250	+$50	+$600
$50	0	+$300	+$250	+$50	+$600
$49	–$100	+$300	+$150	+$50	+$400
$48	–$200	+$300	+$50	+$50	+$200
$47	–$300	+$300	–$50	+$50	0
$46	–$400	+$300	–$150	+$50	–$200
$45	–$500	+$300	–$250	+$50	–$400
$44	–$600	+$300	–$350	+$50	–$600

The Mechanics at Expiration

Every investor who employs this strategy must thoroughly understand its mechanics. Once the mechanics are fully understood, it is possible to determine whether or not this strategy has the potential to meet the investor's objectives. To review the mechanics, a stock price at expiration is selected and then what happens to each component is explained.

Stock Price above $50 at Expiration

With a stock price above $50 at expiration, the short 50 Put expires, and the short 50 Call is assigned. As a result of the call assignment, the owned stock is sold at $50. The final strategy component, the $5,000 cash investment, earns $50 interest. The resulting position is a cash balance of $10,600. This is calculated as follows:

Proceeds from sale of stock:	$ 5,000
Proceeds from sale of 50 Call:	300
Proceeds from sale of 50 Put:	250
Proceeds from $5,000 cash investment (principal plus interest of $50):	5,050
Total:	$10,600

At any stock price above $50, at expiration, the same $600 profit will result. The short put expires; the short call is assigned; the stock is sold; and the investor's resulting position is cash of $10,600. Given this outcome, all capital in cash, the investor is faced with the decision of what to do next. Whatever is decided, a nice profit will have been earned during the 90-day period just ended.

Stock Price below $50 at Expiration

Now consider a stock price below $50 at expiration. The short 50 Call expires, and the short 50 Put is assigned. As a result of the put assignment, a second 100 shares is purchased at $50 per share. The shares are purchased for cash with the proceeds from the maturing cash investment. The resulting position is long 200 shares and $600 in cash ($300 from the call plus $250 from the put plus $50 interest).

At a stock price of $48, at expiration, as Table 14–1 illustrates, there is a profit of $200. This is the result, because 200 shares were purchased at $50 per share, the price of which is now $48. The $400 loss on these shares is more than offset by the $600 option premium and interest. The account equity is therefore $10,200, which is comprised of 200 shares at $48 (value of $9,600) plus $600 in cash.

Table 14–1 also illustrates the break-even point is $47 at expiration. Purchasing 200 shares at $50 loses $600 at a stock price of $47, and this is exactly offset by the $600 option premium and interest.

Stock Price at the Strike Price at Expiration

If the stock is exactly at $50 at expiration, it is assumed that both the call and put expire worthless, and the premiums and interest are kept as income. The resulting position is long 100 shares plus $5,600 in cash.

Do not proceed through the examples which follow until you are thoroughly familiar with the mechanics of this strategy as presented above. If it seems confusing, simply analyze each component before determining the final position.

Similarity to Covered Writing

Readers with experience may notice a similarity between Figure 14–1 and Figure 7–1. The reason for this similarity is another result of the put-call parity concept discussed in Chapter 9. Rather than focus on an explanation of put-call parity, however, the following examples will illustrate how buy stock and write straddle may help investors. The targeted investment objectives depend on an investor's initial position and market forecast.

Case 1: The Income-Oriented Stock Investor

The first investor, John, does not look at the stock market pages every day, but he likes to buy safe, bluechip stocks which pay nice dividends. John's primary goal is to increase his portfolio income, and he is willing to sell stocks at a profit. Right now John has $14,000 in cash and wants to purchase Basic Industries stock which is trading at $70. The 90-day 70 Call is 4, and the 90-day 70 Put is 3. John's forecast is neutral. He expects Basic to continue trading at or near $70 for the next 90 days, and he is debating whether to buy 200 shares now or to buy 100 shares now and wait for a lower price on the second 100 shares. Also, he would be happy to sell 100 shares at $77 and realize a $7 per share profit in 90 days.

Given John's market forecast and his willingness to assume the risk of owning 200 shares at or near $70, the "buy stock and write straddle" strategy might help John get the best of both worlds. John can establish this strategy by purchasing 100 shares now and simultaneously selling both the 70 Call and the 70 Put. The remaining $7,000 cash is left on deposit earning interest. To see how this strategy might achieve John's objectives, consider what happens if the price of Basic is above $70, below $70 or at $70 at expiration.

Basic above $70 at Expiration

If the price of Basic is above $70 at expiration, the 70 Put expires, the 70 Call is assigned, and the owned 100 shares are sold at an effective price of $77, not including commissions or the interest earned on the money market deposit. This is calculated as follows: the call assignment requires John to sell his stock at $70 per share, but he keeps both the call premium and the put premium. $70 + $4 + $3 = $77. This was one of John's initial objectives. He was willing to sell the initial 100 shares and realize a $7 per share profit.

Basic below $70 at Expiration

If the price of Basic is below $70 at expiration, the 70 Call expires, the 70 Put is assigned, and a second 100 shares are purchased at an effective price of $63 (not including commissions or interest). This is calculated as follows: the put assignment requires John to purchase 100 shares at $70 per share, but he keeps both the put premium and the call premium. $70 – $4 – $3 = $63. This was also part of John's initial plan. After purchasing 100 shares initially, his plan was to wait to buy the second 100 shares at a lower price.

Basic at $70 at Expiration

If Basic is exactly $70 at expiration, we can assume both the 70 Call and Put expire worthless and both option premiums are kept as income. This is also consistent with John's original goal of increasing income. If this third possible outcome occurs, John's position is long 100 shares plus $7,700 in cash plus interest from the money market account. He can then choose between buying a second 100 shares, writing another straddle and some other strategy.

Regardless of the stock price at expiration, above, below or at $70, John meets one of his original objectives: to increase income, to realize a $7-per-share profit in 90 days, or to buy a second 100 shares below $70.

Common Objections

As good as all of the above sounds, investors learning about this strategy for the first time have some reasonable questions. First, one might ask: "What if the stock price rises to $80 or $90 or higher?" Second, "Suppose the stock price falls to $60 or $50 or lower?" And, finally, "The $7 profit in 90-days sounds attractive, but how do I know I can earn it again three more times this year?" These questions will be addressed in order.

A "Large" Price Rise

It is true that this strategy, like any strategy involving a covered call, limits participation in a rising market. But remember: John's market forecast and objectives were very specific. Also, what was responsible for the missed rally, the market forecast or the option strategy? Had John forecast a sharply rising stock price, he undoubtedly would have chosen to buy 200 shares initially rather than 100 shares. Consequently, the inaccurate market forecast accounts for the missed opportunity.

A "Large" Price Decline

A similar answer applies to the objection about a sharp price decline. If John had expected the price of Basic stock to decline sharply, he undoubtedly would not have chosen a neutral-to-bullish strategy. John may have decided not to do anything with this stock. Again, any loss must be attributed to an inaccurate stock selection and/or market forecast.

Repeating the Return

Although there is no guarantee that new 90-day options will have the same price as the ones sold by John in this example, the concern over the possibility of repeating the profit misunderstands an important point. Profit calculations are only one element of the subjective investment selection process, and they should not be over-emphasized. The profit potential, remember, is accompanied by the risk of stock ownership. In John's example, he is assuming the risk of owning 200 shares.

Balancing the Positives and Negatives

The most important element of John's decision is his market forecast. Buying Basic stock and writing the 70 straddle matched his forecast; but only John can decide how much confidence he has in his forecast. The objections about potential missed opportunities or negative stock price action should be addressed to the market forecast.

Experienced "buy and hold" stock investors must adapt their style to the two-step thinking required for successful investing with options. The initiation of an option strategy has implications for what happens at option expiration, and that depends on the stock price. Investors who use options must consider all possible outcomes and plan accordingly.

Case 2: The Indecisive Stock Investor with a Gain

Ramona is an investor with a nice problem. Some time ago she purchased 200 shares of Rising Star below $20 per share; the current price is $44. Ramona is bullish and would like to sell her Rising Star at a higher price than $44, but her instincts are telling her to take some profits now. Ramona is considering two alternatives: (1) holding now and selling all 200 shares later or (2) selling 100 shares now and 100 later. A third alternative which Ramona might consider is a variation on the strategy "buy stock and write straddle."

In John's situation described above, he started with $14,000. His initial trade was the purchase of 100 shares at $70 and the sale of the 90-day 70 straddle. After this transaction, John's position was long 100 shares, short the 70 Call, short the 70 Put and $7,000 on deposit. Ramona can create a similar position by selling 100 shares now and simultaneously selling the 90-day 45 straddle.

To see how this strategy might meet Ramona's objectives, first consider what happens if Ramona chooses to hold. Second, consider the implications of selling 100 shares now and 100 later, and, third, examine what happens if the option strategy is used.

If Ramona chooses to hold, she is postponing her sell decision; the ultimate selling price will depend on the future performance of Rising Star's stock. It is impossible to say in advance what the results of holding will be but, as will be seen, the option strategy provides a basis for comparison.

The outcome of the second alternative, selling 100 shares now and 100 shares later, also depends on future price action. The difference between holding now and selling all shares later and selling 100 now and 100 later is the price movement required to achieve the same average selling price. If, for example, Ramona sells 100 shares now at $44 and 100 shares after a $4 price rise to $48, the average price of $46 is equal to holding now and selling all 200 shares after a $2 price rise to $46.

A two-to-one difference also exists if the stock price declines. Holding now and selling all 200 shares at $41, is equal to selling 100 shares now at $44 and the second 100 shares at $38. It is impossible to know in advance which will perform better, but the scenarios can be described. If the price of Rising Star continues to rise, the strategy of selling 200 shares later is best. However, if the price falls to $41 before rising to new highs, then selling 100 shares now at $44 and placing a stop-loss order for 100 shares at $38 would outperform a 200 share stop-loss sell order at $41.

The strategy of selling 100 shares now at $44 and simultaneously selling one 90-day 45 straddle, is not only a third alternative; it also provides additional information for making a decision. The short straddle establishes two prices: a sell price for the second 100 shares and a price at which the sold 100 shares will be repurchased. In Ramona's case, assume the 90-day 45 Call is trading at 2 and the 90-day 45 Put is also trading at 2.

If the price of Rising Star is above $45 at expiration, then the short call is assigned and the second 100 shares is sold at an effective price of $49—the $45 strike price plus the call premium of $2 plus the put premium of $2. The average selling price for all 200 shares under this scenario is $46 1/2 (100 shares at $44 and 100 at $49).

If Rising Star is below $45 at expiration, the short put is assigned and 100 shares are purchased at an effective price of $41 (the 45 strike price minus the two option premiums). The original 200-share position is re-established, but Ramona will have bought back the second 100 shares at a price $3 lower. The $3 per share "savings" on 100 shares equals $1 1/2 on 200 shares.

This strategy, selling 100 shares now at $44 and simultaneously selling the 90-day 45 straddle, offers Ramona a third set of trade-offs. If her short call is assigned, Ramona will have sold her 200 shares at an average price of $46 1/2. If the short put is assigned, she will have a $3 profit on 100 shares or a $1 1/2 profit on her 200 share position. Under what scenario will this strategy perform best?

If the stock stays between $41 and $49, the option premium received increases results. If the stock trades outside this range, and if Ramona is able to make optimal trading decisions, then one of the other alternatives will produce better results. By being aware of this option alternative, however, Ramona has a frame of reference, the $41-$49 range, which she can use as part of the subjective decision-making process in choosing between the three alternatives.

Case 3: Using the Short Straddle to Create a Trading Range

Matthew is a trader whose holdings of Fluctuation Industries has varied during the past twelve months from a low of zero shares to a high of 600 shares. Matthew has been "trading the range," accumulating shares of Fluctuation near $55 and selling near $65. Matthew's current position is long 300 shares which are trading at $60 and $18,000 cash in a money market account. Selling three Fluctuation 60 straddles might assist in Matthew's trading strategy.

Given his current holdings of 300 shares, a stock price of $60, a 90-day 60 Call price of 3 1/2 and a 90-day 60 Put price of 2 1/2, Matthew can consider three alternatives. First, he might wait for the stock price to rise, at which point the owned shares could be sold. Second, he might wait for the price to fall, at which point an additional 300 shares can be purchased. Third, writing a straddle might achieve similar results.

By writing a 60 Call at 3 1/2 for each 100 shares owned, Matthew is assuming the obligation of selling the owned shares at an effective price of $63 1/2. By writing a 60 Put at 2 1/2 for each 100 shares owned, Matthew is assuming the obligation of buying an additional 300 shares, effectively, at $57 1/2.

Writing three straddle contracts, however, expands the range to $66 and $54. With Fluctuation above $60 at expiration, the 60 Puts expire, the 60 Calls are assigned and the owned stock is effectively sold at $66 (the $60 strike price plus the call premium plus the put premium). If Fluctuation is below $60, the calls expire, the puts are assigned and 300 shares are purchased effectively at $54 (the $60 strike price minus both the call and put premiums). Commissions and interest are not included in these "effective" prices.

If Fluctuation is exactly at $60 at expiration, then we assume both the short call and short put expire worthless and Matthew keeps the $1,800 option premium less commissions plus any money market interest. On the downside, the risk is owning 600 shares and having the stock price fall dramatically. On the upside, there is an "opportunity risk" if the stock price rises above $66. In this case, selling the straddle would not perform as well as simply holding the 300 shares and not selling the straddle.

Whether or not writing the straddle performs better than waiting depends on the price action of Fluctuation and Matthew's trading decisions. The short straddle establishes buy and sell prices which meet Matthew's initial objectives, but it is impossible to know in advance if this strategy will perform better than his other alternatives.

Using Leverage

The use of leverage changes the amount of risk in this strategy. Meet Terry, an aggressive trader with $10,000. If Terry purchases 200 shares at $50 and, simultaneously sells two 90-day 50 Calls at 3 and two 90-day 50 Puts at 2 1/2, he has established a buy stock and write straddle position in which cash is not available to purchase stock if the short puts are assigned. Figure 14–2 graphically depicts Terry's position, and Table 14–2 contains the supporting profit and loss calculations.

The differences between Figure 14–1 and Figure 14–2 are the profit potentials and the slopes of the lines. This is the trade-off of leverage: higher profit potential and higher risk.

Figure 14–2 Terry's Buy Stock and Write Straddle

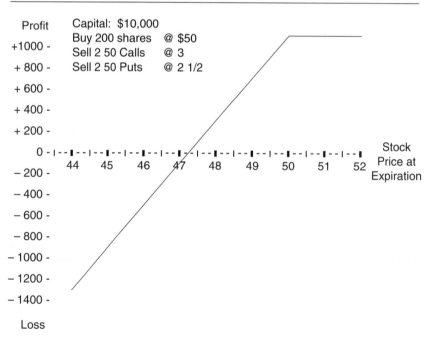

Table 14–2 Terry's Buy Stock and Write Straddle
Profit and Loss Calculations

Stock Price at Expiration	Long 200 Shares @ $50 P/(L)	Short 2 50 Call @ 3 P/(L)	Short 2 50 Put @ 2 1/2 P/(L)	Total P/(L)
$54	+$800	−$200	+$500	+$1,100
$53	+$600	0	+$500	+$1,100
$52	+$400	+$200	+$500	+$1,100
$51	+$200	+$400	+$500	+$1,100
$50	0	+$600	+$500	+$1,100
$49	−$200	+$600	+$300	+$700
$48	−$400	+$600	+$100	+$300
$47	−$600	+$600	−$100	−$100
$46	−$800	+$600	−$300	−$500
$45	−$1,000	+$600	−$500	−$900
$44	−$1,200	+$600	−$700	−$1,300

Expiration Mechanics Explained

At any stock price above $50 at expiration, the short puts expire, the short calls are assigned, and the owned 200 shares are sold. The resulting position is a cash balance of $11,100 ($10,000 from selling 200 shares at $50 plus $600 from selling two calls at 3 each plus $500 from selling two puts at 2 1/2 each). For simplicity, transaction costs and potential interest have not been included.

If the stock price is below $50 at expiration, the short calls expire, the short puts are assigned, and 200 shares are purchased at $50. Assuming sufficient account equity, the purchase of these 200 shares will be financed by margin loans. For example, if the stock price is $48 at expiration, the account equity would be $10,300. This is calculated by taking the initial investment in stock of $10,000, adding the option premium received of $1,100 and subtracting the stock loss of $800 (400 shares purchased at $50 which are now trading at $48).

The break-even stock price at expiration is $47 1/4 (not including commissions). The 400 shares purchased at $50 have a loss of $1,100 at $47 1/4 (400 × 2 3/4), and this equals the total option premium received.

If the stock price is below $50 at expiration, the short puts are assigned and the ending position is long 400 shares with margin debt of $8,900, the $10,000 purchase price of 200 at $50 less the option premium. The maximum theoretical risk is $18,900 (400 shares purchased at $50 minus $1,100 of option premium). The two short puts contribute the increased profit potential and the increased loss potential. This is the double-edged sword of leverage.

Assessing Risk

Some observations can be made about Terry's risk. First, the leverage is equal to buying stock on margin: two units of stock are purchased for each unit of capital. The break-even price, however, is $47 1/4 which is lower than the break-even price of buying stock on margin at $50. Second, the break-even price of $47 1/4 is higher than the break-even price of $47 for covered writing (buy stock at $50 and sell 50 Call at 3). Therefore, the risk of this strategy is somewhere between cash account covered writing and buying stock on margin.

Using the Leveraged Version of Buy Stock and Write Straddle

The existence of leverage makes this an aggressive strategy suited for only those with experience in trading on margin. Because this strategy has limited profit potential, it is an income-oriented strategy. Finally, unless the stock price is exactly at the strike at expiration, assignment of either the short calls or short puts will occur. This strategy, therefore, is likely to involve several transactions and related costs.

A typical scenario over several option expiration cycles is buying stock and selling options, then selling or buying stock through assignment, then selling stock and/or selling more options. Consequently, the leveraged version of buy stock and write straddle is suited only for those traders who are actively involved in watching and managing their investments and who trade in sufficient numbers of shares and options to get volume discounts on commissions.

Furthermore, this strategy is suited only for aggressive traders with experience buying stock on margin, have an income orientation and have a short-term neutral price forecast on a particular stock. Short-term, in this context, means the life of the sold options. One characteristic of this type of investor is decisiveness in cutting losses. As any trader who uses margin knows, the presence of leverage makes losses mount fast, and the only remedy, frequently, is to take action, i.e. sell the stock—or at least buy protective puts to limit the loss.

Readers with option experience will again notice a similarity between Figure 14–2 and Figure 11–1, covered writing on margin. This similarity occurs because of the put-call parity concept.

Summary

In its basic form, buy stock and write straddle involves the purchase of stock with half of the available cash and the simultaneous sale of a call and a put. The remaining cash is left on deposit earning interest and is used to purchase stock if the short put is assigned. This is an income-oriented strategy appropriate for investors with a neutral market forecast.

In its basic form, buy stock and write straddle can be used as a pure income-oriented strategy, or it can be used by indecisive stock investors or by traders who are forecasting a trading range for a stock and want to buy at the low end of the predicted range and sell at the high end. The effective buy and sell prices established by the sold options provide reference points which can be used as part of the subjective decision-making process.

The buy stock and write straddle strategy has a variation involving leverage. This involves using all available cash to purchase stock and, simultaneously, writing straddles. While the short calls are covered by the owned shares, the short puts, if assigned, require the use of margin loans to finance the purchase of stock. Using this leveraged version of buy stock and write straddle has a lower break-even price than buying stock on margin, but it is riskier than covered writing.

SECTION 4

Trading Strategies

Fifteen

Introduction to Trading Strategies

The focus now shifts from using options to achieve investment objectives to short-term trading. This section is designed to help short-term option traders in two ways. First, a method of analyzing market conditions prior to making a trading decision will be presented. Second, traders will be shown how to develop realistic expectations about the results of short-term option strategies. The goal is to improve skills in matching market predictions with appropriate option strategies. An appropriate strategy is one which will yield desired results if the market forecast is accurate. Market forecasting, of course, is an art, not a science, and it is not the intent of this book to explain market forecasting techniques. Investors who implement a strategy should note that a forecast can be correct or incorrect. The risk of any strategy is that the forecast is incorrect. It is therefore important to be fully aware of the risks before choosing to implement any strategy.

OP-EVAL™, the software program which accompanies this text, will be used as a tool to help accomplish the goal of improved strategy selection. Before OP-EVAL™ is described, however, two important points about computers must be made: what computers *can* do and what computers *cannot* do. These are important to identify because traders want to know why they are using the computer, and they do not want to fall into the trap of expecting too much. First, *computers simply make calculations.* Given certain assumptions which option traders enter into a program, the computer will calculate an option value. The most important aspect of this process is that *computers provide consistent information.* But it is the individual using the computer who has the key responsibilities on both sides of the computer's job: the *user* must choose and thoroughly understand the assumptions fed into the program, and the *user* must correctly interpret the results.

Why Use Computers?

191

Second, *computers do not make decisions*. Computer-generated information must be taken by the user with an awareness of its strengths and weaknesses, and it must be incorporated in the proper way into the decision-making process.

The Black-Scholes Option Pricing Formula

How option prices change often seems counter-intuitive. This was one point made in Chapter 4. To review briefly, an option's value depends on six factors: stock price, strike price, time to expiration, interest rates, dividends and volatility. If any of these factors change, the value of the option will change. In the real world, of course, it is common for more than one factor at a time to change as market conditions change. Calculating new option values in one's head is impossible, but the OP-EVAL™ program does the work for you.

OP-EVAL™, given six factors, calculates a "theoretical option value" using a formula known as the Black-Scholes option pricing model. Before proceeding, there are a number of points to be made about the Black-Scholes formula. First, the words "formula" and "model" mean exactly the same thing and are used interchangeably. Second, the Black-Scholes formula involves advanced calculus, and the calculations cannot be carried out on a four-function calculator. Third, it is not necessary to be a mathematician to use the Black-Scholes formula. What is necessary, however, is an understanding of the inputs and how they affect the results from the model.

Fourth, although the Black-Scholes formula is widely used for stock options, it is not the only option pricing formula. Fifth, there is no "best" formula. Like option strategies which offer investors different trade-offs, the different option pricing models have slightly different strengths and weaknesses. For all practical purposes, however, unless one is an advanced mathematician or a full-time professional option trader, the different formulas calculate very similar theoretical values. Sixth, in most cases, how an investor interprets the "theoretical value" calculated by a formula is more important than the value itself. It is more important that an option trader understand the concepts of option price behavior and what goes into the "theoretical value" than it is to be able to calculate the value. Seventh, an investor must understand what "theoretical value" means. Many newcomers to option pricing formulas and to computer-generated theoretical values have misconceptions about what it means

Who Makes the Decisions?

to "buy an option under theoretical value" or to "sell an option over theoretical value." This issue will be dealt with in due course.

The Outline of This Section

An often-heard complaint about short-term option trading is: "I was right on the market, but I lost money in options." It is the goal of this section to address this complaint. Chapters 16–19 explain many aspects of short-term option trading by developing a consistent, disciplined method of estimating option price changes and choosing an appropriate strategy, *given a market forecast*. If the market forecast is wrong, there is little hope, of course, that any strategy will yield positive results.

Chapter 16 introduces OP-EVAL™, the computer program which accompanies this text. Installation of the program, the various screens, inputting assumptions and reading output will all be explained. Chapter 17 presents an analysis technique using OP-EVAL™ which gives traders important information about market conditions so that reasonable assumptions can be made in estimating option prices. Chapter 17 also presents some short-term trading scenarios to illustrate the thinking process which goes into trading decisions. The goal of Chapter 17 is to take a short-term market forecast and determine if a particular option strategy will yield the desired results. Chapter 18, Strategy Comparisons, examines six option strategies, and explains how different market forecasts lead to the selection of each strategy. Chapter 19 discusses index options. In theory, index option trading is not different from standard stock option trading; in practice, however, there are numerous differences which increase the risk under certain circumstances and which change the expected option price behavior under other circumstances. Index option traders must fully appreciate the unique characteristics, risks and potential opportunities which index options offer.

Sixteen

Using OP-EVAL™

his chapter will introduce the OP-EVAL™ program which accompanies the text. After reviewing the installation instructions and disclaimer pages, the calculation page will be explained. How to move the cursor around the calculation page, how to change the input assumptions and how theoretical values are generated will be demonstrated.

Installing OP-EVAL™

Enclosed in the front or back jacket of this book is a 3 1/2″ computer disk labeled: OP-EVAL™ Setup Disk. This disk is designed to work on either DOS or Windows systems. Although the installation instructions are quite easy, if you are a computer neophyte, you may want the help of a more experienced friend. Once the program is installed, as you will see, it is very easy to use.

The installation instructions are as follows:

for WINDOWS:

To Install:
1. Start Microsoft Windows
2. Insert Setup Disk in drive A (or drive B)
3. From Program Manager, select the File menu and choose Run.
4. Type a:\install (or b:\install)
5. Press ENTER and follow instructions

To Run:
1. The "C" Drive must be the default drive. In Windows, this is generally true. If not, go to File Manager (from Program Manager), select the View menu and click on the "C:" icon.

       2. From Program Manager, select the File menu and choose Run

       3. Type c:\op-eval and press ENTER

for DOS:

To Install: 1. Turn on computer

            2. Insert Setup Disk in drive A (or drive B)

            3. Type a:\install (or b:\install)

            4. Press ENTER and follow instructions

To Run: 1. The "C" Drive must be the default drive. If C:\> does not appear when you first turn on the computer, type c:\ and press ENTER

            2. Type c:\op-eval and press ENTER

The first page you see will look like Exhibit 16–1.

Exhibit 16–1 OP-EVAL™ Program Page 1

OP-EVAL DISCLAIMERS and DISCLOSURES

It is important, for your protection as well as ours, that you read and understand the disclaimers and disclosures in this section. Only with fair and accurate knowledge of options and of the limits of this product and the risks that accompany options transactions can you make more appropriate strategy decisions.

SOFTWARE: OP-EVAL is designed for educational purposes only. The goal of the program is to assist in developing a basic understanding of option pricing. OP-EVAL should not be used for pricing actual options or for arbitrage trading.

OPTIONS: Options involve risk, and are not suitable for all investors. Prior to the initial purchase or sale of an option, every investor should read and understand the publication "Characteristics and Risks of Standardized Options." A copy of this publication may be obtained from your broker or from OP-EVAL, Suite 200, 2501 N. Lincoln Ave., Chicago, IL 60614.

Press Any Key to Continue

After reading this page carefully, press any key and the next page you see will look like Exhibit 16–2.

Exhibit 16–2   OP-EVAL™ Program Page 2

TAX CONSIDERATIONS, TRANSACTION COSTS and MARGIN REQUIRE-
MENTS: Options transactions—like other securities transactions—involve tax
considerations and transaction costs that can significantly affect the profit or
loss results of buying and writing options. Certain options transactions also
involve margin requirements which can significantly affect the desirability of the
transaction. None of these factors are taken into account in this program. For tax
considerations, you should seek the advice of a tax professional.

STOCK OPTIONS: OP-EVAL assumes that the dividend flow is continuous and
even throughout the option's life. Actual stocks pay dividends at discrete intervals. The difference between actual ex-dividend dates and the assumption of
even, continuous dividends made by this program can lead to some discrepancies between theoretical values and those observed in the marketplace.

Press Any Key to Continue

After reading this page carefully, press any key and the next page you see
will look like Exhibit 16–3.

Exhibit 16–3   OP-EVAL™ Program Page 3

INDEX OPTIONS: Great care should be taken in selecting the price of the underlying when pricing index options. Sometimes, if there is a futures contract traded
on the index, then price fluctuations of the futures contract above and below theoretical value can impact how options trade in the marketplace. Any prices of
index options calculated by this program should be interpreted very carefully.

FUTURES OPTIONS: Because the cost of carry is included in the futures price,
calls and puts with the same strike price and same expiration date are generally
the same premium when the futures contract is trading at exactly the corresponding strike price. To accomplish this result with OP-EVAL, the dividend rate
should be set equal to the interest rate. If the futures options are subject to
"futures style margining" such as in the U.K., then both the interest rate and dividends should be set to zero.

OP-EVAL IS DESIGNED TO BE USED IN CONJUNCTION WITH TEXTS AND
OTHER EDUCATIONAL MATERIALS—Copyright 1994 OP-EVAL.

For other financial products contact: OP-EVAL #200
2501 N. Lincoln Ave.
Chicago, IL 60614

Press Any Key to Continue

It is important that you read thoroughly the disclosures and disclaimers presented on the first three pages of OP-EVAL™. Only with a thorough understanding of the limitations of this program (or any other program) can you make more informed decisions. If you proceed on your own intuition and uninformed perceptions, you are not likely to do well in any area of investing, let alone option trading. After you have read all disclosures and disclaimers carefully, Exhibit 16–4 illustrates how you will be instructed to press Y if you accept the conditions or any other key to exit.

Exhibit 16–4 OP-EVAL™ Program Page 3 with Statement to Continue or Exit

INDEX OPTIONS: Great care should be taken in selection the price of the underlying when pricing index options. Sometimes, if there is a futures contract traded on the index, then price fluctuations of the futures contract above and below theoretical value can impact how options trade in the marketplace. Any prices of index options calculated by this program should be interpreted very carefully.

FUTURES OPTIONS: Because the cost of carry is included in the futures price, calls and puts with the same strike price and same expiration date are generally th   re-
s   Press Y if you accept these conditions, any other key to exit   ate
s   to
"futures-style margining" such as in the U.K.; then both the interest rate and dividends should be set to zero.

OP-EVAL IS DESIGNED TO BE USED IN CONJUNCTION WITH TEXTS AND OTHER EDUCATIONAL MATERIALS—Copyright 1994 OP-EVAL.

For other financial products contact: OP-EVAL #200
                                    2501 N. Lincoln Ave.
                                    Chicago, IL 60614

Press Any Key to Continue

If you have read and understand the first three pages and are willing to accept the risks you are undertaking by using this option pricing formula with all of its limitations, then press "Y" to indicate your willingness to accept. If you have not read the first three pages and would like to study them again, or if you do not want to proceed for any other reason, then press any other key and the program will terminate. At that point, if you wish, you can restart the program by following the "To Run:" instructions above.

When you have pressed "Y" which means you have read the disclaimers and disclosures and are willing to accept the limitations of the program, you will see a screen that looks like Exhibit 16–5.

Exhibit 16–5   OP-EVAL™ Program Calculation Page—Default Settings

OP-EVAL
Black-Scholes Option Price Solver for DOS
Version 1.2, January 1995

⌐ — · — Inputs to Formula — · — ¬		⌐ — · — Option Estimation — · — ¬		
			Call	Put
Price of Underlying	50.000	Price:	3.051	2.819
Strike Price:	50.000	Delta:	0.542	−0.458
Dividend Yield:	4.000%	Gamma:	0.052	0.052
Volatility:	30.000%	7-Day Theta:	−0.123	−0.105
Interest Rate:	6.000%	Vega:	0.098	0.098
Days to Expiration	90	Rho:	0.055	−0.059

ENTER to Recalculate, Arrows to Move; Q to Quit Program, F1 for Help

This program has limitations; it is for educational purposes only.

You must read the DISCLAIMERS and DISCLOSURES; Press D

Exhibit 16–5 is the main page of OP-EVAL™ and will be referred to as the "calculation page." This page is what you will be using to analyze option price behavior and to gather information which you can interpret for trading decisions.

Inputting Information

This section will describe each area of the calculation page, demonstrate how the input assumptions can be changed and show how the "Option Estimation" (or option theoretical value) changes. In the next section the various outputs will be defined. Chapter 17 will explain how information from the calculation page might be interpreted and used in decision-making.

Moving around the Calculation Page

The highlighted rectangle on the calculation page can be changed either by pressing the arrow keys or by pressing the ENTER key. First, press the arrow keys and the ENTER key to get used to the movement around the calculation page. The down arrow (↓) and right arrow (→) move the highlighted area forward. Forward means down the screen first, then over to the CALL rectangle, then to the PUT rectangle and, finally, back to the "Price of Underlying" rectangle. You will not be able to move the highlighted area to the spaces below the CALL and PUT rectangles. The up arrow (↑) and left arrow (←) move the highlighted area in the opposite direction or backward.

The ENTER key, if pressed one time, will recalculate the call and put values and the other output information. Pressing the ENTER key a second time will move the highlighted rectangle forward.

After familiarizing yourself with movement around the calculation page, press the arrow keys until the "Price of Underlying" rectangle is highlighted. When you first get to the calculation page in OP-EVAL™, you are looking at the "default settings" which appear in Exhibit 16–5. These are 50.000 for the price of the underlying, 50.000 for the strike price, etc. Given these "inputs" OP-EVAL™ has calculated the theoretical value of the 50 Call as 3.051—look on the top line of the right side of the calculation page in the CALL rectangle.

Changing "Price of Underlying"

With the "Price of Underlying" rectangle highlighted, you can input any price from 0.001 to 99,999.999. If a whole number such as 53 is entered, OP-EVAL™ assumes all three numbers to the right of the decimal point are zeros. When the enter key or any arrow key is pressed, the number 53.000 appears, and all output values are recalculated. The three-digit decimal point feature makes it possible to input real United States stock prices in eighths. For example, 50 1/8 is 50.125. 50 3/8 is 50.375, etc.

To Recalculate: Press ENTER or Arrow Keys

When you have entered a new price, you can either press ENTER or any arrow key. If you press ENTER, OP-EVAL™ will calculate a new theoretical value, and the highlighted rectangle will remain the same. If you press an arrow key, OP-EVAL™ will calculate the new theoretical value and highlight the next rectangle either forward or backward depending on which arrow is pressed.

To practice, work through the following example: Assuming the default settings are on the calculation page (as in Exhibit 16–5), 50.000 will appear in the "Price of Underlying" rectangle. Highlight this rectangle, type in "51" and press ENTER. Exhibit 16–6 illustrates what the screen looks like now. The new price, 51.000, appears in the "Price of Underlying" rectangle; and new numbers, 3.614 and 2.391, appear under CALL and PUT respectively. The other outputs—delta, gamma, theta, vega and rho—have also been recalculated. OP-EVAL™ has recalculated all outputs based on the "new" information. In this case, the "new information" is only a change in one input—the price of the underlying—but this one change has caused all the outputs to change.

You can now practice with the different input rectangles and observe how OP-EVAL™ calculates option theoretical values, given your inputs.

Exhibit 16–6 OP-EVAL™ Program—"Price of Underlying" Changed to "51"

OP-EVAL
Black-Scholes Option Price Solver for DOS
Version 1.2, January 1995

Inputs to Formula			Option Estimation		
				Call	Put
Price of Underlying	51.000		Price:	3.614	2.391
Strike Price:	50.000		Delta:	0.594	−0.406
Dividend Yield:	4.000%		Gamma:	0.050	0.050
Volatility:	30.000%		7-Day Theta:	−0.123	−0.106
Interest Rate:	6.000%		Vega:	0.097	0.097
Days to Expiration	90		Rho:	0.061	−0.053

ENTER to Recalculate, Arrows to Move; Q to Quit Program, F1 for Help

This program has limitations; it is for educational purposes only.

You must read the DISCLAIMERS and DISCLOSURES; Press D

Changing "Strike Price"

In option markets in the United States, stock option strike prices on listed options are set at the following intervals:

Stock Price	Strike Interval	Example
Below $25	every $2.50	5.00, 7.50, 10.00, etc.
$25 to $200	every $5.00	25.00, 30.00, 35.00, etc.
Above $200	every $10.00	200.00, 210.00, 220.00, etc.

OP-EVAL™ has the flexibility to set the strike price at any number between 0 and 99,999.999. This feature allows OP-EVAL™ to be used for options on a wide variety of underlying instruments such as commodity futures, financial futures and currency futures.

Changing "Dividend Yield"

Although dividends are paid in discrete payments, the Black-Scholes option pricing formula used by OP-EVAL™ assumes dividends are paid continuously throughout the year. This is one of the limitations described in the Disclosures and Disclaimers pages at the beginning of the program. Because securities valuation involves a process known as "discounting cash flows," this assumption can mean there will be a difference between the values calculated by OP-EVAL™ and prices observed in the real marketplace. This assumption does not diminish the value of OP-EVAL™ for educational purposes. Adapting the program to account for specific dividend payments and specific payment dates would make the program much more cumbersome. This simplification was made for educational efficiency.

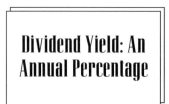

Dividend Yield: An Annual Percentage

To choose a number to put into the Dividend Yield (%) rectangle, you can either take the number in the yield column from your newspaper—if it is there—or you can calculate a rough estimate of the yield yourself by using this simple formula:

Dividend Yield (%) = Total Annual Dividend Payments
÷ Current Stock Price

It is important to note these are the *total annual dividend payments*, not one quarterly payment which is sometimes presented in newspapers. Occasionally, a stock will pay semi-annual dividends or a "special" dividend one time in a year. Special dividends may or may not be in addition to quarterly or semi-annual payments. Consequently, it is important that you fully understand what number is being put into the "Dividend Yield" rectangle, or you will not get meaningful calculations from OP-EVAL™.

To see how a change in the dividend yield affects call and put values, work through the following example: Assuming the default settings are on the calculation page (as in Exhibit 16–5), 4.000 will appear in the "Dividend Yield" rectangle. Press the arrows until this rectangle is highlighted, type "5" and press ENTER. Exhibit 16–7 illustrates what the screen looks like. The number 5.000 appears in the Dividend Yield (%) rectangle and new numbers, 2.988 and 2.873, appear under CALL and PUT respectively. Notice: an increase in the dividend yield lowered the call price and raised the put price. This is consistent with the concepts presented in Chapter 4.

Exhibit 16–7   OP-EVAL™ Program—"Dividend Yield" Changed to "5"

OP-EVAL
Black-Scholes Option Price Solver for DOS
Version 1.2, January 1995

⌐ — · — Inputs to Formula — · — ¬		⌐ — · — Option Estimation · — · — ¬		
			Call	Put
Price of Underlying	50.000	Price:	2.988	2.873
Strike Price:	50.000	Delta:	0.536	−0.464
Dividend Yield:	5.000%	Gamma:	0.052	0.052
Volatility:	30.000%	7-Day Theta:	−0.118	−0.109
Interest Rate:	6.000%	Vega:	0.097	0.097
Days to Expiration	90	Rho:	0.055	−0.060

ENTER to Recalculate, Arrows to Move; Q to Quit Program, F1 for Help

This program has limitations; it is for educational purposes only.

You must read the DISCLAIMERS and DISCLOSURES; Press D

Changing "Volatility"

Volatility, as discussed in Chapter 4, is a statistical concept relating to the range of possible prices. If all other factors are equal, a wider range of possible stock prices (i.e. a higher volatility) means options have a higher theoretical value. It is common practice to express volatility as a percentage, and this same practice is used in OP-EVAL™. The default setting for volatility is 30.000, or 30%. When the "Volatility" rectangle is highlighted, it is possible to enter any number from 0.000 to 999.999. If all inputs are at their default settings (as in Exhibit 16–5), then changing the "Volatility" to 31 and pressing ENTER results in 31.000 appearing in the Volatility rectangle and 3.148 and 2.916, respec-

> ### Volatility:
> ### A Percentage

Exhibit 16–8   OP-EVAL™ Program—"Volatility" Changed to "31"

OP-EVAL
Black-Scholes Option Price Solver for DOS
Version 1.2, January 1995

Inputs to Formula		Option Estimation		
			Call	Put
Price of Underlying	50.000	Price:	3.148	2.916
Strike Price:	50.000	Delta:	0.543	−0.457
Dividend Yield:	4.000%	Gamma:	0.051	0.051
Volatility:	31.000%	7-Day Theta:	−0.126	−0.109
Interest Rate:	6.000%	Vega:	0.098	0.098
Days to Expiration	90	Rho:	0.055	−0.059

ENTER to Recalculate, Arrows to Move; Q to Quit Program, F1 for Help

This program has limitations; it is for educational purposes only.

You must read the DISCLAIMERS and DISCLOSURES; Press D

tively, appearing under CALL and PUT. Take note! An increase in volatility increased both the CALL and PUT values! This is illustrated in Exhibit 16–8. You should experiment with this input rectangle and develop a feel for how changes in volatility affect option prices.

Changing the "Interest Rate"

Interest rates are a factor in the option values, because time and the cost of money are involved in purchasing stocks. The default setting for interest rates is 6.000, or 6%. You should experiment with this input rectangle and develop a feel for how changes in interest rates affect option prices. With experience, you will observe that changes in interest rates have the smallest impact on option values. This is consistent with the concepts presented in Chapter 4.

Interest Rate:
An Annual Percentage

Changing "Days to Expiration"

Time is a well-known factor which affects option prices. Tables 4–1 and 4–3 and Figures 4–3, 4–4 and 4–5 illustrate how the time value portion of option prices erodes as expiration approaches. Chapter 4 also explains how changes in time affect at-the-money options differently from in-the-money and out-of-the-money options.

The default setting for "Days to Expiration" is 90. When counting the days to expiration for equity options, include the current day if it is before or during market hours, but do not include the current day if it is after the market close. Also, be sure to use the third Friday of the expiration month as the expiration day. Even though equity options technically expire on a Saturday, Friday is the last day of trading and the last opportunity to exercise.

Option traders should also be sure to know their brokerage firm's exact exercise deadline on expiration Friday as well as all exercise procedures in case these procedures are ever needed. In addition, option traders should know their firm's *early exercise* procedures, including the daily time deadline, because they are sometimes different. It takes so little effort to learn these details. Not needing something and knowing it is not costly. Needing something and not knowing it, however, could be very costly!

Changing the Call and Put—Estimating Implied Volatility

Given the default setting of inputs (as in Exhibit 16–5), the CALL rectangle will read 3.051. Press the ENTER key or one of the arrow keys until this rectangle is highlighted. Change this number to 3.5 and press ENTER. The first change you will notice is the number in the CALL rectangle is now 3.500. But another change is far more important. Can you tell what it is?

Look at the "Volatility" rectangle. You will observe that the number has been recalculated from 30.000 to 34.607. Exhibit 16–9 shows the computer screen with a call price of 3.5000 and Volatility of 34.607. As will be explained in Chapter 17, 34.607 is the *implied volatility*. If instead of changing the CALL value to 3.500 you had changed the "Volatility" number to 34.607, OP-EVAL™ would have calculated the call value to be 3.500. Chapter 17 explains how using an option price to solve for the implied volatility percentage might assist in making trading decisions.

Exhibit 16–9   OP-EVAL™ Program—CALL Changed to "3.5"

OP-EVAL
Black-Scholes Option Price Solver for DOS
Version 1.2, January 1995

┌─ ─·· Inputs to Formula ─·─·─┐		┌─·─·─ Option Estimation ·─·─·─┐		
			Call	Put
Price of Underlying	50.000	Price:	3.500	3.268
Strike Price:	50.000	Delta:	0.545	−0.455
Dividend Yield:	4.000%	Gamma:	0.045	0.045
Volatility:	34.607%	7-Day Theta:	−0.140	−0.122
Interest Rate:	6.000%	Vega:	0.097	0.097
Days to Expiration	90	Rho:	0.055	−0.060

ENTER to Recalculate, Arrows to Move; Q to Quit Program, F1 for Help

This program has limitations; it is for educational purposes only.

You must read the DISCLAIMERS and DISCLOSURES; Press D

When the value in the CALL rectangle is changed, OP-EVAL™ not only recalculates the volatility, it also recalculates the PUT value using the new volatility percentage and all other outputs as well.

OP-EVAL™ will also calculate a new volatility percentage given a new PUT value. In this case, a new CALL value will be recalculated using the new volatility percentage, and all other outputs will also be recalculated.

Help Pages

From the calculation page, the "F1" key will take you to the first of four "Help Pages." These pages provide support information such as the allowable ranges for the six inputs and definitions of delta, gamma, vega, theta and rho. Pressing any key will move you to the next help page, and you must proceed through all four pages to return to the calculation page.

Practicing with Changing Inputs

Now that all the inputs and how to change them have been reviewed, take out your pencil and paper to practice by creating a table or two of theoretical values. Your goal is to create a table similar to Table 4–1. To assist you, Table 16–1 is a blank table which can be photocopied.

To make this as realistic as possible, select a real stock, choose a real strike price and expiration month and count the days to a specific expiration day. The left-most column of your table should have a range of stock prices. The intervals between prices does not have to be $1. The increments can be half dollars or quarter dollars. For the dividend, be sure to use the annual payments when calculating the dividend yield. Review the formula above if necessary. For now, you will have to guess at the volatility number; the default figure of 30% is good for practice. A method for estimating a more accurate number for volatility will be presented in Chapter 17. The interest rate to use is the current 90-day Treasury Bill rate or, better yet, the Broker Loan Rate if you know it. The Broker Loan Rate is frequently about one-half percent above the 90-day Treasury Bill rate. As you may have discovered when practicing with changing the interest rate, small changes in interest rates do not have a major impact on option prices, so it is only necessary to be close on interest rates.

The days to expiration is, however, very important. Therefore, to practice, choose a real expiration month, verify the expiration date and count the exact number of calendar days (not business days). If now, for example, is

**Table 16–1   Blank Table for Practice with Theoretical Values at Various
Stock Prices and Days to Expiration**

Option Type _____   Strike _____

Interest Rate _____   Volatility _____

	Col. 1	Col. 2	Col. 3	Col. 4	Col. 5	Col. 6	Col. 7
	Stock Price	Days to Exp ___	Days to Exp ___	Days to Exp ___	Days to Exp ___	Days to Exp ___	Exp
Row 11							
Row 10							
Row 9							
Row 8							
Row 7							
Row 6							
Row 5							
Row 4							
Row 3							
Row 2							
Row 1							

Monday morning of expiration week, then it is *five* days to expiration.
Remember, Friday is the day to use as the expiration day. So, from Monday
morning, there is all day Monday, all day Tuesday, etc., and Friday is the fifth
day from now. An expiration calendar can be obtained without charge from
one of the exchanges on which options are traded. The toll-free telephone
numbers of the five options exchanges in the United States are listed in
Chapter 19. Get in the habit of ordering a new expiration calendar every
December for the next year. Make it a present to yourself!

Completing a Practice Table of Theoretical Values

When you have created your table (similar to Tables 4–1 and 16–1), calculated the dividend yield and selected a volatility, you can fill in your table
using OP-EVAL™ by changing the stock price through your selected price
range on a particular day (column). Next, change the number of days to

expiration for the second column and input each stock price in OP-EVAL™ and complete the corresponding cell.

With a little effort, you will have easily completed your first table of "theoretical values," and you can practice checking your intuition with the values in your table. For example, if the stock moves from price 1 on day 1 to price 2 on day 2, how much do you think the option price will change? Now, compare your personal estimate with the value in the table. After a little practice, you will get very good at this, and you can develop realistic expectations when estimating option prices.

Summary

The purpose of this chapter has been to introduce the OP-EVAL™ computer program which accompanies this text. After installing the program, you must read carefully and thoroughly understand the three pages of disclaimers and disclosures before practicing with the calculation page.

Starting with the default settings on the calculation page, you may change any one or more of the six inputs. When the ENTER key is pressed, OP-EVAL™ recalculates all outputs and leaves the highlighted rectangle the same. Pressing the ENTER key a second time moves the highlighted rectangle forward. When one of the arrow keys is pressed, OP-EVAL™ recalculates all outputs and moves the highlighted rectangle forward or backward, depending on which arrow is pressed.

If the CALL or PUT value is changed, OP-EVAL™ recalculates the volatility percentage. Simultaneously, the PUT or CALL value is recalculated using the new volatility percentage. All other outputs are also recalculated.

It is important to practice changing inputs with OP-EVAL™. One way to practice is to create tables of theoretical values, each row being a different stock price and each column being a different number of days prior to expiration. The purpose of practicing with theoretical value tables is to develop realistic expectations when estimating changes in option prices.

For additional copies of OP-EVAL™, please send $10.00* per disk plus $1.50 per order for shipping and handling to:

OP-EVAL
Suite 200
2501 N. Lincoln Avenue
Chicago, IL 60614

Please make checks payable to: OP-EVAL

Allow 3–4 weeks for delivery

*Illinois residents please add 0.80 per disk (8% Illinois sales tax)

Seventeen

Trading Examples

This chapter will demonstrate an analysis technique designed with the goal of increasing the chances of making successful trades. This technique estimates an option price in the future based on a market forecast and historical option price information. The concept is that better decisions can be made if they are based on concrete, consistent information. Profitable results, of course, are not guaranteed. Market forecasting, after all, is an art, not a science, and it is the most important element in successful trading! Commissions and other transaction costs are not included in the examples presented in this chapter, but they must be considered when analyzing real trades.

The Importance of Implied Volatility

Of the six factors affecting option values, five can be objectively identified. The stock price, the strike price, the days to expiration, the dividend yield, and the interest rate can all be observed independently. Only the volatility number is unknown. As a result, option traders must decide for themselves what volatility number to use.

As illustrated in the preceding chapter, OP-EVAL™ can be used to calculate implied volatility by entering a price in the CALL or PUT rectangle. OP-EVAL™ works the Black-Scholes option pricing formula in reverse and calculates the volatility percentage which, if input into the formula, would calculate the input option price. This process—calculating the volatility percentage which produces a given option price—is known as calculating the implied volatility of an option.

Implied volatility is the volatility percentage which the market forces of supply and demand have agreed on in determining the current market price of an option. When selecting strategies, traders can make more informed decisions by observing what the market has done in the past.

Implied Volatility and P/E—An Analogy

For a rough analogy, consider the price/earnings (P/E) ratio and how it is used by some stock analysts. A stock's per-share earnings and price range for previous years are known. This information and earnings estimates are used by analysts to forecast stock prices.

For example, assume a stock is currently trading at $17. If last year's earnings were one dollar per share and the price range of the stock was from $15 to $22, then the P/E ratio went from a low of fifteen to a high of twenty-two and is currently seventeen. If an analyst predicts this year's earnings will rise to $1.25, that analyst could reasonably forecast that the stock will trade between $18 3/4 (fifteen times the predicted earnings) and $27 1/2 (twenty-two times the predicted earnings). Of course, many other factors are involved, and the stock price can act differently from what is expected, even if the earnings prediction is accurate. Nevertheless, this is a common practice in stock market analysis and forecasting.

In options trading, implied volatility can be used in a similar way, starting with an analysis of past levels and making forecasts. If options on a particular stock, for example, have traded historically at implied volatility levels between 25% and 30%, it is reasonable to predict they may trade in that range, under normal circumstances, in the future. Of course, market conditions change, and there is risk making predictions this way. Nevertheless, many options traders believe this is a reasonable process.

Trading Example #1

Assume that Greg, a successful real estate broker in Los Angeles, has been watching the stock of a telecommunications company, Phoneco, for some time. Greg thinks the time is right for the price of Phoneco to rally from $58 1/2 to $60 or $61 over the next two weeks. Today is 49 days to April expiration, and the Phoneco April 60 Call is offered at 1 7/8. Greg is trying to decide whether or not to buy this call.

First, Greg must do a little research. Because he is a regular trader, he has saved some business sections from past Friday and weekend papers. Looking at five past issues selected at random, Greg gathers the information in the Option Fact Sheet presented as Table 17–1.

Observe that on Jan 13, Jan 27 and Feb 17 Greg obtained the closing price of only one option. On Feb 3 and Feb 24 he found information on two options with different expirations. Although it is very rough, Greg will use

Table 17–1 Greg's Option Fact Sheet on Phoneco (with Preliminary Information)

Dividend Yield (%) 1.91   Interest Rates (%) 4.65

Date	Stock Price	Exp Mo. & Strike	Days to Exp	Option Price	Implied Volatility
Jan 13	62 1/4	MAR 60	63	3 3/4	
Jan 27	63 3/4	MAR 65	49	1 1/2	
Feb 3	63	MAR 65	42	1 3/8	
Feb 3	63	APR 65	77	2 1/8	
Feb 17	61	APR 60	63	3	
Feb 24	59 3/4	MAR 60	21	1 1/4	
Feb 24	59 3/4	APR 60	56	2 1/8	
Today	58 1/2	JUN 60	49	1 7/8	

this information, along with his market prediction, to decide whether or not to buy the April 60 Call.

In addition to the stock and option information in Table 17–1, Greg must supply the interest rate and the dividend yield. He finds the latest 90-day Treasury bill rate to be 4.65%, and, from the stock tables, he finds Phoneco's annual dividend is $1.12. Dividing the dividend by the stock price, he calculates the dividend yield percentage to be 1.91% (1.12 ÷ 58.50 = 0.0191).

Using OP-EVAL™ to Calculate Implied Volatilities

Greg inputs the information in each row of Table 17–1, along with the interest rate and dividend percentages, in the OP-EVAL™ program to calculate the implied volatility percentage for each option price. Exhibit 17–1 shows how Greg has input the information from Table 17–1, row one (Jan 13) into OP-EVAL™. When the stock price of $62 1/4, the strike price of 60, the dividend yield of 1.91%, the interest rate of 4.65%, the days to expiration of 63 and the call price of 3 3/4 are entered, OP-EVAL™ calculates an implied volatility of 22.58%.

The same process is repeated for the remaining rows, including the "Today" row which has the information about the April 60 Call Greg is con-

Exhibit 17–1   OP-EVAL™ Screen with Data from Table 17–1, Row 1 (Jan 13)

OP-EVAL
Black-Scholes Option Price Solver for DOS
Version 1.2, January 1995

Inputs to Formula		Option Estimation		
			Call	Put
Price of Underlying	62.250	Price:	3.750	1.234
Strike Price:	60.000	Delta:	0.687	–0.313
Dividend Yield:	1.910%	Gamma:	0.057	0.057
Volatility:	22.582%	7-Day Theta:	–0.136	–0.107
Interest Rate:	4.650%	Vega:	0.091	0.091
Days to Expiration	63	Rho:	0.064	–0.034

ENTER to Recalculate, Arrows to Move; Q to Quit Program, F1 for Help

This program has limitations; it is for educational purposes only.

You must read the DISCLAIMERS and DISCLOSURES; Press D

sidering buying. The Option Fact Sheet with all implied volatilities is presented in Table 17–2.

Comparison of Implied Volatilities

Greg makes an interesting observation from the implied volatility column of Table 17–2. The option prices observed from January 13 to February 27 have implied volatilities ranging from a low of 22.36% to a high of 24.63%. The option price in the "Today" row, however, has an implied volatility of 28.58%, substantially higher than the high observed from January 13 to February 24. Greg must wonder: what are the implications of this?

To answer this question, Greg can clearly state his market forecast and then test some scenarios using OP-EVAL™.

Table 17–2 Greg's Option Fact Sheet on Phoneco
(with Implied Volatility Levels)

Dividend Yield (%) 1.91   Interest Rates (%) 4.65

Date	Stock Price	Exp Mo. & Strike	Days to Exp	Option Price	Implied Volatility
Jan 13	62 1/4	MAR 60	63	3 3/4	22.58
Jan 27	63 3/4	MAR 65	49	1 5/8	22.36
Feb 3	63	MAR 65	42	1 1/2	23.45
Feb 3	63	APR 65	77	2 1/8	24.63
Feb 17	61	APR 60	63	3	23.17
Feb 24	59 3/4	MAR 60	21	1 1/4	23.22
Feb 24	59 3/4	APR 60	56	2 1/8	22.87
Today	58 1/2	APR 60	49	1 7/8	28.58

Greg already has a stock price forecast and a time forecast. He is predicting a stock price of $60 to $61 in two weeks, which will be 35 days prior to April expiration. He assumes that the other factors, dividends and interest rates, will remain static; so the question becomes, "what will the implied volatility be?" Greg might assume, based on the information in the Option Fact Sheet, that implied volatility will return in two weeks to a "more normal" 23%. Alternatively, he could assume the implied volatility will remain at, or near, its current level.

Greg can use OP-EVAL™ to estimate the price of the April 60 Call based on his different assumptions about the volatility. Table 17–3 shows the completed Option Fact Sheet with Scenario #1, implied volatility of 23%, and Scenario #2, implied volatility of 28%.

Under Scenario #1, implied volatility of 23%, Table 17–3 shows a 60 Call price of 1 3/4 or 2 3/8 with a stock price of $60 or $61, respectively, in two weeks. The conclusion: if volatility decreases to 23% and if the stock price is $60 or $61 in two weeks, then the 60 Call, purchased today for 1 7/8 is expected to be 1 3/4 or 2 3/8. Buying the 60 Call now and selling it in two weeks, therefore, could be expected to result in a 1/8 loss or a 1/2 profit (not including commissions).

Under Scenario #2, implied volatility of 28%, Table 17–3 shows a 60 Call price of 2 1/8 or 2 3/4 with a stock price of $60 or $61, respectively, in two weeks. The conclusion: if volatility is 28%, a purchase of the 60 Call

**Table 17–3 Greg's Option Fact Sheet on Phoneco
(with Possible Scenarios)**

Dividend Yield (%) 1.91   Interest Rates (%) 4.65

Date	Stock Price	Exp Mo. & Strike	Days to Exp	Option Price	Implied Volatility
Jan 13	62 1/4	MAR 60	63	3 3/4	22.58
Jan 27	63 3/4	MAR 65	49	1 5/8	22.36
Feb 3	63	MAR 65	42	1 1/2	23.45
Feb 3	63	APR 65	77	2 1/8	24.63
Feb 17	61	APR 60	63	3	23.17
Feb 24	59 3/4	MAR 60	21	1 1/4	23.22
Feb 24	59 3/4	APR 60	56	2 1/8	22.87
Today	58 1/2	APR 60	49	1 7/8	28.58
Scenario #1: Volatility—23%					
in 2 weeks	60	APR 60	35	1 3/4	23.00
in 2 weeks	61	APR 60	35	2 3/8	23.00
Scenario #1: Volatility—28%					
in 2 weeks	60	APR 60	35	2 1/8	28.00
in 2 weeks	61	APR 60	35	2 3/4	28.00

today for 1 7/8 and sale in two weeks could be expected to result in a 1/4 profit or 7/8 profit (not including commissions).

Greg must now decide if the chances favor success on this trade. The more conservative forecast is Scenario #1 in which implied volatility declines to 23%. Under this scenario, the range of outcomes does not seem to Greg to be worth the risk: $1 7/8 at risk to make 1/2 under the most optimistic stock price forecast. The most profitable outcome, earning 7/8 in Scenario #2, only occurs if the most optimistic forecast for volatility and stock price is realized.

To summarize Greg's situation: the more conservative scenario could result in a loss, and the most optimistic outcome is expected to make a profit of 7/8 not including commissions. The chances of success do not seem very high to Greg. What he wants is a scenario in which a conservative forecast shows a small profit and an optimistic forecast shows a substantial profit. Greg decides to forego buying this call.

Trading Example #2

In this trading example, Catherine, a management consultant in Miami, has been following the stock of a large discount retailer, Saleco, currently $29 1/2. She is considering whether or not to buy the September 30 Call (with 28 days to expiration) which is offered at 5/8. Catherine is forecasting a price rise to $30 3/4 in two weeks.

Table 17–4, an Option Fact Sheet for Saleco, offers the necessary information to analyze this situation. Catherine draws information in the first five columns, "Date" through "Option Price," from newspapers, and calculates the implied volatility percentages using the OP-EVAL™ program.

Table 17–4　Catherine's Option Fact Sheet on Saleco (Completed)

Dividend Yield (%) 0　　　　Interest Rates (%) 4.20

Date	Stock Price	Exp Mo. & Strike	Days to Exp	Option Price	Implied Volatility
Jun 30	31 1/8	AUG 30	39	3 3/4	27.09
Jun 30	31 1/8	SEP 30	77	1 5/8	30.04
Jul 14	30 3/8	AUG 30	35	1 1/2	29.86
Jul 14	30 3/8	SEP 30	63	2 1/8	28.84
Jul 28	29 1/8	SEP 30	49	3	29.26
Today	29 1/2	SEP 30	28	5/8	24.74
Scenario #1: Volatility—28%					
in 2 weeks	30	SEP 30	14	11/16	28.00
in 2 weeks	30 3/4	SEP 30	14	1 1/8	28.00
in 2 weeks	31 1/4	SEP 30	14	1 1/2	28.00
Scenario #2: Volatility—24%					
in 2 weeks	30	SEP 30	14	9/16	24.00
in 2 weeks	30 3/4	SEP 30	14	1 1/16	24.00
in 2 weeks	31 1/4	SEP 30	14	1 7/16	24.00

Saleco pays no dividend, and Catherine found that current 90-day Treasury bills yield 4.20%.

From the completed Option Fact Sheet, Catherine observes that implied volatility levels from June 30 to July 28 for the August 30 Call and September 30 Call have ranged from 27.09% to 30.04%. Today, however, the September 30 Call is offered at an implied volatility level of 24.74%. On the surface, Catherine sees an attractively priced option. To complete her analysis, however, she must create some market scenarios and estimate the change in price of this call.

According to Scenario #1 in Table 17–4, if the price of Saleco rises, as forecast, to 30 3/4 in two weeks, and if the implied volatility rises to 28%, then OP-EVAL™ calculates a 30 Call price of 1.137, approximately 1 1/8, or nearly double the purchase price of 5/8. To see what happens under a broader range of outcomes, Catherine also estimates the option price if the stock is at $31 1/4 or $30. With a stock price of $31 1/4, OP-EVAL™ estimates the 30 Call to be 1.509 or approximately 1 1/2. With a stock price of $30, the estimate is 0.68, or 11/16.

Scenario #2 makes a more conservative forecast of volatility. With a volatility of 24% in two weeks, OP-EVAL™ estimates call prices of 9/16, 1 1/16 and 1 7/16 if the stock price is $30, $30 3/4 or $31 1/4 respectively.

Of course, Catherine should also consider the risks of Scenario #3 (not shown) in which volatility drops to 20%, a level below both the historical observations and the current level. Such an occurrence is a possibility! With a volatility of 20% in two weeks, OP-EVAL™ estimates call prices of 1/2, 1 and 1 3/8 if the stock price is $30, $30 3/4 or $31 1/4 respectively.

Looking at the range of outcomes in scenarios #1, #2 and #3, Catherine favors buying this call. The first scenario suggests a doubling of the option price, and a more conservative scenario also leads to an option price rise. Only if the stock price rises by 1/2 or less, or falls, and if implied volatility remains static or falls does a loss result.

Trading Examples #1 and #2 Compared

Keeping in mind that their stock forecasts could be wrong and therefore cause losses, Greg and Catherine's examples offer some important points to look for and some others to avoid. First, a review of implied volatility levels in the past provides a basis for making a personal judgment as to whether a current option price is "relatively good" or "relatively poor." Second, estimating an option price using the time and price forecast for the stock along with a forecast of volatility leads to an estimate of profit or loss. Finally, a range of forecasts provides more information and must be considered. Since a number of factors affect option values, various elements of a forecast should be experimented with so as to get "a feel" for the possible outcomes.

For Greg, a return to "normal" implied volatility levels (in his opinion) led to the conclusion that buying the April 60 Call will not yield a desirable profit even if his forecast is realized. Consequently, he did not buy the call. In contrast, for Catherine, her forecast, whether or not the implied volatility level returns to "normal," yields an acceptable profit. Catherine, therefore, buys the September 30 Call, because she is willing to accept the risk of her stock forecast being incorrect.

Table 17–5 is a blank Option Fact Sheet which can be photocopied and used for analysis of real trading decisions. Although the examples presented in this chapter were created for illustration purposes only and do not include commissions and other transaction costs which can affect results, Catherine's situation is the type to look for.

Summary

Implied volatility is the volatility percentage which justifies the current market price of an option. Given the market price of a call or put and the other inputs, the OP-EVAL™ program works the Black-Scholes formula in reverse to solve for implied volatility. Option Fact Sheets which include closing stock and option prices, days to expiration, interest rates and dividend yield can be used to analyze implied volatility levels in the past.

Experimenting with market predictions helps traders to understand how changes in one or more factors affect option prices. Most importantly, this process helps develop realistic expectations. The goal of this process is to choose those option strategies which are most likely to yield positive results.

Market forecasting is an art, not a science. Profitable results, therefore, are not guaranteed. Commissions and other transaction costs must be included when creating scenarios and estimating results.

Table 17–5   Option Fact Sheet

Dividend Yield (%) _____   Interest Rates (%) _____

Date	Stock Price	Exp Mo. & Strike	Days to Exp	Option Price	Implied Volatility

Eighteen

Strategy Comparisons

arket forecasting, when option strategies are involved, must involve several specifics: a specific price forecast for the underlying stock, a specific time forecast during which the price movement will occur and a specific forecast for the volatility level of the option. Given the many combinations, it is impossible to cover all possibilities, but it is possible to create scenarios that cover a range of outcomes with the greatest potential.

Buying the "Right" Option

A commonly asked question is this: "Which is the 'right' option to buy?" This broad question, of course, is difficult to answer. In fact, there will be no "right answer," but if all of the market forecast variables are placed in a framework that allows the results to be compared, strategies with high *expected* results will emerge. This analysis does not guarantee profitable results, however, because, if any part of the forecast (market price, timing, implied volatility level) is incorrect, a loss may result. But the goal is clear: to gather valuable, relevant information for the purpose of enhancing the decision-making process.

In the following discussion, the task of strategy selection is accomplished in three steps. First, theoretical value tables for different strategies will be created. The purpose of the tables is to facilitate strategy comparisons. Second, some typical market forecasts will be presented with a discussion of what each forecast should include. Third, the process of matching an appropriate strategy with each forecast will be described in detail. After these steps are completed, some general observations will be made about which strategy fits which type of market forecast.

221

Strategies and Theoretical Value Tables

The six tables at the end of this chapter, Tables 18–1 through 18–6, were developed using the OP-EVAL™ program. The theoretical values which OP-EVAL™ expresses in decimal-point form were rounded to the nearest 1/8 to better simulate the real options market. For all strategies, the following assumptions were made: stock price range, $48–$57; time to expiration, 90 days to zero days at 15-day intervals; volatility, 27%; interest rates, 5%; and dividends, none. Tables such as these will provide valuable information when analyzing strategy alternatives.

The tables present theoretical values for (1) the 50 Call, (2) the 50 Put, (3) the 55 Call, (4) the 50–55 Call Spread, (5) the 50 Straddle and (6) the 50 Covered Write. The values for the 50 Call, 50 Put and 55 Call were taken from OP-EVAL™ and rounded to the nearest eighth. The 50-55 Call Spread values were created by subtracting the 55 Call value from the 50 Call value in the corresponding square. The 50 Straddle values are sums of the 50 Call and 50 Put values, and the 50 Covered Write values are stock prices minus 50 Call values.

Making a Forecast

A market forecast, when option strategies are contemplated, must be more specific than when purchasing a stock to hold for the long term. Such a forecast must include a specific price forecast for the underlying stock or index, and a specific time period for the price forecast to be realized. The forecast should also include a forecast of implied volatility. Consequently, "being bullish" is not a sufficient market forecast. A more specific forecast is "the stock will rise from $49 to $53 in four weeks with volatility unchanged."

The trader must also declare a risk attitude and an intention regarding the underlying stock. A statement about risk might be, "I am willing to risk $2,000" or "I am willing to buy stock at $48 1/2." The second of these statements indicates a willingness to assume the risk of stock ownership which includes the theoretical risk of the stock price falling to zero. A statement regarding the stock might be, "I am willing to sell at $52" which indicates a target selling price or "this is a trade; I do not want to own the stock," which means the trader intends to close the option position prior to expiration when exercise or assignment is most likely to occur.

With these components, a specific market forecast and statements about risk and intention regarding the underlying stock, an appropriate strategy can be selected. The following discussion will present some market forecasts and strategy analyses. Commissions and other transaction costs are not included, but these costs can significantly affect the desirability of any transaction and should be included when analyzing real strategies. Commission calculations are especially important when multiple-option and/or stock-and-option orders are involved.

Forecast #1 (Adam)—90 Days to Expiration, Stock Price $50

"I believe the stock price will rise to $54 in the next four to six weeks. I am willing to risk approximately $2,400, not including commissions, but I do not want to buy the stock. I cannot decide whether to buy eight 50 Calls at 3 each, thirteen 50–55 Call Spreads at 1 7/8 each or twenty-one 55 Calls at 1 1/8 each."

Adam's next step is to estimate the profit and loss of each strategy assuming his market forecast is realized. To do this, Adam could look either at Tables 18–1, –3, and –4 or use OP-EVAL™ to estimate the price of each strategy under the new assumptions, 30 days later (which is 60 days to expiration), a stock price of $54, etc.

For ease, we will follow Adam as he uses the theoretical value tables to reach his decision. First, note that the three alternatives are nearly equivalent in cost (not including commissions) and potential risk (i.e., the entire amount invested is lost):

Quantity	Strategy	Cost
8	Buy 50 Call at 3	$2,400
13	Buy 50–55 Call Spd at 1 7/8	$2,438
21	Buy 55 Call at 1 1/8	$2,363

Outcomes at $54, 30 Days Later (60 Days to Expiration)

Strategy	Initial Price	Ending Price	Unit Profit	$ Profit per Unit	×	# Units	=	Total Profit
Buy 50 Call	3	5 1/8	2 1/8	212	×	8	=	$1,696
Buy 50–55 Call Spread	1 7/8	3	1 1/8	112	×	13	=	$1,456
Buy 55 Call	1 1/8	2 1/8	1	100	×	21	=	$2,100

Outcomes at $54, 45 Days Later (45 Days to Expiration)

Strategy	Initial Price	Ending Price	Unit Profit	$ Profit per Unit	×	# Units	=	Total Profit
Buy 50 Call	3	4 3/4	1 3/4	175	×	8	=	$1,400
Buy 50–55								
Call Spread	1 7/8	3 1/8	1 1/4	125	×	13	=	$1,625
Buy 55 Call	1 1/8	1 3/4	5/8	62	×	21	=	$1,302

This analysis is most enlightening. Different readers, undoubtedly, will have had different inklings about the "best" strategy. Some may have thought they are approximately equal. These calculations, however, illustrate the different results. If the passage of 30 days is assumed, so that it is then 60 days to expiration, the 55 Call results in a profit $404 higher than the second place strategy, buying eight 50 Calls. If the passage of 45 days is assumed, the call spread has the highest profit by over $200. This analysis leads Adam to purchasing the 50–55 Call spread.

Since Adam does not want to buy the underlying stock, his strategy must also include plans to close the position prior to expiration if either or both of the calls are in the money. Exactly when to close the position is a subjective decision which Adam must make himself.

Adam's situation should be an eye opener to traders who "automatically buy at-the-money calls" or who "automatically buy out-of-the-money calls." Buying call spreads is a viable alternative given an appropriate forecast. Commissions, of course, must be considered when analyzing real trading situations.

Forecast #2 (Barbara)—30 Days to Expiration, Stock Price $52

"I've got a hunch this stock will rise to $57 or higher at expiration. I am willing to risk approximately $1,500 on a speculative basis, and I don't know whether to buy five 50 Calls at 2 7/8 each or nineteen 55 Calls at 3/4 each."

Barbara's prediction meets the requirement of being specific. She has a short-term price forecast and a stated willingness to risk the loss of approximately $1,500. Furthermore, she has expressed no interest in owning the underlying stock. The two alternatives are nearly equivalent in cost (not including commissions) and risk:

Quantity	Strategy	Cost
5	Buy 50 Call at 2 7/8	$1,438
19	Buy 55 Call at 3/4	$1,425

Again, we will watch Barbara as she uses the theoretical value tables to estimate the expected profit from each strategy and as she makes a choice between these two alternatives. From Tables 18–1 and 18–3, Barbara gets an estimate of option prices if her forecast is realized, and she calculates the expected profit of each strategy (not including commissions) as follows:

Outcomes with the Stock at $57 at Expiration

Strategy	Initial Price	Ending Price	Unit Profit	$ Profit per Unit	×	# Units	=	Total Profit
Buy 50 Call	2 7/8	7	4 1/8	412	×	5	=	$2,060
Buy 55 Call	3/4	2	1 1/4	125	×	19	=	$2,375

Given Barbara's specific forecast, these figures indicate to her that buying the 55 Calls is the slightly better choice. Further analysis reveals, however, that with a stock price of $56 at expiration buying the 50 Calls is more profitable. At a stock price of $56 at expiration, the five 50 Calls are worth 6 each for a profit of $1,562 {(600 – 287.50) × 5} versus a profit of $475 from the 19 55 Calls worth 1 each {(100 – 75.00) × 17}. Barbara, therefore, must be extremely confident of her forecast for a stock price rise to $57 or higher to justify buying the 55 Calls.

Forecast #3 (Charles)–60 Days to Expiration, Stock Price $51

"I am not too excited about the market right here, but I have $4,900, and I am willing to buy stock at $49 or below. If I miss buying the stock this time, I feel confident it will dip again in the not-too-distant future."

This forecast may not seem very specific. It does, however, reveal Charles' willingness to buy stock at a specific price. His forecast, therefore, leads to a specific strategy, but it does not lead to numerous strategy comparisons.

Because Charles wants to buy stock at or below $49, he can sell one 50 Put at 1 1/2 (Table 18–2). If the stock price is below $50 at expiration, his short put will be assigned, requiring him to use his cash-ready reserve to buy the stock at $50—but his effective purchase price is only $48 1/2. Charles will be happy owning the stock at that price, and, if the stock price is not below $50 at expiration, he will have earned a profit by keeping the put premium.

Forecast #4 (Dione)—75 Days to Expiration, Stock Price $52

"Something is up with this stock, but I don't know what. I smell something in the air about the up-coming earnings report, and I think the stock will be up or down $4 in the next two weeks. I am deciding whether or not to buy the 50 Straddle for 5 3/8 now and, hopefully, sell it at a profit in two weeks."

To buy the 50 Straddle for 5 3/8, Dione must buy both the 50 Call for 3 7/8 (Table 18–1) and the 50 Put for 1 1/2 (Table 18–2). Two commissions, of course, are involved and must be included in an analysis of real options. A study of Table 18–5 reveals much about the way straddle prices behave. Dione's forecast says, specifically, that the stock will be at $56 or $48 in two weeks, which is approximately 60 days prior to expiration in this example.

With the stock at $56 at 60 days, Table 18–5 indicates a straddle value of 7 1/8. Buying the straddle at 5 3/8 and selling it at 7 1/8 results in a profit of 1 3/4 (or $175.00 per straddle) *before transaction costs*. While many traders would consider $4 a good-sized price move for a $50 stock, Dione sees that the straddle may not be an appropriate strategy for this specific forecast, because she also estimates the straddle value if there is a $4 down move. With the stock price at $48 at 60 days, Table 18–5 indicates a straddle value of 4 1/2. Purchasing a straddle for 5 3/8 and selling it at 4 1/2 results in a loss of 7/8 per straddle. The $4 stock price decline from $52 to $48 is estimated to cause a larger decline in the 50 Call price than a rise in the 50 Put price. Dione decides, therefore, that the purchase of a straddle in this instance is not justified.

Forecast #5 (Evan)—75 Days to Expiration, Stock Price $50

"I like this stock, but I can't decide between a covered write and buying the stock outright. I don't think anything 'big' is going to happen, but if the stock is up $3 in two months, how much will I lose on the short call?"

Theoretical Value Table 18–6 assists in answering this question. If Evan buys the stock at $50 and sells the 50 Call for 3 (Table 18–1), his initial Covered Write Value will be $47 as indicated in Table 18-6. Two months later, at 30 days to expiration, with the stock price at $53, Table 18–6 indicates a Covered Write Value of 49 3/8, an increase of 2 3/8. The outright stock purchase would have an increase in value of 3 according to the forecast. Consequently, the short call "cost" 5/8 in terms of underperformance, although Evan still realized a profit of $2 3/8.

Determining whether or not this underperformance is, in some sense, worth it depends on Evan's certainty about his price forecast and willingness to realize a profit (i.e. sell the stock). Remember, the covered write strategy is a different strategy than buying stock outright. The covered write entails the benefit of lower cost, from the sold call, and the obligation to sell if the call is assigned. Buying the stock has a higher cost and no obligation to sell. Therefore, no direct comparison can determine which is "better." After obtaining all available information, Evan must make a subjective decision about which strategy better fits his specific forecast.

General Observations about Strategies

Theoretical Value Tables 18–1 through 18–6 reveal much about the kind of market forecast required to justify particular strategies. Newcomers to options should study these tables, or similar tables they create themselves.

Consider Table 18–1, theoretical values for the 50 Call, and assume this call is purchased for 3 with the stock at $50, 90 days prior to expiration (not including commissions). According to the table, in order for this call buyer to break even, the underlying stock price must rise by nearly $1 in the first 30 days and by slightly more than $1 in the second 30 days. There are times, of course, when $50 stocks move much more than this. But there are also times when they do not. Having a table such as Table 18–1 helps call buyers to understand, specifically, the estimated market price action required to make the desired profit.

Comparing At-the-Money Calls to Out-of-the-Money Calls

In order to make a meaningful comparison of Tables 18–1 and 18–3, it is necessary to make an assumption about how capital is managed. If an equal quantity of options (i.e., 5 Calls) is purchased, the 50 Call buyer will always have greater risk and greater profit potential. If, however, the same amount of capital (i.e. $2,000) is assumed, then the strategies will appear to have very similar percentage profits in many instances. For example, consider a stock price rise from $51 to $54 between 75 days and 45 days. The 50 Call, according to Table 18–1, rises from 3 1/4 to 4 3/4, a 46% rise. The 55 Call rises by a similar percentage from 1 1/4 to 1 3/4 , a 40% rise; the difference is due to the rounding involved in eighths and quarters.

The strategic concern in selecting at-the-money calls versus out-of-the-money calls depends on the size of the move around a particular strike and the proximity to the expiration date. For example, if a stock price rises from $52 to $55 from 45 days prior to expiration to the expiration is forecast, then the in-the-money 50 Calls are preferred. Buying six 50 Calls at 3 1/4 each (total cost $1,950 not including commissions) would result in a profit of $1,050 if they are sold for 5 each with the stock at $55 at the expiration (again, not including commissions).

The strategy of buying twenty 55 Calls for 1 each, however, would have disastrous results. With the stock at $55 at expiration, the total cost of $2,000, not including commissions, would be lost when the options expired worthless.

A different market forecast, however, given the same initial circumstances, would favor buying the twenty 55 Calls over the six 50 Calls. If a stock price rise from $52 to $58 were forecast and occurred, the twenty 55 Calls would rise to $3 each for a profit of $4,000 (not including commissions). The six 50 Calls, worth $8 each with a stock price of $58 at expiration, would have a lower profit of $2,850 not including commissions. The conclusion is that out-of-the-money calls offer more leverage, given the same amount of capital at risk. For the purchase of these calls to be more profitable than purchasing at-the-money calls, however, there must be a sufficiently large price change in the underlying stock.

Summary

Theoretical value tables such as Tables 18–1 through 18–6 are valuable tools for strategy analysis and selection. Similar tables can be created with the OP-EVAL™ program. The tables can be used to estimate whether the results of a predicted stock price move will justify selecting a particular strategy. Also, the tables can be used to compare the results of different strategies.

Table 18–1 50 Call Theoretical Values at Various Stock Prices and Days to Expiration (Volatility, 27%; Interest Rates, 5%; No Dividends)

Stock Price	90 Days	75 Days	60 Days	45 Days	30 Days	15 Days	EXP
$57	8 1/8	7 7/8	7 5/8	7 1/2	7 1/2	7 1/8	7
$56	7 1/4	7	6 3/4	6 1/2	6 1/4	6 1/8	6
$55	6 3/8	6 1/8	5 7/8	5 5/8	5 3/8	5 1/8	5
$54	5 5/8	5 3/8	5 1/8	4 3/4	4 1/2	4 1/4	4
$53	4 7/8	4 5/8	4 3/8	4	3 5/8	3 1/4	3
$52	4 1/8	3 7/8	3 5/8	3 1/4	2 7/8	2 1/2	2
$51	3 1/2	3 1/4	3	2 5/8	2 1/4	1 3/4	1
$50	3	2 5/8	2 3/8	2	1 5/8	1 1/8	0
$49	2 3/8	2 1/8	1 7/8	1 1/2	1 1/8	5/8	0
$48	2	1 3/4	1 1/2	1 1/8	3/4	3/8	0

Table 18–2 50 Put Theoretical Values at Various Stock Prices and Days to Expiration (Volatility, 27%; Interest Rates, 5%; No Dividends)

Stock Price	90 Days	75 Days	60 Days	45 Days	30 Days	15 Days	EXP
$57	1/2	3/8	1/4	1/8	1/16	0	0
$56	5/8	1/2	3/8	1/4	1/8	0	0
$55	7/8	5/8	1/2	3/8	1/4	1/16	0
$54	1	7/8	3/4	1/2	3/8	1/8	0
$53	1 1/4	1 1/8	7/8	3/4	1/2	1/4	0
$52	1 5/8	1 1/2	1 1/4	1	3/4	5/8	0
$51	2	1 3/4	1 1/2	1 1/4	1	5/8	0
$50	2 3/8	2 1/4	2	1 3/4	1 1/2	1	0
$49	2 7/8	2 5/8	2 1/2	2 1/4	2	1 5/8	0
$48	3 3/8	3 1/4	3	2 7/8	2 5/8	2 1/4	0

Table 18–3   55 Call Theoretical Values at Various Stock Prices and Days to Expiration (Volatility, 27%; Interest Rates, 5%; No Dividends)

Stock Price	90 Days	75 Days	60 Days	45 Days	30 Days	15 Days	EXP
$57	4 1/2	4 1/4	3 7/8	3 1/2	3	2 1/2	2
$56	3 7/8	3 1/2	3 1/4	2 7/8	2 3/8	1 7/8	1
$55	3 1/4	3	2 5/8	2 3/8	1 7/8	1 1/4	0
$54	2 3/4	2 3/8	2 1/8	1 3/4	1 3/8	3/4	0
$53	2 1/4	2	1 5/8	1 1/4	7/8	1/2	0
$52	1 3/4	1 1/2	1 1/4	1	5/8	1/4	0
$51	1 1/2	1 1/4	1	5/8	3/8	1/8	0
$50	1 1/8	7/8	5/8	3/8	1/4	1/16	0
$49	7/8	5/8	1/2	1/4	1/8	0	0
$48	5/8	1/2	3/8	3/16	1/16	0	0

Table 18–4   50–55 Call Spread Theoretical Values at Various Stock Prices and Days to Expiration (Volatility, 27%; Interest Rates, 5%; No Dividends)

Stock Price	90 Days	75 Days	60 Days	45 Days	30 Days	15 Days	EXP
$57	3 5/8	3 3/4	3 7/8	4	4 1/4	4 1/2	5
$56	3 3/8	3 1/2	3 5/8	3 3/4	4	4 1/4	5
$55	3 1/8	3 1/4	3 1/4	3 1/4	3 1/2	3 7/8	5
$54	3	3	3	3 1/8	3 1/4	3 3/8	4
$53	2 1/2	2 5/8	2 5/8	2 3/4	2 3/4	2 7/8	3
$52	2 3/8	2 3/8	2 3/8	2 3/8	2 1/4	2 1/4	2
$51	2 1/8	2 1/8	2	2	1 7/8	1 5/8	1
$50	1 7/8	1 3/4	1 5/8	1 1/2	1 3/8	1 1/8	0
$49	1 5/8	1 1/2	1 3/8	1 1/4	1	5/8	0
$48	1 3/8	1 1/4	1 1/8	7/8	3/4	3/8	0

Table 18–5 50 Straddle Theoretical Values at Various Stock Prices and Days to Expiration (Volatility, 27%; Interest Rates, 5%; No Dividends)

Stock Price	90 Days	75 Days	60 Days	45 Days	30 Days	15 Days	EXP
$57	8 5/8	8 1/4	8	7 5/8	7 3/8	7 1/8	7
$56	7 7/8	7 1/2	7 1/8	6 3/4	6 3/8	6 1/8	6
$55	7 1/4	6 7/8	6 1/2	6	5 1/2	5 1/8	5
$54	6 3/4	6 1/4	5 3/4	5 1/4	4 3/4	4 1/4	4
$53	6 1/4	5 3/4	5 1/4	4 3/4	4 1/8	3 1/2	3
$52	5 3/4	5 3/8	4 7/8	4 1/4	5 3/8	2 7/8	2
$51	5 1/2	5	4 1/2	4	3 1/4	2 3/8	1
$50	5 3/8	4 7/8	4 3/8	3 3/4	3 1/8	2 1/4	0
$49	5 1/4	4 7/8	4 3/8	3 3/4	3 1/8	2 1/4	1
$48	5 1/4	4 7/8	4 1/2	4	3 3/8	2 5/8	2

Table 18–6 50 Covered Write Theoretical Values at Various Stock Prices and Days to Expiration (Volatility, 27%; Interest Rates, 5%; No Dividends)

Stock Price	90 Days	75 Days	60 Days	45 Days	30 Days	15 Days	EXP
$57	48 7/8	49 1/8	49 3/8	49 1/2	49 1/4	49 7/8	50
$56	48 3/4	49	49 1/4	49 1/2	49 5/8	49 7/8	50
$55	48 5/8	48 7/8	49 1/8	49 3/8	49 5/8	49 7/8	50
$54	48 3/8	48 5/8	48 7/8	49 1/8	49 1/2	49 3/4	50
$53	48 1/8	48 3/8	48 5/8	49	49 3/8	49 3/4	50
$52	47 7/8	48 1/8	48 3/8	47 3/4	49 1/8	49 1/2	50
$51	47 1/2	47 3/4	48	48 3/8	48 3/4	49 1/4	50
$50	47	47 1/4	47 5/8	48	48 3/8	48 7/8	50
$49	46 5/8	46 7/8	47 1/8	47 1/2	47 7/8	48 3/8	49
$48	46	46 1/4	46 1/2	46 7/8	47 1/4	47 5/8	48

Nineteen

Index Options

Introduction

The theory of index options is simple: investors and traders can focus on the overall market rather than specific stocks. In theory, index options work the same as regular stock options; and, in theory, index options can be traded exactly the same way as regular stock options. The reality, of course, is somewhat different than the theory.

This chapter is not meant to be a definitive treatise on index options. Rather, given the background developed on stock options, this chapter will explain some of the unique aspects of index options and offer pointers for short-term traders. After briefly reviewing available index options, this chapter will first explain the important differences in contract specifications between index options and regular stock options. Second, some theoretical pricing differences from regular stock options will be presented. Third, how OP-EVAL™ can be used and what adjustments should be made when valuing index options will be covered. Finally, some practical complications will be explained.

The Basics

Index options have been designed to be easy to understand and easy to trade. Most shorter-term index options such as the popular OEX, SPX and XMI index options have strikes every five index points (450, 455, 460, etc.), although strike intervals vary for longer-term index options. Also, index option prices are quoted just like regular stock options: whole dollars and eighths above three dollars and whole dollars and sixteenths below three dollars. The actual dollar value of an index option is 100 times the quoted price,

233

just like stock options. For example, the price of an OEX December 500 Call trading at "4 1/2" is $450, not including commissions.

Options on Several Indices Are Available

The popularity of index options has led to the introduction of options on more and more indices. The following list is by no means complete, but it includes most of the popular index options:

Index Symbol	Description of Underlying	Where Traded
OEX	Standard and Poor's 100 Index	Chicago Board Options Exchange (CBOE)
SPX	Standard and Poor's 500 Index	CBOE
XMI	Major Market Index	American Stock Exchange
VLE	Value Line Index	Philadelphia Stock Exchange
NYA	NYSE Composite Index	New York Stock Exchange
RUT	Russell 2000 Index	CBOE
MID	Mid-Cap Index	American Stock Exchange
TPX	U.S. Top 100 Index	Philadelphia Stock Exchange
WSX	Wilshire 200 Index	Pacific Stock Exchange
XII	Institutional Index	American Stock Exchange
NDX	NASDAQ 100 Index	CBOE
XOC	National OTC Index	Philadelphia Stock Exchange

In addition, options are traded on several industry indexes such as UTX, the Utility Industry Index, and BGX, the Biotech Industry Index. Also, at least 10 country indexes have options available. The list of index options, as well as other products, being traded is constantly expanding. Investors who want to keep abreast of the latest product introductions or who have questions can call the toll-free numbers below:

Exchange	Toll-Free Phone Number
The American Stock Exchange	800-THE AMEX
Chicago Board Options Exchange	800-OPTIONS
The New York Stock Exchange	800-NYA NYSE
The Pacific Coast Stock Exchange	800-TALK PSE
The Philadelphia Stock Exchange	800-THE PHLX

Stock Index Options versus Options on Stock Index Futures

The stock index option contracts listed above should not be confused with futures contracts or with options on futures contracts which are traded at the Chicago Mercantile Exchange or the Kansas City Futures Exchange. The index option contracts listed above can be traded through brokers licensed by the Securities and Exchange Commission (SEC), the same brokers who handle stock transactions. Futures contracts and futures options can only be traded by futures brokers who are licensed by the Commodity Futures Trading Commission (CFTC).

Cash Settlement

A significant difference between index options and regular stock options is what is delivered and received when an option is exercised. For equity options, of course, the underlying is the stock itself. For index options, however, the underlying is an index which consists of various numbers of shares of the different stocks in the index. Delivery of the individual shares which make up the index would be cumbersome and expensive. For this reason, the concept of cash settlement was developed.

Cash settlement means that, upon exercise, the in-the-money amount is paid by the option writer to the option buyer. The "in-the-money amount," in real dollar terms, is $100 (the index multiplier) times the intrinsic value of the exercised option. In the case of an index call, this is calculated by subtracting the option strike price from the index settlement value and multiplying the result by $100. In the case of a put, the in-the-money amount is calculated by subtracting the index settlement value from the strike price and multiplying the result by $100. Settlement value may be determined after an afternoon market close, as it is for OEX options (known as "p.m. settlement") or after an expiration Friday morning opening, as it is for SPX options (known as "a.m. settlement").

Consider an example in which Sam, an index option trader with a bullish opinion purchases an OEX March 440 Call for 6 1/2, or $650, and holds it until expiration. If the index settling price is 454.00 at expiration, Sam's call will be exercised. Sam will receive $1,400, which is the in-the-money amount of 14.00 times $100. Sam's profit, in this case, is $750 ($1,400–$650). Alternatively, if the index settles at 443.00 at expiration, Sam receives $300 (3.00 × $100) when the call is exercised. This produces a loss of $350 ($650–$300). A third possible outcome is the index settling below 440 at expiration. In this case, Sam's call expires worthless, resulting in a total loss of the $650 Sam paid.

When Sam exercises, who is assigned? Just like regular stock options, writers of index options receive assignment notices, and they must fulfill the terms of the option contract. In the case of index options, a randomly assigned writer pays the in-the-money amount in cash.

The High Leverage of Index Options

Leverage means that two related securities experience different percentage price changes. Consider a stock trading at $50 and a 50 Call on that stock trading at $3. If the stock price rises 10% to $55 at expiration, the 50 Call, at $5, will have risen approximately 67%. Similarly, a 10% decline in the stock price to $45, at expiration, would result in the 50 Call expiring worthless, a 100% loss in value. The call is, therefore, "leveraged" relative to the stock.

Understanding the concept of leverage is important, because price comparisons are frequently made between index options and regular stock options. The absolute price of index options often is greater than the absolute price of stock options, but such a comparison does not take into consideration the percentage of underlying value and the potential leverage.

The difficulty of comparing index options and stock options will be illustrated by considering a 500-strike index call trading at 10.00, or $1,000, when the index is at 500.00 and a 50-strike stock call trading at 3, or $300, when the stock price is $50. The 500-strike index call may initially, appear more expensive than the 50-strike stock call. However, after considering the option price in terms of a percentage of the underlying value and the potential leverage, the index option appears cheaper, relatively, than the stock option.

First, the 50-strike stock call, at 3, is six percent of the underlying stock's price. The 500-strike index call, at 10, however, is only two percent of the underlying index. Second, if the index level rises 10% to 550 at expiration, the 500 Call will be worth 50, or $5,000, a 400% increase from 10. If the stock price rises 10% to $55 at expiration, the 50 Call will be worth 5, approximately a 67% increase from 3.

Despite its higher absolute dollar cost, the price of the 500-strike index call is a lower percentage of the underlying value than is the 50-strike stock call, and it is more highly leveraged. Why this situation exists will be explained next.

The Lower Volatility of Index Options

Consider this question: is it more likely, less likely or equally likely for a typical stock to rise or fall 10% or for a typical index to rise or fall 10%?

Specific events affect individual companies and general events affect the whole market. The price of an individual company may rise or fall 10% in response to a specific or general event; but general events do not affect all companies the same way. Therefore, in order for an index to change by 10%, some stocks in the index would have to move by more than 10%. Consequently, the likelihood of an individual stock price moving 10% is greater than the likelihood of an index moving 10%.

Since options are similar to insurance policies, as explained in Chapter 3, and since indices are less likely than individual stocks to have a "big move," as explained above, index options are "cheaper" than stock options. "Cheaper," not in absolute dollar terms, but in percentage terms. The 500-strike index call described above was two percent of the underlying index value while the 50-strike stock call was six percent of the underlying stock value. As a result, index options have higher potential leverage than stock options. Percentage terms are only one way of describing relative value. Another, more mathematically sophisticated, comparison takes into account potential price movement, or volatility.

"Cheapness" versus Leverage

While the higher leverage of index options may appeal to short-term traders who buy options, there is a corresponding higher risk to writers of index options. The speculative writing of index options, therefore, is an activity which should not be undertaken lightly. The risks of writing index options, as well as the risks of selling any uncovered options, should be thoroughly examined and understood prior to engaging in this strategy.

American Style versus European Style Index Options

The popular OEX Index options are American style which means early exercise is permitted. Other index options such as the SPX and XMI index options are European style where early exercise is not permitted. Since exercise style varies by index option contract, it is crucial for index option traders to fully understand the risks involved in strategies involving short index options.

"Covered" and "Uncovered" Index Options

The cash settlement feature has significant implications for writing American style index options. Written, or short, index options may not be covered, even though, in similar stock option strategies, those options could be covered.

Traditionally, a covered call is a short call position which exists in conjunction with at least one of three other positions: long stock, long another call of a lower strike or long another call of an equal strike. If the short call is assigned, delivery can be fulfilled by either delivering the owned stock or by delivering stock purchased from exercising a call (although even this may not be possible in rare circumstances such as a tender offer that is expiring). With equity options, price fluctuations do not pose a risk for the covered call writer, because shares are delivered regardless of intervening price fluctuations.

Consider, for example, a stock option spreader named Floyd who purchased an XYZ 50 Call for 3 and sold an XYZ 55 Call for 2, the total spread cost being 1, or $100. Assume that on a morning two weeks prior to expiration when XYZ closed at $70 the day before, Floyd receives an assignment notice on the short 55 Call. If the 50 Call had closed at 20 and the 55 Call closed at 15, Floyd would have a paper profit of 4, or $400, on the 50–55 Call spread. If on that morning XYZ opens at $62, down $8 from the previous close, the 50 Call is likely to open around 12, a decline of 8 from the previous close. Such an event is of no concern to Floyd, because his assignment requires him to deliver stock at a price of $55; and the 50 Call gives him the right to buy stock at $50. In this situation, Floyd buys stock at $50 via exercise and delivers it to meet the assignment at $55. Consequently, Floyd realizes the profit of $4 per share even though the stock price dropped sharply overnight.

If a similar situation were to occur in cash-settled American style index options, however, the result would be very different. A short American style index option is not considered to be covered by an owned index option with a lower strike because day-to-day fluctuations in the underlying index affect the amount of cash received or delivered. An assigned index option writer cannot exercise an owned index option until the next day when, in all likelihood, the index level has changed.

As an example, assume that Floyd, instead of spreading XYZ stock options, had purchased a 450 American style index call for 3.00, and sold the 455 Call for 2.00, and thus created the 450–455 index call spread for 1.00, or $100.

If the index closed on that fateful day at 470 and the 450 and 455 Calls closed at 20.00 and 15.00, respectively, and if the short 455 Call were assigned, then Floyd would be required to pay 15.00, or $1,500, in cash to the owner of the 455 Call. Because Floyd did not receive notice of the assignment until the next morning, however, he could not exercise his long 450 Call and be guaranteed of receiving the 20.00, or $2,000, based on yesterday's index settlement price of 470. The cash amount received from Floyd's exercise today will be determined by today's index settling price. If the index settles today unchanged at 470 (or higher), then exercise of the 450 Call results in the receipt of 20.00 (or more), a sufficient amount to meet the assignment from the previous day. If, however, the index declines sharply on day two and settles at 462, for example, exercise of the 450 Call results in the receipt of only 12.00, or $1,200, an insufficient amount to cover the assignment of $1,500.

If this outcome occurred (i.e., the index settling at 462), the index call spread purchased for 1.00, or $100, would result in a loss of $400! The 450 Call purchased for 3.00 and closed at 12.00 (by exercise), resulted in a profit of $900. The 455 Call, however, was sold for 2.00 and closed at 15.00 (by assignment), resulting in an $1,300 loss. The net loss was, therefore, $400— $100 paid to initiate the spread and a net $300 paid when assignment of the short 455 call and subsequent exercise of the 450 call occurred.

Vertical Spreads with European Style Index Options

The possibility that the loss from a vertical spread could exceed its cost is one of the reasons European style index options were developed. Since early exercise is prohibited by the option contract, the problem described above and others caused by early exercise do not exist with European style index options of the same expiration month. Consequently, traders who are exploring the strategy of spreading index options, either buying or selling the spread, might be well advised to start with European style index options. There are, however, a few additional considerations to keep in mind.

First, because the early exercise feature has value, American style index options frequently trade at a higher price than corresponding European style options. Index option spread traders may discover, therefore, that spread prices for European style index options are lower than for American style index options. Buyers of index spreads will, undoubtedly, find this an advantage, but spread sellers will find it a disadvantage.

European Style Options—Unique Pricing Characteristics

The lack of early exercise has implications for deep in-the-money European style options which may trade at a discount to parity even when there is considerable time to expiration. An option trading at parity is an in-the-money option with no time value, or an option trading exactly at intrinsic value. For European style options, it is possible to trade *below* intrinsic value because arbitrageurs, unable to exercise early, will bid and offer for options at prices which are tied to the cost of carry.

It is beyond the scope of this book to explain cost of carry and arbitrage, but deep in-the-money European style index options can trade below parity. This can be observed by using OP-EVAL™. With the default settings on the calculation page, lower the "Price of Underlying" to 25.000 and press ENTER. This results in a value of 0.000 for the 50 Call and a value of 24.527 for the 50 Put. The 50 Put is 0.473 below intrinsic value. Thus, an arbitrageur, in theory, could buy the 50 Put for 24.527 and buy the stock for 25.00 and earn a riskless profit of 0.473 plus dividends at expiration in 90 days. However, since 0.473 plus dividends is equal to the 90-day interest cost of financing the purchase of the stock and the 50 Put, an arbitrageur would actually bid at a lower price for the 50 Put. The important concept index option traders must understand is that theoretical values of European style options can be less than intrinsic value.

It is important for non-professional option traders to be aware of these concepts, because the difference in pricing in the marketplace of European style options relative to American style options should be taken into consideration when choosing a strategy and anticipating results.

Using OP-EVAL™ to Price European Style Index Options

As discussed in Chapter 3, option values depend on six inputs: stock price, strike price, time to expiration, dividends, interest rates and volatility. OP-EVAL™ can be used to price European style index options by entering the appropriate information. American style index option prices, however, can vary from the OP-EVAL™ theoretical values, sometimes significantly so. Under normal market conditions, the theoretical price of an American style option should not trade for less than its intrinsic value or for less than the theoretical price of the corresponding European style option.

In theory, using OP-EVAL™ to price European style index options is simple. There are, however, a few practical complications.

Strike Price and Days to Expiration

The easiest inputs to determine are strike price and time to expiration, because index options are identified by their expiration month and strike. OP-EVAL™ users need only count the days to expiration.

Interest Rate

Although dividends and interest rates are complicated to determine in theory, users of OP-EVAL™ can easily find satisfactory approximations. In theory, the correct interest rate is the cost of funds, or borrowing rate, used by index arbitrageurs who buy or sell the underlying stocks in the index and sell or buy index options in the hope of profiting from "price discrepancies." A close approximation to this rate is the 90-day Treasury Bill rate which is widely published in business journals. Users of OP-EVAL™ should know how to find the 90-day Treasury Bill rate and be sure to use a current rate.

Dividends

Calculation of the dividend yield of an index is complicated in theory, because individual stocks pay dividends on different schedules. The Black-Scholes pricing model used by OP-EVAL™ assumes dividends are paid continuously and evenly throughout the year. While this difference may sound significant, fortunately it generally is not. Dividends are spread out sufficiently so as not to invalidate the assumption made by the Black-Scholes model. Users of OP-EVAL™ can use the index dividend yield numbers presented on Mondays in *The Wall Street Journal, Investor's Business Daily* or *Barron's*.

"Price of Underlying"

Much care should be taken when selecting the appropriate value for "Price of Underlying" when valuing index options with OP-EVAL™. For regular stock options, the price of the underlying stock is readily observable. With index options, however, the situation is more complicated. Although the current level of the underlying index is readily observable and can be used most of the time, there are times when this is not the appropriate number. A detailed explanation of pricing index options is beyond the scope of this book. However, a brief discussion of the complicating factors is warranted.

The concept of put-call parity mentioned in various chapters is that the prices of calls, puts and the underlying stock must have a certain relationship with each other or there will be arbitrage opportunities. Whenever prices are "out of line," professional traders will adjust their bids and offers and force prices "back in line." Although it is beyond the scope of this book to explain them in detail, there are also arbitrage relationships between stock index options and stock index futures contracts. Consequently, price fluctuations of stock index futures contracts above and below theoretical value can impact stock index option prices.

As long as stock index futures contracts are "fairly priced," which means in line with theoretical value, then stock index options can be priced using the current index level as the "Price of Underlying." However, if supply and demand conditions in the stock index futures markets cause these contracts to trade sufficiently above or below theoretical value, then professional option market makers may make bids and offers for stock index options based on arbitrage relationships with the futures contract. Consequently, the index option prices will appear "out of line" if the current index level is used as "Price of Underlying" in option pricing models. When this occurs, index option traders must adjust the "Price of Underlying" and be very careful how they interpret the information from OP-EVAL™.

In order to understand how to make the necessary adjustment to "Price of Underlying," the following brief explanation of stock index futures pricing is necessary.

Calculating a "Fair" Stock Index Futures Price

In a simplified form, the "fair value" of a futures contract is:

$$\text{Spot Price} + \text{Cost of Carry} = \text{Futures Price}$$

If a futures contract is "over valued," arbitrageurs will borrow money, buy the underlying instrument and sell the futures contract. On the futures delivery date, they will deliver the underlying cash commodity, receive cash equal to the sold futures price and pay off the loan with interest. The difference is their profit.

If a futures contract is "undervalued," purchasers of the underlying instrument will profit by buying futures and earning interest rather than paying cash for the underlying and storing it.

For stock index futures contracts, the existence of dividends requires an adjustment to the formula shown above. Dividends received by arbitrageurs are income which, effectively, reduce the cost of carry. Consequently, the formula for stock index futures is:

Spot Price + Cost of Carry – Dividends = Futures Price

Cost of carry and dividends are generally presented in annual rates and must be adjusted to fit the specific time period in question. For a specific time period, the formula for stock index futures is:

$$\text{Spot Price} + [\text{Spot Price} \times (\text{Cost of Carry} - \text{Dividends})$$
$$\times \frac{\text{Days to Expiration}}{\text{Days per Year}}] = \text{Futures Price}$$

A Specific Example

For example, to use the formula to get a rough estimate of the "fair value" of an index futures contract, make the following assumptions:

Days to expiration:	47
Treasury Bill rate:	5.2%
Dividend yield on the index:	2.8%
Cash value of index:	440.00

A rough estimate of the "fair value" of the index futures contract is:

$$440.00 + [440.00 \times (.052 - .028) \times \frac{47}{365}] = 441.36$$

Interpreting the Information

If the futures contract is trading approximately at 441.36, as calculated above, then the current index level of 440.00 can be used in OP-EVAL™ as "Price of Underlying." The 440 Call with 47 days to expiration should be approximately 1.36 greater in value than the 440 Put with 47 days to expiration. Also, if the actual market prices of the index options are typed in, OP-EVAL™ will calculate accurate implied volatility numbers.

However, if the index futures contract is not trading near 441.36, then the price of the underlying must be adjusted accordingly. If, for example, the index futures contract is trading at 443.36, two points above "fair value," then, in theory, the "Price of Underlying" typed in OP-EVAL™ should be raised to 442.00. In theory, the option prices will now be consistent with put-call parity.

Practical Problems in the Real World

While all this is good in theory, there are some real world practical problems. When futures contracts are trading at a significant premium or discount to "fair value," then market conditions are probably very hectic. "Very hectic" means erratic price fluctuations and possible delays in order processing due to a heavy volume of orders. Consequently, it may be difficult for a trader without constantly updated information to tell exactly at what price index futures are trading or exactly where the underlying cash index level is, because both are changing rapidly and erratically. While such a situation is theoretically impossible, there are occasions when hectic trading activity causes stock index futures and stock index options to trade at prices significantly different from those implied by the theory of futures and option pricing. Index option traders must be aware of the risks of such market action and prepare themselves accordingly.

Inability to Profit from "Price Discrepancies"

Even if the price discrepancies described above are detected, it is virtually impossible for non-professional traders to take advantage of such a situation. The only "riskless" method of profiting from a price discrepancy is to create an arbitrage. But this is impossible for non-professional traders for at least two reasons. First, commissions and other transaction costs for a non-professional trader would, almost certainly, be greater than any profit potential from an observed price discrepancy. Second, entering orders and getting executions at the observed prices is highly unlikely due to hectic market conditions.

The Fallacy of Buying "Undervalued Options"

The belief that one can take advantage of price discrepancies by purchasing "undervalued options" is based on a misunderstanding of option price theory. An option (either a stock option or an index option) will appear undervalued at one particular moment, only because a pricing model, at that moment, yields a higher "value." A trader who purchases this option would profit only if the option returns to "theoretical value," and *all other things remain constant.* But all other things never remain constant, especially in the hectic market environments described above.

"Undervalued," in the context used above, refers to an option with an implied volatility below expected volatility. "Returning to theoretical value," in such a case, means the implied volatility of the option rises to the expected level. This is known as the "vega effect," vega being the change in option price attributable to a change in volatility. It is possible, however, that the price of the underlying index could change adversely even though the implied volatility may be changing to the expected level. The change in option price attributable to a change in price of the underlying is called the "delta effect." The buyer of the "undervalued option" could lose money if the delta effect is greater than the vega effect.

Index Options and Changing Volatility

An additional complicating factor in trading index options is the changing levels of volatility. Implied volatility, it will be recalled, is the volatility percentage which justifies an option's current market price. Implied volatility, is, in some sense, the "market's opinion" of possible movement. Consequently, as the market's opinion changes, the implied volatility level changes. Constantly changing implied volatility levels is a characteristic of index options.

CBOE's Volatility Index—The VIX

One measure of the level of implied volatility in index options is CBOE's Volatility Index (VIX). This index is calculated by taking a weighted average of the implied volatilities of eight OEX calls and puts. The chosen options have an average time to maturity of 30 days. Consequently, the VIX is intended to indicate the implied volatility of 30-day index options. It is used by some traders as a general indication of index option implied volatility. Five years, 1990–1994, of the VIX, calculated daily, are presented in Figure 19–1. This information about the VIX reveals that implied volatility levels in index options change frequently and substantially.

Three-Part Forecasting

Keeping in mind the complications of trading index options discussed above, three components of an option's value most subject to change are: price of the underlying, time to expiration and volatility. Option traders

**Figure 19–1   CBOE Volatility Index (VIX) January 2, 1990
               through December 30, 1994.**

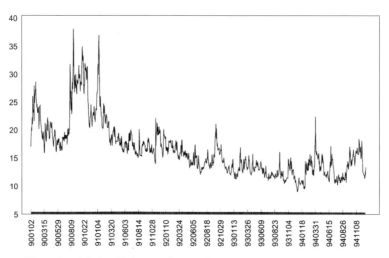

Source: Chicago Board Options Exchange—Past results are not an indication of future performance.

should attempt to forecast all three, not just the price of the underlying. For long-term options, changes in interest rates also have a substantial impact and traders of these options should add this fourth element to their forecast.

A three-step process to follow when contemplating an index option trade is as follows: First, use the current option price and time to expiration to determine the implied volatility. This can be done with OP-EVAL™, assuming normal market conditions when stock index futures contracts are trading approximately at "fair value." Second, forecast the extent of the move, the expected time period over which the move will occur and the implied volatility level at the end of the move. Third, use OP-EVAL™ to estimate the option price after the predicted move. If a loss or insufficient profit is indicated by this process, then the trade should not be made.

The three-step process just described involves gathering information, making a specific forecast and estimating results. This is a careful, thoughtful process rather than a haphazard, impulsive one.

Summary

Options can be traded on a variety of market indices, allowing investors and traders to focus on the overall market rather than specific stocks. In theory, index options are exactly the same as regular stock options. The cash settlement feature of index options and the existence of stock index futures contracts, however, mean that there are real-world, practical differences between index and stock options.

OP-EVAL™ can be used to value index options, but traders must know the "fair value" of the relevant futures contract and the current market price of that contract. If the two are approximately equal, then the current index level can be used in OP-EVAL™ as the "Price of Underlying." Otherwise, an adjustment must be made.

The volatility component of index option prices fluctuates and is an important factor to be considered. The CBOE's Volatility Index (VIX) is a 30-day weighted average of the implied volatility of eight OEX calls and puts and can be used as a measure of the current implied volatility level. When trading short-term index options, traders should forecast the index level, the time period and the volatility level. Traders of long-term index options should also include a forecast of interest rates.

SECTION 5

Getting Started

Twenty

Choosing Strategies That Work for You

Every investor should have a comprehensive investment plan. This maxim is especially true for options, because the range of possible uses is so wide for options that an investor who blindly plunges into the market without analyzing how a strategy fits into a comprehensive plan is courting disaster. Of course, creating such a plan is so personal and so individual that there are no "right" or "wrong" ways to do it. There are, however, some guidelines which all investors, regardless of experience, should know. This chapter will present some advice for newcomers to options and/or investing, review the traditional approach to investing, discuss strategies that four different types of investors might find most appropriate and, finally, describe an organized method for strategy selection.

Thoughts for Beginning Investors

Options are not a first step in investing. Beginning investors must first learn about the financial markets in general and the stock market specifically: basic experience in investing in stocks is an absolute requirement. Prior to the first option trade, an individual should have, to some extent, "suffered the slings and arrows" and the various "outrageous fortunes"—both good and bad—that are an inevitable part of investing.

Acquiring the knowledge to get to the point of buying individual stocks is not the overwhelming, time-consuming task that many newcomers fear. The first thing to do is learn about some companies, the history of their stock prices, their past earnings performance, their products and markets and their prospects. This can be accomplished by reading the newspaper business section once or twice per week, calling for—and reading—annual reports and raising the subject of investing in conversation. Many people have good ideas and enjoy talking about investing but are reluctant to raise the topic because there seems to be a perception that "few people invest" or

"nobody wants to talk about the market." But frequently, it only takes some-
one to break the ice, and a new, interesting area of conversation is opened!

Learning about investing is a gradual process, but beginning investors
must learn an important lesson: patience. As the cliche goes: "Rome wasn't
built in a day." Neither can "learning about the market" be accomplished in
a short time.

Second, have a good method of picking stocks. Whether it be a fundamental approach, a technical approach, or a combination of the two, a stock
selection method coupled with experience in market prediction will add
confidence to an investor's decision-making abilities. Without these basics,
anyone new to options is doomed to fail, but with some practice and
patience most people can gain an opportunity to improve results in the
world of options. As an added plus, the judgement and decision-making
skills that are developed will be valuable personal assets throughout life—
and not only in investing!

The Spectrum of Investments

The risk/reward spectrum covers a range of investments from low-risk-low-
reward (such as certificates of deposit and Treasury Bills) to high-risk-high-
reward (such as high-risk stocks, some speculative option strategies and
"junk" bonds). A related, but different, concept is that of investment goals,
i.e., "income oriented" or "growth oriented."

Traditionally, financial advisors suggest that investments be spread
across the risk-reward spectrum and diversified among investment goals in
accordance with individual situations. They also suggest that limits be set,
both for risk and for the percentage of assets invested in one particular
investment and in one type of investment. Some of the goals and related
types of investments are the following:

Goal of Investment	Examples
"Aggressive" Capital Growth	New Issues, Speculative Investments
"High-Quality" Capital Growth	Growth-Oriented Blue Chip Stocks
Balanced Capital Growth and Income	Stocks with Increasing Dividends
"High" Income	Utility Stocks, Corporate Bonds
Conservation of Capital and Income	T-Bills, CD's

The Hierarchy of Risk

Typically, financial planners suggest that more investments be oriented to less risk and fewer be oriented to greater risk as illustrated in Exhibit 20–1. Although the exact percentage in each category varies, the concept is that investments should be spread across a "hierarchy of risk" in accordance with individual goals and risk tolerance. For example, a young person saving for retirement in 30 years may have a larger percentage in growth-oriented investments, and an older individual approaching or in retirement may have a larger portion in income-oriented and conservation-of-capital investments.

Options and the Hierarchy of Risk

Some might think that options fit only the top tier, Level 5, of the hierarchy of risk. Not so!

The cash account option strategies discussed in Chapters 6–10 can be used to pursue the objectives of *all levels of risk*. Covered writing (Chapter 8), the strategy in which stock is purchased and calls are sold on a share-for-share basis, for example, is an income-oriented strategy involving stock ownership. Depending on the "riskiness" of the underlying stock, covered writing might be either a Level 2 or Level 3 risk.

Exhibit 20–1 The Hierarchy of Investment Risk

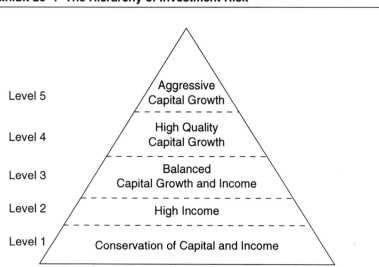

Buy Call plus Treasury Bill (Chapter 7) is a short-term risk management technique of acquiring stock. Remember, the investment or speculative orientation of using calls depends on an investor's willingness and ability to purchase the underlying stock. This strategy, therefore, could be used for investments in Levels 2, 3 or 4.

The option strategies which fit into the highest level of risk are the margin account strategies in Chapters 12–15 and the trading strategies in Chapters 17–19.

Four Broad Categories of Investors

Since there is a wide variety of investment goals, risk preferences, and financial conditions, it is not possible for one set of guidelines to apply to all investors. Therefore, four distinct types of investors will be defined and appropriate strategies will be suggested. The four types of investors are: *the beginning investor, the income-oriented investor, the growth-oriented investor,* and *the well-capitalized investor.*

The Beginning Investor

Definitely lacking in experience and potentially lacking in investment funds, the beginning investor must first establish goals. The exact amount of investment capital required before a beginning investor might select a strategy involving options is difficult to determine. Many financial advisors recommend, however, that beginners first have some liquid savings—for the proverbial rainy day. After that, advice typically runs along the lines of: "choose your investments carefully with an eye to long-term growth." An Individual Retirement Account (IRA) is frequently recommended to young investors because of the favorable tax treatment.

Covered writing is an appropriate strategy for beginning investors for at least two reasons. First, it is stock oriented which means success is most likely if the underlying stock is chosen wisely. Covered writing, therefore, capitalizes on the skill developed while learning about the market. Second, if the static and if-called returns are known (and deemed acceptable), a covered write will have a definite goal and an easily measured result. These are important attributes for beginners to have at anything. Also, covered writing is a good beginning strategy, because the time element of two to four months or longer teaches beginning investors to be patient. Also, covered writing is allowed in tax-deferred IRA accounts where many young people have long-term savings.

Covered writing also helps beginning investors gain decision-making experience. At every expiration a decision must be made. If the stock price is below the strike at expiration and the call expires, a decision must be made between simply holding the stock, selling another covered call, and selling the stock and making another investment. If the stock price is above the strike as expiration approaches, a decision must be made whether or not to roll the call as explained in Chapter 8. If early assignment occurs, a decision must be made whether to repurchase the stock or move into something else. During the first year of covered writing, a beginning investor's experience will increase dramatically. This investor will have made three or four investment decisions while a buy-and-hold investor will have made only one.

When does a beginning investor buy calls? One situation is when the necessary funds to buy a stock are anticipated, but not currently available. In this case, an at- or in-the-money call is purchased. The expiration month is chosen so that the required funds to pay for the stock in full are available at or before the expiration date. After acquiring stock via this method, it is not necessary that options be used again on this particular holding, because the goal of "adding a good long-term stock to the portfolio" has been achieved.

Please note that no trading or speculative strategies have been suggested for beginning investors who should spend their time studying the market in search of good quality investments. Options can play a role in this long-term plan, when appropriate, by helping investors pursue their risk-management or income-enhancement objectives.

The Income-Oriented Investor

Income-oriented investors may be in retirement or experiencing high short-term expenses such as a child in college. Whatever the reason, the need for income-oriented investments points not only to covered writing. Writing puts on a non-leveraged basis (Chapter 13) is a second income-oriented strategy, and buying stock and writing straddles, without using margin loans, (Chapter 14) is a third. Return calculations must include all transaction costs, and investors must remember that these strategies involve the risk of owning the underlying stock. Stock selection and managing one's investments, therefore, play as important a role as ever.

The Growth-Oriented Investor

Growth-oriented investors have many opportunities to use options to pursue their investment objectives. When entering higher-risk Level 4 or Level 5 stocks, the investor can use Buy Call Plus Treasury Bill to pursue the goal of short-term risk management. As explained in Chapter 6, the call is used as a limited-risk way of participating in a forecasted price rise. If the forecast is correct, the stock can be purchased via exercise of the call and paid for with the funds invested in Treasury Bills. During the life of the call, the investor can rest easier knowing that risk is limited to the premium paid for the call.

If an investor is indecisive about selling a stock, regardless of risk level, the Protective Put strategy (Chapter 10) also pursues the goal of short-term risk management.

When the forecast calls for a neutral market, growth-oriented investors might write puts and buy Treasury Bills (Chapter 13) as an alternative to placing limit buy orders below the current market price of stocks they want to purchase.

Buy Stock with Ratio Call Spread (Chapter 9) pursues the goal of increasing profits over a limited stock price rise without increasing risk. Growth-oriented investors who understand this strategy may find times when it is possible to add a ratio call spread to a stock position which, given their market forecast, offers an opportunity to increase profits. The strategy need not be implemented on an entire position. If, for example, 200 shares are owned, options might be used as follows: buy one at-the-money call and sell two out-of-the-money calls. This ratio call spread involves only half of the holdings in this example. If the stock price rises as predicted, then profits can be increased over a limited price range on those shares. Transaction costs must be considered, and if the stock price is above the strike price of the short calls at expiration, then shares will be sold when exercise of the long call and assignment of the two short calls occurs. This possibility must be anticipated and planned for.

The Well-Capitalized Investor

This investor is assumed to have a variety of investments with varying objectives and risk levels. Unfortunately, many people in this situation start by asking the wrong question. They frequently want to know: "How much of my money should be in options?" This is the wrong question, because the focus should be on investment objectives, market forecasts and opinions of specific investment opportunities. Rather than think of options as a separate investment vehicle, these investors should view options in the context of how they might accomplish the investment objectives of the portfolio.

The full range of option strategies discussed in this book can be used by the well-capitalized investor where appropriate. For the income-oriented portion of their assets, covered writing, writing puts and buying Treasury Bills and buying stock and writing straddles—all on a non-leveraged basis—pursue the goal of income.

When a market forecast calls for short-term risk management, buying calls and Treasury Bills or protective puts are the appropriate strategies to consider. Buy stock with ratio call spread can be used on growth-oriented holdings to add leverage over a limited price rise.

For Level 4 and Level 5 risk investments, the well capitalized investor can use the margin account strategies discussed in Chapters 11–15 and the trading strategies discussed in Chapters 16–19.

Strategy Selection Framework

All four types of investors described above should know their priorities and think carefully about the selection of any strategy. The following discussion presents a simple, four-step approach for selecting strategies. The goal is to help all investors and traders think clearly with realistic expectations so that an appropriate strategy can be chosen, given a specific forecast.

The four steps are: (1) know your situation, (2) state clearly your market forecast, (3) identify your specific objective and, finally, (4) choose a strategy that will meet your goal if the forecast is accurate.

Know Your Situation

Many investors take for granted that they know a situation. Since the use of options requires specific thinking, however, it is worth reviewing some examples. "I'm bullish" is not a situation; it is a forecast. "I would like to increase income" is not a situation; it is a goal. A situation is "I have cash to invest," or "I own stock with a profit that I am willing to sell," or "I own stock with a loss." These different situations, given the same forecast, may lead to the selection of different strategies.

State Clearly Your Market Forecast

The idea of stating a market forecast clearly has been discussed before. Being "bullish" is not specific enough for the purposes of investing or trading with options. "The stock price will rise from $51 to $54 in the next three to five weeks," or "the stock price will trade at or below $40 between now and expiration" are clear market forecasts.

Identify Your Specific Objective

This is much different than what is required of a typical "buy-and-hold investor." Examples of specific objectives are "I want to sell my stock at $51 3/8," or "I would like to leverage my investment without increasing risk if the stock price rises as I predict," or "I am willing to buy stock at $28 3/4." In contrast, just wanting to "make money" is not specific enough to lead to the selection of a particular option strategy.

Choose a Strategy That Meets Your Goal

The three elements described above may or may not lead to the selection of an option strategy. Exhibit 20–2 illustrates how situations, market forecasts and goals might lead to selection of a strategy. The concept is presented in a conceptual manner and can be used in real situations only after actual prices and commissions have been considered.

Line 1 in Exhibit 20–2 illustrates that for an investor who owns stock and has a neutral market forecast, selling a covered call pursues the goals of increasing income or selling at a higher price. Notice that Line 1 can start from either owning stock with a profit or owning stock with a loss.

Line 2 starts at "Have cash to invest." For an investor in this situation with a neutral market forecast, writing puts and buying Treasury bills pursues the objectives of increasing income and buying stock below the current market price. Line 3 starts in the same place as Line 2, but the neutral/bullish forecast and the different objective of adding leverage without more risk leads to the strategy "buy stock with ratio call spread."

Line 4 illustrates that this process does not always lead to the selection of an option strategy. For a very bearish investor who owns stock, either with a profit or a loss (Line 4 has two starting points) and who has the objective

Exhibit 20–2 A 4-Step Approach to Strategy Selection

Situation*	Market Opinion*	Goal*	Strategy*

———————————— Line 1
···················· Line 2
– – – – – – – – – – Line 3
– · – · – · – · – · Line 4

* This is not a complete list. Investors and traders can adapt this approach in decision making to fit their own circumstances.

of eliminating risk, selling the stock is the logical strategy. A protective put, remember, if exercised, would result in a lower effective selling price for the stock than the current market price and therefore would not eliminate risk.

Exhibit 20–2 does not present a complete list of situations, market opinions, goals or strategies. Investors and traders can expand these lists to fit their own circumstances.

Summary

Options are not a first step in investing. Investors must have an understanding of the financial markets in general and the stock market specifically before considering options.

Options can be used to pursue the investment objectives of all levels in the hierarchy of risk. Covered writing is income-oriented and may be appropriate for risk levels 2 and 3. Buy call and Treasury Bills and the protective put strategies are short-term risk management ways of acquiring stock and can be used to acquire investments in risk levels 2, 3, and 4. The margin account strategies in Chapters 11–14 and the trading strategies in Chapters 16–19 are potentially risk Level 5 strategies.

Beginning investors should consider starting with covered writing, because it is conservative and stock oriented. Covered writing and writing puts and buying Treasury bills pursue the goals of income-oriented investors. Buy stock with ratio call spread might help growth-oriented investors leverage investments on part of a position, and buy call plus Treasury Bills is a short-term risk management technique to be considered when entering new positions. The entire range of option strategies is available to well-capitalized investors, because their investments are diversified across the hierarchy of risk and involve many different goals.

A simple, four-step strategy selection process promotes organized thinking and realistic expectations. The four steps are: (1) know your situation, (2) clearly state your market forecast, (3) identify your goal and (4) select a strategy that meets your goal if the forecast is accurate.

This book has followed a proven outline for learning to use options. Learn to draw profit and loss diagrams and master the mechanics of exercise and assignment first. Understand the difference between investing and speculative uses second. Third, commit yourself to adapting to the psychological differences between investing with stocks and investing with options. Fourth, define a specific goal up front, and choose a strategy which will achieve that goal if your market forecast is correct. Finally, traders must develop realistic expectations about option price behavior prior to expiration.

By keeping these guidelines in mind, by gaining experience and nurturing patience, and by selecting stocks and strategies with a reasoned approach, any investor can succeed in the world of options.

Index